PATTING
THE
SH/\RK

Tim Baker is the bestselling author of *Bustin' Down the Door*, *High Surf*, *Occy*, *Surf for Your Life* (with Mick Fanning), *Surfari*, *Century of Surf* and *The Rip Curl Story*. He is a former editor of *Tracks* and *Surfing Life* magazines. He has twice won the Surfing Australia Hall of Fame Culture Award and been nominated for the CUB Australian Sports Writing Awards. His work has appeared in *Rolling Stone*, the *Sydney Morning Herald*, the *Australian Financial Review*, the *Bulletin*, *Inside Sport*, *Playboy*, *GQ*, the *Surfer's Journal* and *Qantas: The Australian Way*, as well as surfing magazines around the world.

PATTING THE THE SHARK

TIM BAKER

A SURFER'S JOURNEY:
LEARNING TO LIVE
WELL WITH CANCER

EBURY
PRESS

EBURY

UK | USA | Canada | Ireland | Australia
India | New Zealand | South Africa | China

Ebury is part of the Penguin Random House group of companies
whose addresses can be found at global.penguinrandomhouse.com.

Penguin
Random House
Australia

First published by Ebury, 2022

Copyright © Tim Baker, 2022

The moral right of the author has been asserted.

'Medicine' from *The Book of Longing* by Leonard Cohen published by
Penguin Books. Copyright © Leonard Cohen 2006, published by Viking 2006, Penguin
Books 2007. Reprinted by permission of Penguin Books Limited.
Front cover photography by Benjamin Ono
Back cover photography by SurfChimp, courtesy of UrbnSurf
Cover design by Adam Yazxhi
Typeset in 12.3/18pt Bembo Std by Midland Typesetters, Australia

Printed and bound in Australia by Griffin Press, part of Ovato, an accredited
ISO AS/NZS 14001 Environmental Management Systems printer

 A catalogue record for this
book is available from the
National Library of Australia

ISBN 978 1 76089 891 5

penguin.com.au

We at Penguin Random House Australia acknowledge that Aboriginal and Torres Strait
Islander peoples are the Traditional Custodians and the first storytellers of the lands
on which we live and work. We honour Aboriginal and Torres Strait Islander peoples'
continuous connection to Country, waters, skies and communities. We celebrate
Aboriginal and Torres Strait Islander stories, traditions and living cultures;
and we pay our respects to Elders past and present.

To Kirsten, Vivi and Alex
for weathering the storm
and providing the most profound
motivation to remain healthy

CONTENTS

MEDICINE

My medicine

Has many contrasting flavours.

Engrossed in, or perplexed by

The difference between them,

The patient forgets to suffer.

Leonard Cohen, 'Medicine' in *Book of Longing*

FOREWORD

'There is, one knows not what sweet mystery about
this sea, whose gently awful stirrings seem to speak
of some hidden soul beneath.'

Moby Dick, Herman Melville

WHEN I FIRST CONNECTED with Tim, I was struck by the aura
of a man with something to say, about something much bigger
than could readily be grasped.

On the surface, his is no ordinary success story. An award-
winning author and journalist, he has also carved a career
as the world's best-known anthropologist of surfing culture,
having penned titles including *The Rip Curl Story, Occy,
High Surf, Bustin' Down the Door, Surf for Your Life, Australia's
Century of Surf* and *Surfari*. While his bibliography suggests a
full-time occupation in long-form writing, Tim is also the

former editor of *Tracks*, *Surfing Life* and *Slow Living* magazines, and a two-time winner of the Surfing Australia Hall of Fame Culture Award. The entrancing children's book *The Surfer and the Mermaid* is also the product of Tim's creative energy, and has been harnessed for stage play and performed to sell-out audiences.

In surfing lexicon, he's a literary wave-riding guru.

But below the wave, where souls seldom find the freedom to arch, he's a man coming to terms with advanced prostate cancer.

When Tim recounts the day of his diagnosis, in July 2015, you can almost visualise a man being dropped to surf Cape Fear, without a leash. He eloquently describes the rising wave of panic, the anxiety of uncertainty, the paralysis of shock, and the anger of abandonment by a health system that in his experience was beset by fragmented care, systemically uninterested in what patients think.

His story hands a mirror to those of us who labour within the healthcare arena, reminding us of what we already know, but struggle to change. Faced with a grim diagnosis, Tim pivots from the perspective of a man who has worn an unconventional path in life, approaching his diagnosis and treatment with open-mindedness and a sceptical, inquiring mind.

He writes openly about the impact of prostate cancer treatment on all aspects of his life, and considers an alternative clinical reality, where prescriptions embrace lifestyle and complementary therapies that can satisfy the evidence benchmarks of scientific rigour. He concedes he is unqualified beyond his own experience, and writes of worrying that some may accuse him of being anti-science, while gently pleading for necessary consideration of strategies that might help us realise a higher quality of life throughout the challenges of cancer treatment.

If we accept that the beginning point for all medical and scientific wisdom is knowing simply that we don't know all the answers, then Tim's solitary quest can be read as a deep embrace of the scientific method. Indeed, he concedes, with raw honesty, that his own mortality depends on it.

Tim's experience reveals a man in search of the ultimate wave, balancing the acceptance of what is with the hope of what may be.

Professor Suzanne Chambers, AO, PhD, FCHP
Centre for Research Excellence in
Prostate Cancer Survivorship

INTRODUCTION

I KNOW HOW IT feels to pick up a book like this, in the bewildering days or weeks or months after you or someone you love has received a cancer diagnosis, in a desperate search for answers, hope, guidance. So, I'll cut straight to the chase.

This is not a book about how to cure cancer. I'm not a doctor and I'm not qualified to give medical advice. I have, however, lived with stage four metastatic prostate cancer for seven years and I'm still fit, active and healthy – still surfing, writing, being a dad and husband, with a full and rich life. This book is primarily about maintaining quality of life, managing the ravages of cancer treatments and their often-devastating side effects, and facing this mortal threat with some semblance of equanimity.

I also know the crippling sense of overwhelm from information overload, the bewildering blizzard of medical advice,

1

treatment options, dubious folk remedies and whacky and expensive alternative therapies, which the newly diagnosed cancer patient can all too easily become lost in.

So, allow me to synthesise what I've learnt over the past seven years about cancer self-care into one short, handy mantra:

Remember to take your M.E.D.S.

Meditation. Exercise. Diet. Sleep.

These have become the pillars of my self-care, in no way intended to replace, but rather to' complement, conventional treatments. Meditation is the foundation of this approach. The ability to cultivate a clear and calm mind, to find a place of inner peace and stillness you can access at any time, is critical to managing the stress and uncertainty of a cancer diagnosis. Exercise is increasingly being recognised as a vital element of cancer care with numerous benefits, from alleviating stress, fatigue and depression to enhancing cardiovascular health and bone strength. Diet is something most oncologists don't talk about, chiefly because they receive little or no training in nutrition, but the virtues of a predominantly plant-based diet have been validated in numerous studies. And quality sleep is now well established as one of the most fundamental determinants of good health. If I can tick each of these boxes each day, I feel like I am on the right path and in my healing zone.

To this you can add whatever lifestyle strategies work for you and personalise your cancer self-care from a metaphorical spice rack of therapies. Music, art, immersion in nature, social support, a good psychologist, birdwatching, gardening, nude sunbathing, swing dancing, whatever floats your boat.

But I would caution against blindly following all the strategies I've employed here, without proper medical guidance. Psychedelic therapy, in particular, which I turned to out of desperation for relief from crippling depression, shows great promise but I imagine could be dangerous for some people and without proper oversight. The sooner these sorts of therapies become legal and mainstream, with proper regulation, the safer they will be.

What I'm most passionate about here is advocating for a more integrative approach to cancer care, to see an end to the false dichotomy that cancer patients must make an agonising choice between the ravages of conventional treatment, and the often expensive and unproven lottery of alternative therapies. Integrative oncology is not about spurious miracle cures but rather an embrace of evidence-based complementary therapies alongside mainstream oncology to increase the efficacy of treatment, mitigate its side effects, and improve quality of life and, in some cases, even the prognosis of cancer patients.

In 2020, 1.4 million men were diagnosed with prostate cancer worldwide, and over 375,000 men lost their lives. Prostate cancer is the most common cancer in men and the second most deadly, behind lung cancer. In Australia, one in seven men will be diagnosed with prostate cancer. Prostate cancer survivorship and quality of life issues have been identified as a national health priority by the Prostate Cancer Foundation of Australia. Mainstream oncology is slowly recognising that its ability to keep men with advanced prostate cancer alive has outstripped its ability to manage the often soul-crushing side effects of treatment.

In particular, the frontline treatment euphemistically known as hormone therapy, or androgen-deprivation therapy – that effectively amounts to chemical castration – causes great misery and suffering among many men with prostate cancer. While hormone therapy is effective in suppressing testosterone, which prostate cancer feeds on, it does so at great cost to the patient's physical and mental health, sense of self, ability to work and family life.

It shouldn't be seen as controversial or anti-science to suggest that evidence-based complementary and supportive therapies have a role to play in helping men with prostate cancer deal with these devastating side effects. While there's growing evidence for the use of complementary therapies to support men during prostate cancer treatment, in reality, few oncologists make any specific recommendations to their patients, mainly because they have almost no training in this area. The need for a multi-disciplinary team – nutritionist, exercise physiologist, psychologist, oncology masseuse, acupuncturist – should be self-evident. Yet even chronically over-worked and stressed oncologists guard their turf intently, fearful of their patients seeking unproven, expensive and dangerous alternative treatments. As I argue within these pages, by bringing credible supportive therapies within the oncology tent, the snake oil salespeople will be left exposed as the charlatans they are and patients will receive better, more holistic care. And time-poor oncologists will be relieved of the role of advising patients on supportive therapies they are unqualified for.

Prostate cancer treatment protocols were developed for a mainly elderly patient population, but in recent years there has been a pronounced increase in the numbers of younger men being diagnosed, though no one seems to know why. Yet there has been no adjustment to these protocols to recognise the very different and often extreme challenges this younger subset of patients face. Younger men generally experience greater distress and more aggressive disease because their natural testosterone levels are usually higher, so hormone therapy and the abrupt collapse in testosterone levels hits younger men hardest.

For younger men with advanced prostate cancer, I'd like to see a new protocol developed that at least offers the possibility of intermittent hormone therapy to reduce the side effects of treatment. Where men are otherwise young, fit and motivated they should not be given the message, as I was repeatedly, that there is nothing they can do to improve their own prognosis. A discerning use of lifestyle strategies might equip these men with the means to better manage their own health and quality of life.

I'm not a cancer researcher and do not have their years of specialist study and clinical experience. But if I'd ask anything of people who do, it would be that they more fully investigate the roles of exercise, diet, meditation, certain herbs and supplements, and off-label drugs that show promise as adjuvant therapies. To improve the quality of life of men going through hormone therapy, everything should be on the table – medicinal cannabis, psychedelic assisted therapy, and other supportive therapies.

Research on cancer survivorship is usually undertaken by career academics, often psychologists. While theirs is valuable and important work, this academic approach can miss many of the subtleties and nuances of individual cancer patients' lived experience. In the case of prostate cancer, men often exhibit a reluctance to open up around the impact of hormone therapy on sexuality and masculinity. As Paul Kalanithi, a medical doctor who eventually died from advanced lung cancer, writes in his cancer memoir *When Breath Becomes Air:* 'Science may provide the most useful way to organize empirical, reproduce-able data, but its power to do so is predicated on its inability to grasp the most central aspects of human life: hope, fear, love, hate, beauty, envy, honour, weakness, striving, suffer-ing, virtue.'

This is not an instructional or how-to book. It is a raw and candid account of my own cancer journey, with as much honesty and vividness as I can muster, despite the discomfort of this process, cancer-related fatigue and the deleterious impacts of treatment on cognitive function. After a wide reading of the genre, it seems to me cancer memoirs tend to fall into one of two categories – the miraculous cancer survivor who has defied all odds and the tragic cancer victim bravely facing end of life.

My interest is in documenting the sizeable space between these two extremes, which I'd argue occupies the attention and energy of most of us living with cancer – the day-to-day business of getting up each morning and trying to live a worthwhile life while coming to terms with the dire prog-nosis hanging over our heads.

My focus is not how to 'beat' or 'conquer' cancer, to win some metaphorical battle. I came to a realisation some time ago that if survival is my only goal, I will be forever on tenterhooks, agonising over every blood test and scan result in the hope of defying the medical orthodoxy and achieving an unlikely long-term remission. However diligent I may be in this quest, no matter how disciplined I am in following mainstream or alternative cancer treatments, no matter how karmically blessed I may or may not be, I accept that there is much here that is out of my hands.

If my focus is quality of life, identifying lifestyle interventions that might provide relief from the side effects of treatment, that support and enhance my enjoyment of life in the here and now, to evolve to a state of consciousness in which death holds little or no fear, then this is a quest I have more control over and can work on every day.

Buddhism teaches us that our life's work is to prepare for death, yet for most of us it is the homework we put off until the last minute. A cancer diagnosis is a wake-up call to do your homework. In many ways, this book is about me doing my homework, to live a 'good life', however I might come to define that, while accepting the certainty of my own mortality. I aspire to use my experience to inform and benefit others and for my journey not to be a burden but rather a profound shared experience with my family and inner circle of close friends.

Ultimately, it is about cultivating the tools to navigate a good death, at peace, accepting, able to offer comfort and solace to my loved ones, having lived a full life, whatever its duration. This endeavour, undertaken in tandem with a creative writing PhD scholarship from Griffith University, is also an act of optimism that my good health and cognitive function will endure long enough to see it through to completion, that I am sending a powerful message to myself, my spirit, and my body that I have important and compelling reasons to not just survive but thrive well into the future. Having strong reasons to live and a powerful sense of purpose are widely recognised as important elements in improving outcomes for cancer patients. This writing project then is, in itself, an act of self-care, a strategy for maintaining quality of life and a sense of meaning through the travails of my cancer journey.

We have an amazing health system in Australia, and I remain incredibly grateful for the dedicated care and expertise I have received from a wide range of health professionals. But when it comes to cancer care, the provision of supportive services lacks coordination and consultation between disciplines. The newly diagnosed cancer patient is left to navigate a confounding maze of mainstream and alternative treatment options and fend for themselves when it comes to maintaining quality of life. Modern medicine is typically something that is done to patients by doctors. I choose to regard my cancer treatment as a collaboration between myself, my oncologist and a range of allied health professionals. Together, we make decisions about my cancer treatment and manage the multi-layered challenges of my diagnosis to mind, body and spirit.

Ultimately, I am advocating for a more integrative and holistic approach to cancer care that treats the whole person and not just the tumour, one that offers agency and dignity to the patient and places an appropriate emphasis on quality of life.

1

PUNCHING THE SHARK

A LONE FIGURE SITS astride their surfboard, like a rider on a horse, calmly balanced, scanning the horizon, searching the vast blue undulations for telltale signs of an approaching swell. It's a scene played out on thousands of beaches by countless surfers every day. But this particular scene is being witnessed by millions of viewers around the world, transfixed by a sporting contest about to transform into a mortal, human drama.

Suddenly, a boiling eruption of water, a flash of grey, the shocking appearance of a large dorsal fin so close to the surfer he can touch it. The surfer grips the rails of his surfboard like a rodeo rider, before he's bumped off just as a passing wave obscures him from view.

We are left agonising over his fate for ten long seconds that feel like an eternity. When the wave passes, we see him swimming desperately towards the beach, before he stops, turns 180 degrees towards the horizon, treading water, as if deciding to face his attacker.

Some 11,000 kilometres away, I wake to the rowdy song of rainbow lorikeets in the golden winter morning glow of our Currumbin treehouse on the southern Gold Coast. Shafts of sunlight pierce the canopy of towering ironbarks. The radically altered nature of my reality gradually seeps through my semi-consciousness, like waking after a big night with ashtray brain and an empty wallet, times a thousand.

Old routines offer some small comfort. I make coffee, reach for my phone, check messages, socials, emails. It's an odd way we choose to ease ourselves into the new day, the jolt of caffeine, the sensory onslaught of the world at our fingertips – every global disaster, every silly cat meme, every political scandal or disgraced celebrity, all mainlined through our own pocket-sized tower of babble.

But *this* morning is different. This morning there appears to be only one topic on everyone's minds. And it does nothing to allay my own recently acquired case of acute existential dread.

'Aussie Surf Star in Shark Attack,' the headlines blare.

I'm wide awake. Mind racing. Who? Where? Brushes with mortality seem to be the theme de jour. The clip is everywhere across every conceivable digital platform, pro surfing finally cutting through to the mainstream but not in the way anyone would have wanted.

Soon enough my questions are answered. The who is my old mate, three-time world surfing champion Mick Fanning.

The where is the notoriously sharky waters of Jeffreys Bay, South Africa. Six years earlier, I'd been holed up in a spare room of Mick's luxurious beachfront rental at that very spot. Mick had been bundled out of the event early and embarked on an enthusiastic bender while I worked on his memoir titled, ironically enough, *Surf for Your Life.*

The footage is hard to watch, but harder not to. It's the final of the J-Bay Open and Mick is up against his good friend and compatriot Julian Wilson, who's just caught a long ride down the famed point. Mick sits alone and waits for a wave, all composure and steely focus, when there's a sudden turbulence next to him. He looks confused, then alarmed. Then we see it. A large grey dorsal fin abruptly surfaces next to him as the turbulence intensifies. Mick is thrown from his board as the shark thrashes about, apparently (we later learn) tangled in his legrope. The surfing world holds its collective breath while the passing wave obscures him for long, drawn-out seconds. In that moment, I figure I have a better idea how he's feeling than your average surf fan.

At Jeffreys Bay, the local beach commentator blasts the contest hooter to sound the alarm. Mercifully, Mick is plucked from the water by a jet ski unharmed, just as Julian Wilson has made the bold decision to paddle towards Mick and the white pointer menacing him, rather than away.

'I figured I had my board, I could try and stab it or something,' Julian offered afterwards.

All good, courageous, Aussie mateship at its finest.

But what really interests me is what Mick does in those few moments when he's confronted with his mortality, when it's just him and the shark thrashing about, before the cavalry arrives.

'It was right there. I saw the whole thing and I was being dragged under by the legrope,' Mick recounts on camera, only minutes later, still pinging on adrenalin. 'I punched it a couple of times . . . I was swimming in and I had this thought, what if it comes to have another go at me? So I turned around so I could at least see it coming.'

When Mick flies home to Coolangatta, a media scrum is waiting, every bit as carnivorous as that apex marine predator. Everyone wants to know how he felt, what was going through his mind, how long it will take before he gets back in the water, if he will ever get back in the water (silly question, of course he will). News crews with satellite trucks camp out on the verge of his large, beachfront home. The inevitable *60 Minutes* exclusive and silly internet memes soon follow.

I've never had a close shark encounter myself. But I do feel like I'm living through a slow-motion version of weirdly parallel events that began twelve days before Mick's well-publicised brush with death. And I'm still thrashing about trying to work out how I might survive.

My great white shark is a balding, bespectacled urologist dispassionately informing me that not only do I have prostate cancer, but the cancer has already spread to my lymph nodes, my right femur (thigh bone) and left seventh rib. Or rather, my shark is those clusters of mutant cells swimming about in my blood stream and colonising my bones. There is the initial panic, the incomprehension, the wild flailing, the trying to process my dire situation, the desperate fight for survival.

I've known Mick since he was fifteen, and have written a book and dozens of magazine articles about him and his courageous rise to surfing greatness, hurdling one potentially career-ending injury or personal tragedy after another. As I watch those extraordinary images from Jeffreys Bay over and over, I think I might need to borrow a bit of inspiration from the champ. However much I want to flee, I'll turn and face my shark, get a few punches in, do whatever I can to prevent it getting its teeth into me.

But there are no jet skis or rescue boats coming to pluck me out of my confrontation with mortality, no global audience witnessing my desperate struggle for survival. My fight for life will be played out privately, over years not seconds, and I will have to learn to live with this thing swimming around inside me for whatever time I have left.

What I remember most clearly is my wife squeezing my hand so tight I thought my fingers would break.

The last time Kirst nearly crushed my fingers we were in this same building, though back then the trigger for her vice-like grip was the superhuman effort of bringing new life into the world. This time round it's the threat of a drastically reduced lifespan for the father of those children she so heroically birthed. Each time, tiny clusters of cells dividing brought us here.

John Flynn Hospital rises symmetrically from a fold in a low ridge of hills, all gleaming glass, concrete and steel. Both our kids were born here, within view of Coolangatta's famous point breaks. Thirteen years ago, our daughter Vivi entered the world after a long and difficult birth, at twenty minutes past midnight on a crisp autumn night. Kirst lost a lot of blood, and probably should have had a transfusion. Our first-born slept on my chest sucking insistently on my little finger while my wife lay exhausted beside us. I remember feeling like a little boy who'd successfully smuggled his new puppy into bed.

Nine years ago, our son Alex arrived at 4 am on a glorious spring morning. I bathed him while the first hint of dawn began to creep across Coolangatta Bay, and windswept lines of swell wrapped around Snapper Rocks.

Now, Kirst and I are sitting in a urologist's office as he slides a bone scan onto his wall-mounted lightbox and takes up a pen to indicate a large white smudge where my right femur should be.

'This more or less confirms our suspicions,' he announces, deadpan.

Time stands still like a record needle stuck in a groove, a feedback loop of dissonance. This can't be happening. This is happening. This can't be happening. This is happening.

Kirst is first to gather her thoughts.

'Hang on, can we just back up for a minute?' she asks, a rising note of panic in her voice, neatly mirroring my internal state. 'Are you saying that is cancer in Tim's leg?'

The urologist seated at the other side of a wide, timber desk nods without any trace of emotion. It must be tough delivering this kind of news for a living, and our guy's coping strategy seems to involve acting as a clinical, emotionless dispenser of information. With the aid of a small model prostate on his desk – a walnut-sized object mounted on a wooden stand like a trophy, inscribed with the name of a pharmaceutical company – and some handy laminated diagrams, he explains that once the cancer has spread beyond the prostate and metastasised in the bone as mine has, 'the horse has bolted', a metaphor that does nothing to calm my mounting sense of dread. The prognosis? Incurable, ultimately fatal, but can be 'managed' for an indeterminate period with a range of debilitating treatments.

It's curious how quickly the mind defaults to cliché. 'How long have I got?' is the first coherent thought I manage to vocalise, just like in the movies. Doctors don't like to give definitive cancer prognoses these days because they're often accused of pointing the bone, of seeding a self-fulfilling prophecy. There's a vague assurance that we are talking years, maybe five, maybe more, depending how well I respond to treatment.

'We'll get you started on hormone therapy straight away and I'll refer you to an oncologist who can explain further treatment options,' he says, busily scribbling on sheafs of paper. 'I'll also get you to see an orthopaedic surgeon in case we need to pin the leg to prevent a pathological fracture.'

That doesn't sound good. But then nothing about this unfolding nightmare sounds good. He hands over a wad of scripts and referrals and attempts a thin-lipped smile to indicate our appointment is over. *What the fuck are we supposed to do now?* I want to scream. *Is that it? We're supposed to just, what? Keep calm and carry on?*

Kirst and I step blinking out of his office into the reception area, where the outside world appears to be operating normally despite our world being abruptly tilted off its axis. The mainly elderly clientele thumb through trashy magazines or gaze at daytime TV patiently. A smiling receptionist seizes the referrals and begins briskly making appointments for me by phone, cheerily asking if particular dates and times suit me. I have the disconcerting sense of being sucked into a large machine over which I have little control.

'Can we bulk bill Mr Baker please?' she asks whomever is on the other end of the phone, then stage whispers to me, 'That will save you a few dollars.' Lucky me.

She hands me back my referrals with a couple of appointment cards and a handy booklet from the Cancer Council titled, 'Understanding Prostate Cancer'. She flashes another sympathetic smile that seems to suggest we should now get on with what remains of our shattered lives.

We shuffle out into the hall gripping our wad of prescriptions, referrals and brochure. I collapse back against the wall of the long, white corridor, exhaling heavily. 'Fuck' is all I can mutter as Kirst and I stare helplessly at each other. I feel like I've been smacked in the face with a baseball bat. Thirteen years ago, we left here carrying our first-born in a baby capsule wondering how we would manage this daunting new challenge, gripped by a mixture of exhaustion, excitement, joy and anxiety. This time, all we're leaving with is pure, undiluted terror.

The elevator ride is a blur. I don't register whether there is anyone else in the lift with us. We march solemnly through the vast hospital car park back to Kirst's VW Passat, now a little too closely resembling a hearse for my liking.

Once we make it to the privacy of the car, we both burst into tears, barely able to speak. I don't know how long we sit there for, bawling uncontrollably, unable to offer each other any comfort. Eventually, Kirst picks up her phone and rings her dad, Ken, and through barely coherent jumbles of words between breathless sobs she manages to convey the general nature of our news. My father-in-law, bless him, says he'll meet us at our place and get the kids out of the house for the afternoon to give us some time to process the information we've been given.

Again, I don't know how long we sit there trying to compose ourselves and formulate a plan for what to tell the children. At ages nine and thirteen, it's difficult to judge through our own panic how much they need to know. We settle on a vague plan to explain we've had some news about my health and we just need a bit of time to make sense of it. Mercifully, Ken is already there by the time we get home, cheerily explaining to the kids they're going to have an afternoon with Grandpa. They look at us inquiringly as I stifle tears and dispense hugs. 'Everything's going to be okay, Mum and I just need to have a chat,' I offer meekly, though as an explanation of our fraught state it feels wholly inadequate.

The kids appear to take this unexpected development in their stride, smile at us uncertainly but go along with the plan happily enough. An unscheduled afternoon with Grandpa at his classic, old fibro beach house is a welcome treat, sure to involve a relaxation of normal dietary guidelines. Only the sight of their ashen-faced parents tempers their glee.

For several hours, Kirst and I work through my prognosis and treatment options – reading the brochure, consulting Dr Google – but whatever way we look at things, it's hard to escape one ultimate conclusion. I'm fucked.

We're still unsure how candidly to communicate all this to the kids when Ken delivers them home. But Alex solves the dilemma for us. He marches up and stands in front of me seated on the couch, looks me straight in the eye and asks bluntly, 'Do you have cancer, Dad?'

I don't know if he's overheard something or somehow intuited the nature of my distress. Either way, there is nowhere to hide.

'Yeah, mate. Yeah, I do,' I manage haltingly.

2

A BETTER WAY

WHEN KIRST AND I first got together, I used to joke that she'd been seduced by my grey water system – a bit of dodgy (and illegal) home plumbing a mate constructed for me to release all the household sink, shower and bath water into my garden through a series of trenches and ag piping. It wasn't designed to attract a mate, but it seemed to do the trick nicely anyway. Now my own dodgy plumbing poses a threat to marital harmony and a happy life together.

Kirst struck me then as a kind of classy eco-chick who'd studied permaculture and lived in a tent in Lillian Rock in the hinterland of northern New South Wales. She had a part-time job in the kitchen of an upmarket health retreat, preparing healthy vegetarian food for its wealthy guests, while also working as an acupuncturist. We were both in other relationships when we met – she was friends with my housemate

Mary and would often drop by, so we got to know each other first as friends. I remember chatting to her at a party on a friend's front porch and putting my hand on the railing, accidentally placing it on top of hers. I hurriedly removed it as if I'd received a mild electric shock, horrified that my body had betrayed my attraction to her so publicly.

Soon after, we both found ourselves newly single. We used to see each other at the local yoga centre and one day Kirst rang and asked me if I'd like to share a ride to class. As I later said at our wedding, I didn't read too much into this – I just thought it was some kind of yogic, eco-friendly car-pooling deal. Within the space of two years, we'd moved in together, become engaged, married and were expecting our first child. Before the wedding, Kirst's mother Sharon told her if she'd been a boy, she would've been called Tim. This all seemed like fate. Then my mum arrived from Melbourne for the big day with a letter she had sent to her mother when she was pregnant with me. 'If it's a boy it will be Tim, if it's a girl it will be Kirsten,' she'd written in her elegant cursive script. Identical spelling and all. In her speech at the wedding, my teary mum shared this story and declared, 'And now I do have a daughter called Kirsten.' There were audible gasps in the crowd, and barely a dry eye in the place.

We had two beautiful kids – a 'pigeon pair' three and a half years apart – a comfortable home close to the beach, careers that appeared to be progressing nicely, a great community of friends. The kids did well at school; Viv distinguished herself as a budding poet, and Alex was my little surfing and guitar buddy. We had much to be grateful for – the full domestic dream. But we both still harboured a sense of adventure, with family trips to the Maldives, Japan, Italy. In 2011, when the kids were nine and five, we pulled them out of school and towed a caravan around the country, 27,000 kilometres in eight months, enjoying the most delicious sense of freedom I've ever experienced in my life. I never imagined our charmed lives could be derailed in a moment, all our hopes and dreams for the future set ablaze by a few words from a urologist: 'This more or less confirms our suspicions.' One of the first thoughts I had when I received my diagnosis was, *I'm so glad we did that trip around Australia.*

I once heard author Tim Winton say, 'The human condition is to be T-boned by life.' At the time I thought this an overly pessimistic assessment, until it became my reality. You can be watching the road up ahead for potential dangers like a hawk, casting a cautious eye in the rear-view mirror at regular intervals, but it will be the unseen threat that comes out of nowhere and sideswipes you that'll do the damage. They say you never see the shark that attacks you, never hear the bullet that takes you out. Before all this, I'd honestly never given a moment's thought to the risk of developing cancer.

I don't know if anything could have made that awful day in the urologist's office any less traumatic. But I've had a lot of time to think about it, and I have a few suggestions. How might a compassionate, integrative healthcare system interested in treating the whole person best deliver this diagnosis and prepare the patient for the challenges ahead? Obviously, it's too late for me to turn back the clock, but my hope is that others in my situation might be met with a more humane, empathetic and holistic approach to the delivery of this daunting diagnosis and explanation of the rocky path ahead.

It's well established that stress is terrible for cancer patients' physical and mental health, that it can suppress the immune system, increase production of the stress hormone cortisol and cause cancer cells to spread and metastasise in other parts of the body more quickly.

In a 2010 article published in the *Future Oncology* journal, 'Impact of Stress on Cancer Metastases', the authors note:

> Cortisol is secreted by the adrenal cortex in response to stress. Social support and stress reduction are associated with lower cortisol levels. A number of studies have demonstrated that stress can disrupt neuroendocrine circadian rhythms in ways that favor tumor growth and metastasis . . . Chronic stress results in the activation of specific signalling pathways in cancer cells and the tumor microenvironment, leading to tumor growth and progression.

So, the way a cancer diagnosis is delivered would seem to be key to how the newly diagnosed patient manages their new reality. In many cases, the abrupt and insensitive nature of this process plunges the patient and their loved ones into a state of crisis they may never fully recover from. The sudden descent into traumatic and toxic treatments only exacerbates this distress.

A 2016 study of 174 cancer patients found 74 per cent experienced severe distress after their diagnosis (I can't help wondering what the other 26 per cent experienced) and 55 per cent were found to be suffering post-traumatic stress disorder. A 2019 study 'Are We Missing PTSD in Our Patients with Cancer?' answered its own question with a resounding yes, with gravely negative impacts on patient outcomes.

> Multiple studies have reported that psychological distress, including cancer-related PTSD, can negatively impact patients' health, treatment and quality of life. Within cancer, the avoidant behaviours of PTSD may exhibit themselves as missed appointments, failing to complete treatment or withdrawing from friends to avoid speaking about the cancer . . . Cancer-related PTSD is often missed by a patient's clinical team, and can impact treatment outcomes, recovery, and quality of life post-treatment.

The study found cancer patients with PTSD often lived in fear, tended to avoid painful reminders of their cancer diagnosis and treatment and suffered high levels of stress and isolation.

My urologist knew on that day he was going to be delivering news that would radically up-end my life and that of my family, plunging us into a world of physical, psychological and financial stress. In a large, busy hospital, similar scenarios are played out daily. One of the most disorienting aspects of this whole experience is being treated with a kind of cool, detached professionalism or a forced cheeriness by health professionals when life as you know it has just been irretrievably altered, that no one acknowledges the dire nature of what has transpired. Let's roll back the tape and consider the possibility of a different approach.

Take 2: Now, Kirst and I are sitting in a urologist's office as he slides a bone scan onto his wall-mounted lightbox and takes up a pen to indicate a large white smudge where my right femur should be.

'This more or less confirms our suspicions,' he announces, deadpan.

Time stands still like a record needle stuck in a groove, a feedback loop of dissonance. This can't be happening. This is happening. This can't be happening. This is happening.

Kirst is first to gather her thoughts.

'Hang on, can we just back up for a minute?' she asks, a rising note of panic in her voice, neatly mirroring my internal state. 'Are you saying that is cancer in Tim's leg?'

Our urologist removes his glasses, looks at us with an expression of grave concern and sympathy. 'Look, I know all this must come as a hell of a shock, and yes, this is a very serious diagnosis requiring aggressive treatment and it comes with an uncertain prognosis,' he says, in a softer, kinder voice. 'But we will offer support through every stage of treatment, can provide the tools and health professionals to help offset the side effects of treatment, and there is much you can do to improve your own outlook.'

Our mounting sense of dread is soothed a little by his comforting words. 'I've taken the liberty of booking the hospital social worker and a specialist prostate cancer nurse to spend some time with you, to answer any more questions you might have, and to explain some of the support systems we would like to put in place. Does that feel like something you'd like to do? Of course, if you'd prefer to just spend time with family and discuss all this privately, that is completely fine, and we can make these appointments for another time.'

Kirst and I exchange glances. Even in the midst of our shock and trauma we both instantly recognise that we need all the help we can get. Kirst nods and says quietly, 'Yes, I think that would be helpful, thank you.' The social worker is summoned and soon appears at the door of the urologist's office, a soft-spoken woman in her forties with a gentle smile. 'Hi, I'm Sue. Let's find somewhere quiet we can chat and get you a cup of tea,' she suggests. Kirst and I are reeling, with no idea what to do next, so we're entirely open to suggestion and follow her obediently.

Sue leads us to a quiet lounge area, offers us a seat on a comfortable couch and places a box of tissues on the coffee table in front of us while she makes us a cup of tea. We both reach for the tissues and dissolve into tears. Sue takes up an armchair across from us. 'There's no way round it, this is awful news, but we're going to assemble a team to help you deal with every aspect of your diagnosis,' she begins. 'Chris, our prostate cancer nurse, will join us shortly to talk to you about treatment options until you get to see your oncologist, but let me explain some of what we can do for you in the meantime.'

Kirst and I gradually compose ourselves, dabbing at our eyes, clutching each other's hands, as Sue leads us through a menu of supportive therapies and specialists she'd like to put in place, the 'medical and emotional scaffolding' as she puts it, to help us navigate the path ahead. 'Your diagnosis triggers what we call a coordinated healthcare plan, which entitles you to five free referrals to any of a number of allied health professionals. What I'd like to propose is that we also organise a mental health care plan for you both to see a psychologist, individually or together, as you choose, to work through the trauma of your diagnosis and provide some coping tools and strategies.'

Sue recommends a meditation practice, and sessions with a nutritionist, exercise physiologist, even an oncology masseuse (who knew there was such a vocation?). 'I know there's a lot to take in but please feel assured there is a great deal we can do to support you on this journey.' She suggests a short breathing exercise we can do here and now to reduce our stress levels, then attempts to explain the path ahead. She discusses the difficult conversations to be had with our children and other family members and the support services we can access, particularly for the kids.

We are soon joined by Chris, the prostate cancer nurse, a smiling, thirty-something bloke with the fit, tanned look of a surfer, who works exclusively with men with prostate cancer. Together, they carefully explain our treatment options, the benefits of early chemo-therapy and concurrent hormone therapy to stop the cancer in its tracks, the role of exercise, diet and meditation to maintain physical and mental health during the rigours of treatment.

'You're relatively young and fit. You should tolerate treatment pretty well, and we can design a comprehensive healthcare plan to help you best maintain your health and fitness,' Chris offers encour-agingly. 'And happily, plenty of surf time is probably one of the best things you can do for yourself at this stage.' I smile for the first time since receiving my diagnosis. He goes on to explain the role of medicinal cannabis in assisting with sleep, stress reduction and offsetting any potential nausea and loss of appetite during chemo, and asks if I'd like a referral to a specialist medicinal cannabis doctor.

With a pen and paper, Chris illustrates the statistical 'bell curve' of advanced prostate cancer survival times. It rises steeply just after the five-year mark and peaks around the six- or seven-year mark, before declining again in a neat symmetry. This hump indicates most men might expect to live for another six to eight years post-diagnosis. 'But the thing to notice about the bell curve is that it has a long tail,' he points out with his pen, the long extension along the horizontal axis, indicating the small number of men who live far beyond the statistical average, for ten, fifteen, even twenty years. 'This is where you want to be,' he suggests, underlining this section of the graph with his pen.

'We don't have definitive studies around why these men fare so well, and it's difficult to do that research retrospectively, but given the evidence it seems reasonable to predict that those who embrace a supervised self-care plan and the recommended approach to diet, exercise, and stress reduction through a mediation or mindfulness practice tend to do better over time. Is this something that appeals to you?' he asks.

I nod vigorously. Just give me something, anything, I can do to improve my prognosis and I'll do it. Kirst squeezes my hand, more with encouragement than panic this time. There is at least a source of hope we can focus on, and that feels like all we need at this stage. 'We are really only just beginning to understand the emotional dimensions of a cancer diagnosis, but increasingly we are seeing real benefits in quality of life and improved survival times with this supportive, integrative approach,' Chris says.

He begins to sketch out the fundamentals of this plan – a predominantly plant-based diet, taking whatever steps I feel capable of to reduce my consumption of red meat, dairy, sugar, wheat and alcohol, and instead favouring fresh fruit and vegetables, nut and seeds, fish and seafood. High intensity interval training to offset the potential loss of bone density and cardio-vascular health from hormone therapy. Utilising effective strategies for stress reduction to minimise the role of the stress hormone cortisol in potentially accelerating the spread of cancer. There's a lot to take in and Sue suggests another appointment to follow up with any more questions that may arise, as well as financial counselling to assist us with issues around work, health insurance and Centrelink support. I wouldn't claim the sun has entirely come out from behind the clouds and birds are merrily singing in the trees, but I can feel my sense of panic slowly subsiding.

'Prostate cancer is often spoken of as a couple's disease because it can impact the partner of the one with the diagnosis so acutely, so we want to make sure we support you as much as Tim,' Chris says to Kirst. He explains some of the implications of hormone therapy for our sexual relationship and intimacy, and suggests a referral to a men's sexual health specialist whenever we feel ready.

We're still in shock but it feels at least as if the healthcare system is circling the wagons to try to insulate us from some of the most severe impacts of our new reality. We're asked if we want to call anyone or just take some time to ourselves, and Chris assures us he will be our lynchpin to coordinate this supportive care throughout my treatment and beyond. He mentions local prostate cancer support groups and cancer exercise studies that I might want to participate in to kickstart my new regime.

When we've eventually exhausted all our questions, Chris prints out our tailored healthcare plan and presents it to us with several referrals for our supportive therapies. We're breathing a little easier now, looking at each other with a sense of shared mission and purpose. Finally, after taking a little time just to sit and process everything we've learnt, and to discuss how to communicate the basics of all this to the kids, we feel ready and prepared to step back out into the world.

It's a nice fantasy. In the absence of such supportive therapies, the newly diagnosed cancer patient is left to fend for themselves, to wade through the maze of spurious alternative therapies, overpriced supplements and other unproven 'healing modalities'. By identifying those complementary therapies with a sound evidence base, the cancer patient can be spared all this desperate searching. Because there is plenty of evidence to support a sensible 'middle path' through the maze.

Several studies are currently exploring the benefits of high intensity interval training (HIIT) and nutrition to address cancer-related fatigue, one of the most debilitating side effects of hormone therapy. A 2019 study, 'Diet and Lifestyle Considerations for Patients with Prostate Cancer', reviewed clinical trials of diet and lifestyle interventions for prostate cancer patients and concluded:

> A wide variety of lifestyle practices may be beneficial in slowing prostate cancer progression, mitigating the adverse effects of prostate cancer treatment, and improving QOL . . . A habit of healthy eating, regular exercise, and psychological well-being confers the best outcomes among patients with prostate cancer and strategies to disseminate the evidence and implement best practices will have great impact.

A 2017 study, 'Nutrition Therapy with High Intensity Interval Training to Improve Prostate Cancer-Related Fatigue in Men on Androgen Deprivation Therapy: A Study Protocol', found that cancer-related fatigue (CRF) was a distressing and prolonged symptom of prostate cancer treatment and its management was critcal to improving quality of life:

> Nutrition therapy and exercise prescription have the potential to improve CRF and other prostate cancer disease- and treatment-related side effects . . . Currently CRF is managed primarily with medications. Natural therapies such as diet and exercise provide a multi-faceted approach to managing CRF, which may in turn improve other associated side effects seen from ADT (e.g. metabolic and cardiovascular risk).

Despite all this evidence, we're offered no advice or guidance in accessing supportive therapies to help withstand the rigours of treatment.

I'm fortunate that my wife is an acupuncturist and well-connected and informed in the worlds of evidence-based, complementary therapies and quickly helps me assemble my own team – physiotherapist, nutritionist, naturopath, psychologist, oncology masseuse. And we have the financial means and private health insurance to (just) afford these allied health services. Many men in my position are not so fortunate. This is not about offering unfounded, miracle cures but rather giving the newly diagnosed patient, reeling with this dire news, some sense of empowerment, agency and control to at least improve their lot and take charge of their health. The message I'm consistently given is that there is literally nothing I can do to improve my own prognosis and my most prudent option is to hand all power and decision-making over to my oncologist, and to obediently follow treatment protocols, without muddying the waters with any far-fetched alternative therapies.

Having navigated a maze of helpful and dubious supportive therapies, I am convinced cancer care needs to move to an integrative model. The worlds of mainstream and alternative or complementary medicine seem to expend more time and energy fighting a turf war, trying to demonise and discredit each other, than finding a sensible common ground that would best support their patients.

By dismissing all complementary therapies, while offering nothing but toxic and debilitating treatments with no prospect of a cure, the medical mainstream pushes patients, desperate for hope and gripped by an intuitive sense there must be something more they can do to support their own health, towards unproven, overpriced therapies.

The alternative medical world, with its far-fetched conspiracies, its anti-science rhetoric, its nonsensical claims that a particular leaf or berry or herb is '10,000 times more powerful than chemotherapy', dissuades patients from undergoing conventional treatments that may save or extend their lives.

I have no doubt that we will look back in ten or twenty years' time and see the current generation of cancer treatments, and general approach to cancer care, as primitive and barbaric. Nothing oncologists offer supports a patient's overall health and well-being; all of it comes with serious and damaging side effects, much of it with questionable benefits and inadequate consideration of quality of life. Promising medical break-throughs take years, even decades, to percolate through the system to become accepted as a part of standard care.

The gold standard of proof – double-blind, randomised clinical trials with vast patient populations staged over years or even decades – costs millions of dollars and can only be justified if there's a payback in the form of highly profitable new drugs as an end point. The system is gamed in favour of pharmaceutical solutions.

Unexplained, so-called radical or spontaneous remissions are dismissed as statistical anomalies rather than inspiring case studies to be learnt from. Treatments like chemotherapy that wreak such havoc on a patient's health clearly need a very high bar of evidence to support their use. But perhaps a lower bar could be set for supportive therapies that struggle to attract research funding, such as those related to diet, exercise, emotional support, the use of medicinal cannabis and medita-tion, as they don't really have a downside, even if their impact on a patient's prognosis may be questionable.

I'm reminded of the famous climate change cartoon by US cartoonist Joel Pett. In it, he depicts a climate change summit with a bespectacled speaker extolling the many virtues of climate action – 'energy independence, preserve rainforests, sustainability, green jobs, livable cities, renewables, clean water, air, healthy children, etc. etc.' A heckler in the audience calls out, 'What if it's a big hoax and we create a better world for nothing?'

Similarly, the medical orthodoxy seems to protest, 'What if complementary or lifestyle therapies are all a big hoax and we create a healthier, happier, less stressed patient with a better quality of life and it's all for nothing?'

Mainstream oncology focuses on killing or excising cancer cells through surgery, chemotherapy and radiation – the old cut, poison, burn paradigm – at the expense of a more holistic approach to human health. An integrative oncologist once told me, 'Most oncologists regard their patients as delivery systems for their tumours.' The war on cancer – the trillions of dollars in research, the biggest morning teas and the bandanas, ribbons and pink days – has delivered slim advances in survival times or less toxic treatment options.

I remain convinced there has to be a better way.

3

THE SURF WRITER

My new life still feels surreal – the six-weekly blood tests; the six-monthly scans; the rollercoaster ride of hope and despair as results inevitably fluctuate; the search for clarity amid the maze of sensationally reported medical breakthroughs; the deluge of whacky folk remedies from well-meaning friends and acquaintances, and ill-qualified webinars and podcasts; the hazy brain fuzz of chemo; the fatigue and occasional descent into outright depression brought on by hormone therapy.

It's not supposed to be this way. Some kind of awful mistake appears to have been made; perhaps my medical records have been mixed up with someone else's. I'm the surf writer guy, the carefree idealist who forfeited earnest career goals and material wealth to follow his passion, to live the dream. I hadn't just pursued my bliss, I'd caught the slippery bugger. I might not have amassed a fortune from the uncertain returns of surf writing, but I sure as hell wasn't meant to develop a chronic, incurable disease.

When people ask me how I became a surf writer, I tell them a surf story literally changed my life. I'd been on a diligent maths/science path all through high school to 'keep my options open', with no idea what I wanted to do for a career. My father was an industrial chemist who managed oil refineries for petroleum giant BP, my entire childhood funded by fossil fuels. The primacy of the 'hard' academic subjects was imparted to me by osmosis. That all changed with one unlikely bolt of inspiration during my Year 12 Higher School Certificate English exam.

Seated in neat rows at desks in the school library, we'd been required to write four essays in three hours, in the days when 100 per cent of your final mark was based on this intense, pressure-cooker, end-of-year exam. You could ace a subject all year but blow the exam and you were toast. I banged out earnest literary analyses of the prescribed texts, Orwell's *1984*, Austen's *Pride and Prejudice*, and the thematic topic, the Nature of Justice, in reasonable time, one eye on the clock.

Then I turned the page of my exam paper with thirty minutes to go and saw the general essay topic: 'Early morning experiences'. This was the pay-off, my chance to wax lyrical and indulge a nascent creative instinct. I instantly knew what to write about. An eager but frustrated surfer dry-docked far from the coast, I hurriedly penned a heartfelt account of my determined missions to reach the beach, the pre-dawn surf checks from the craggy clifftops of my favourite surfing locale, Phillip Island, emptying my bladder in a glorious arc, 'marking my territory like a dog'. My pen moved across the page in a feverish scrawl, as if with a will of its own, barely keeping up with my half-formed thoughts. I was convinced this was what passed for edgy, literary expression in the otherwise drab reality of eighties suburban Melbourne. Everything dropped away. The exam room. The earnest warnings that this was the most important exam of our lives. The conspicuous ticking clock on the library wall. The dour exam supervisors peering over glasses, arms folded, alert to any signs of cheating. I was in my own happy little story-telling bubble oblivious to their stern surveillance.

Once they called time and snatched up our pens and papers, I stepped blinking back into the harsh daylight of the school-ground, no longer so sure about my mad creative impulse. What on earth had I just done? Pissing off a cliff, marking my territory like a dog? What was I thinking? This was the exam that would determine my life's path, what university course I could get into, my future career prospects, prosperity, whether I'd ever find a mate and be able to procreate. And I'd blown it all with a silly, ill-conceived rush of blood to the head.

Six weeks later, when our HSC results arrived by snail mail, I waited anxiously by the front door until the postie slipped a slim official-looking envelope into our mailbox. I raced to retrieve it, ripped it open and quickly scanned my scores for maths, physics, chemistry. Sweet. I'd done well enough to be offered a place in my chosen uni courses of forestry or agricultural science. Noble instincts but no great passion guided these choices – I was either going to reforest or feed the world. Then I saw my English result. One hundred per cent. Damn. What did that mean?

It took me quite a while to process this information. The rush of blood to the head, the spontaneous, stream-of-consciousness outpouring, the unrestrained writing from the gut, apparently this was all a *good* thing. This very official piece of paper on a Victorian Education Department letterhead proved it. I'd always loved writing but had never seen it as a potential career. I didn't know anyone who had a creative vocation in suburban Blackburn. That privilege was reserved for far cooler people leading much more interesting lives in bohemian inner-city environs, like Fitzroy or St Kilda. Writers didn't come from Blackburn. But if writing was what I was best at, and what I most enjoyed, perhaps that was what I ought to do with my one precious life.

Buoyed by this unexpected development, I fired off an official change of preference form to study journalism at the grandly titled Royal Melbourne Institute of Technology. I'd left it too late to apply for a newspaper cadetship (which was the norm, in tandem with uni studies) and so mowed lawns for a year to support myself until I managed to score a cadetship at the old Melbourne *Sun News-Pictorial* a year later. There in the hurly-burly of the daily metropolitan newspaper world, I tackled everything from shipping movements to fruit and vegetable prices to five-point sports results (the pages and pages of tiny type at the back of the paper covering country lawn bowls and horse racing). Eventually I graduated to the grisly world of police rounds, chasing ambulances and asking relatives of the recently and dramatically deceased how they felt, before landing in the sports department, destined for the life of an Australian Rules footy reporter, which suited me just fine.

And yet I tossed it all in for the far-fetched fantasy of working for a surfing magazine in Sydney. And not just any surfing magazine but the legendary newsprint surf mag I'd grown up with, *Tracks*, the so-called bible of surfing, celebrated for its subversive counterculture roots. I answered an ad for an associate editor's position on a whim, with as much expectation as buying a scratchy from the newsagent, but somehow I landed the job.

For five glorious years I lived the surf magazine dream in Sydney, before I was poached by the opposition and moved further north to the Gold Coast to take up the editor's role at new surf mag upstart *Surfing Life*. My staunchly Melburnian brother Rick observed that I was seeking out progressively more hedonistic, less cerebral environments, and predicted my next career move would be running a bar in Manila.

Surfing Life offered me more money, a desk with a view of Burleigh point, a publisher who surfed, and creative free reign that led to some truly absurd reportage of the pro surfing world of the early nineties. In a regular column called 'Life's Great Mysteries' we asked pro surfers to tackle the big questions, like 'Is it okay to wee in the shower?'. Legendary three-time world champ Tom Curren was emphatic in his views but guilty of a certain mission creep in his answer.

'Weeing in the shower is fine but pooing in the shower is a definite no-no.'

Okay. Thanks Tom. Good to know.

These were heady, hedonistic, hard-working days, and the magazine flourished, but after nearly a decade of monthly magazine deadlines, and as my thirties loomed, I hit the wall.

I quit my job, by then as editorial director for a stable of eight action sports magazines, ostensibly on the offer of a publishing contract to write a biography of 1978 world surfing champion Wayne 'Rabbit' Bartholomew.

Privately I was suffering acute burnout that made it harder and harder to drag my weary body into the office on time each day or to remotely give a shit about the rapidly expanding suite of youth culture or active lifestyle magazines we churned out. I discovered I loved to write books, to spend a year focused on one big writing assignment rather than dozens of little ones or overseeing budgets and brutal publishing schedules. While the media world began moving online and catering to shorter attention spans, I opted for the shrewd career move of heading in the opposite direction, going long form and remaining stubbornly print-based. I may as well have pursued a vocation as a cooper, hand-making wooden wine barrels.

So began my precarious existence as a freelance surf journalist, working from home, surfing whenever I felt like it, discovering a belated enthusiasm for weed, puffing on a sly joint for inspiration if productivity waned, and sweating on the arrival of each sporadic contributor cheque to keep poverty at bay. But I sensed an existence here that held the promise of almost perfect freedom and creative fulfilment, despite its tenuous economic basis.

In a premature midlife crisis I formed a band, the Frothies, that played appalling three- and four-chord beer-drinking anthems, the chief virtue of which was our genuinely talented Maori rhythm section. I recall complaining to our bass player Wayno about the financial insecurity of my chosen path. 'All I want to do is surf, write and play music,' I whined, after a surf. He looked at me blankly.

'That's what you do,' he pointed out helpfully.

The flipside to this dreamy existence was near-constant financial stress and the gnawing sense I'd somehow failed to grow up and forge a sensible and viable career. An old school friend used to regularly berate me that I could have been anything and had squandered my talents on surf journalism. Yet surf writing has taken me around the world, introduced me to many of my heroes, financed a home walking distance to the beach, allowed me to not only attract a highly desirable mate and start a family, but to take that family on fancy junkets to the Maldives (twice) and an ambitious, eight-month, round-Australia road trip. It has earnt me awards and bestseller status, writers' festival lanyards and goodie bags, and the singular highlight of sitting next to Thomas Keneally at a publisher's dinner (he seemed to regard surf writing as a fine and noble profession despite my acute case of imposter syndrome). Still, I harboured a lingering guilt I was getting away with some sort of elaborate ruse that would one day be called out, that I'd get a tap on the shoulder from the fun police and sternly warned to get a proper job.

The starving artist thing had a certain romance as a single bloke in my early thirties, playing in a band and cultivating pot in my backyard; not so much as a fifty-year-old with a family, a mortgage, two cars and a dog.

Turning fifty with little in the way of super or savings feels like a wake-up call. I need to get serious, dial down the far-fetched passion projects and become more pragmatic and mercenary. On cue, I receive an email out of the blue from the folks at Red Bull who are rapidly expanding into a media production empire.

Would I be interested in scripting a series of online action sports and youth culture documentaries, which will of course carry their conspicuous logo and be edited in a rapid-fire style to inculcate viewers with a sudden, mysterious desire to swill their sweet, red elixir to give them wings? I wouldn't dream of letting my own children near their product, but the pay is good and at this point I figure I need the money more than any sense of moral virtue. And so I sign up to enjoy the legendary largesse of Red Bull's Austrian billionaire owner Dietrich Mateschitz, to help him move the estimated 7.5 billion cans of his sickly sweet and highly caffeinated product sold annually.

Writing, it hardly needs spelling out, can be a tough way to earn a crust. Not tough like digging ditches or cleaning toilets or teaching or performing brain surgery, but gruelling in its insecurity, the yawning time lag between doing the work and getting paid (if you get paid at all), the nagging self-doubt and the low contempt with which freelancers are treated. The chief pay-off is in lifestyle and flexible work hours, the exquisite luxury of staying in your pyjamas all day if you damn well feel like it, checking the web cams incessantly to monitor surf conditions and ducking out for a wave whenever the wind swings offshore or the crowd thins out.

If you don't ever have the Big Hit, the runaway international bestseller and subsequent movie deal and super-sized advances, it can be a desperate existence. Yet I've been saved, granted my Hollywood moment by the purveyors of a toxic cocktail that makes good on its promise to bestow upon me the power of flight. Before I know it, I'm winging my way to LA, where I am met by an Uber driver and installed in a suite at the beachfront Pacific Edge Hotel in fashionable Laguna Beach. I shop for the essentials, and stock my bar-fridge with Sierra Nevada Pale Ale and a large tub of spicy Mexican salsa to accompany a jumbo bag of corn chips. Major food groups sorted. I have already made a start on several of the scripts, and I'm teamed up with a gregarious and talented South African filmmaker, Peter Hamblin, to bring my words to life.

Sure, my big break has arrived relatively late in life but perhaps it is just as well. If I'd had my Hollywood moment in my hedonistic twenties or early thirties I may have done myself permanent injury. As it stands, Peter and I fang up and down the Pacific Coast Highway in his red Mustang convertible rental with minimal debauchery, diligently recording interviews with notable characters from the US action sports and youth culture industries. Steve Van Doren from Vans, Bob McKnight from Quiksilver, Bob Hurley from, well, Hurley, obviously, and friends, family and colleagues of the late Sean Collins, founder of Surfline and father of modern surf forecasting.

But amid this delightful and lucrative gig, I notice a disturbing development. At Surfline's offices in Huntington Beach, where we spend several days filming interviews, one has to request a key from the friendly receptionist to use what Americans politely refer to as the restroom. I find myself having to ask the friendly young woman at reception for the key so frequently she must think I have chronic fatigue; I require such regular rests. Within minutes of relieving myself, I have to go again. It gets to the point where I start hanging around outside the men's room waiting for someone else to go in or out so I can duck through the open door. It's a wonder I'm not reported to security. If I knew the location of a nearby key cutter, I'd sneak off and get one cut. On the flight home, I make sure I score an aisle seat so I can access the loo without repeatedly clambering over my slumbering fellow passengers.

Kirst has noticed I'm getting up during the night more often, but I haven't thought too much of it – just another unfortunate side effect of turning fifty. But the LA experience convinces me it's time to visit my friendly GP for that overdue, post-turning-fifty check-up, and the daunting prospect of an unwelcome digit up the date.

First up, the doc checks my weight – 95 kilos. Jesus. How'd that happen? 'You could afford to lose some weight,' he suggests bluntly. Really? I consider myself solidly built, big-boned, chunky even, but hardly in need of Jenny Craig's services. 'When you first came to see me twelve years ago you were 83 kilos,' he points out. One kilo for every year of parenthood. Yikes! Somewhere along the way I've acquired a dad bod.

After the routine check of temperature, blood pressure and heart rate with no sounding of alarm bells, it's time to drop my strides, lie on my side on the examination table and hug my knees up to my chest while my grim-faced medico dons the rubber glove. I wouldn't queue up to repeat the experience, though it is less traumatic than I expect, and relatively pain free, if a little unsettling. But something has caught my doctor's attention. 'It's definitely enlarged,' he announces, 'and abnormally hard.'

I've never given a moment's thought to the prostate and its function, or even its location, but something about my doctor's tone suggests I'm about to become a whole lot better acquainted with this particular organ. The prostate, it turns out, is a small walnut-sized gland that sits below the bladder and produces the creamy white semen that acts as a carrier for sperm when we attempt to procreate, or even when we give our appendage an especially vigorous rub in the shower.

He orders blood tests and an ultrasound. Hilariously, I assure him I'm not pregnant, a wisecrack I'm almost certain he's never before heard in his life. The wait for test results is agonising, but I try to reassure myself that all will be fine. I'm a reasonably fit fifty-year-old surfer who does a bit of yoga, doesn't smoke, tries to eat well and drinks moderately. But my return visit to the GP for results does nothing to allay my fears. The ultrasound confirms the prostate is enlarged, making it difficult for the bladder to completely empty itself, hence the frequent trips to the loo. And the blood test shows my PSA, or prostate-specific antigen level (the main biomarker for prostate cancer) is worryingly high. I've never even heard of a PSA, so the number means nothing to me, but it is high enough for my GP to promptly refer me to a urologist for closer investigation.

I get a phone call later that day from the urologist's reception-ist, a note of urgency in her voice as she informs me they've had a cancellation and they've been able to get me an appointment that very afternoon. This is impressive, if slightly alarming, efficiency. But shit is about to get a whole lot more alarming. When I meet with the urologist, he calmly explains that a normal PSA score is three or under, a score of ten rings alarm bells. Mine is 120. I have to ask him to repeat this bit of information, as my brain struggles to compute the grave implications. He orders yet more tests – an MRI and a bone scan.

We are due to fly to my old hometown of Melbourne the next day for the kids' school holidays to visit family and I don't want to extend this torturous uncertainty any longer than is necessary. Can I get the scans done in Melbourne? This poses no problem and I'm able to make an appointment at a radiologist in Richmond, the suburb I was born in as it happens. Will my death sentence be confirmed in my birthplace, I wonder?

The usual delight of seeing family – my mum, brothers, their partners and kids, is tinged with this gnawing anxiety, but Kirst and I keep it to ourselves for now. No point worrying them unnecessarily until we know for sure what we are dealing with. I consult Dr Google and am reassured that the PSA is a notoriously unreliable marker, more useful for monitoring once prostate cancer is confirmed rather than as a diagnostic tool. Prostate-specific antigen is an enzyme the prostate secretes, and a high PSA is no guarantee of cancer – it can be caused by nothing more alarming than an infection, requiring only antibiotics to put it right. That must be it, I reason. I'm far too young, fit, handsome and karmically-endowed for such a fate, surely.

On the appointed day, I make excuses to the family and venture into town alone for my appointment at the radiologist, just a short hop from the hallowed turf of the MCG. I lie on the narrow, padded mattress as I slide in and out of the large donut of the MRI machine, attempting to keep perfectly still as requested. I take an odd pride in my ability to follow instructions precisely in such circumstances, and after about thirty minutes of this joyless in-and-out action the friendly young technician comes in and informs me we are done, congratulating me on lying so still.

'They are really nice, clear scans,' he assures me. Radiologists are forbidden to discuss scan results with patients – that solemn duty falls to the specialist who ordered the tests, and I will have to wait another week until I'm back home on the Gold Coast for the big reveal. But I manage to convince myself this is the technician's sly way of reassuring me there's nothing to worry about. Nice. Clear. Scans. Code for all okay, surely! I latch on to those three words, replaying the comment over and over in my head, examining it for telltale clues of tone and expression in a desperate effort to convince myself all is well.

To dissipate my anxiety before returning to the family I go for a walk down Brunswick Street, Fitzroy, where I'd first encountered Melbourne's fascinating inner-city bohemia as an easily impressed teenager from the white-bread, middle-class outer eastern suburbs. I was what great Aussie troubadour Dave Warner famously immortalised as 'just a suburban boy' back in the late seventies, quickly seduced by the multicultural charms of the inner city.

The Black Cat Café and Polyester Records and reinvigorated corner pubs that had surpassed their working-class roots seemed unfathomably hip to me back then, full of exotic and unfamiliar foods and fashions and sounds and humans. Now I walk through its increasingly gentrified environs gazing enviously at its well-heeled citizens happily going about their everyday indulgences – grazing on empanadas and vegan bowls and overpriced pizza in cafes and restaurants, sipping mid-arvo beers, foraging through books and records and vintage clothes. Such exquisite simple pleasures. Why do they get to go about their carefree lives so happily while I'm trapped in this intolerable limbo?

By the time I get back to the Gold Coast and see my urologist I've convinced myself that he is going to report cheerfully there is nothing to worry about – he'll write me a script for antibiotics and send me on my way. When he fails to play his part in this happy narrative, when something far more dire comes out of his mouth, that 'this confirms our suspicions' and 'the horse has bolted', I have difficulty processing his words. His lips are moving but the words coming out are all wrong. So begins a spiralling descent into a new nightmare world that nothing has prepared me for, and no amount of mental gymnastics can extricate me from. I have advanced metastatic prostate cancer and I'm off to the oncologist.

The small formality of a biopsy, the gold standard of diagnostic tools, is all that's left to finalise matters. This procedure sounds like a barbaric process but, I'm assured, a necessary one to put the matter beyond any doubt. An incision will be made in my perineum, the little patch of skin between the anus and the genitals, through which a needle will be inserted to extract a dozen or more core samples from the prostate itself to confirm with certainty the presence of cancer, its extent and severity. Treating a diseased organ by stabbing it repeatedly with a needle seems like a questionable practice and is not without risks: the possibility of infection, blood in the urine, the inherent hazards of a general anaesthetic and, most worryingly, the prospect of spreading cancer cells (though the fact that they're almost certainly already circulating through my system offers some cold comfort).

In a matter of days, I'm wheeled into surgery by a bloke who looks familiar. Turns out, he's a builder who did some work on our place a couple of years ago who's opted for a career change due to an old injury and retrained as a hospital orderly. We stare at each other with what I imagine are similar expressions of bewilderment, each trying to place the other. I watch him turn ashen faced as I tell my story. He's clearly seen a bit of this sort of thing in his time here. His reaction seems to say, *You poor, poor bastard*, and only heightens my anxiety

I'm mercifully oblivious to the procedure and wake with no apparent ill-effects other than a slight grogginess and a certain tenderness between my legs. But that's the least of my worries. The aggressiveness of prostate cancer is measured by something called a Gleason score and mine registers as nine out of ten, reflecting the condition of the cells within the prostate. This is one exam for which you don't want to earn a distinction. With aggressive advanced prostate cancer confirmed, it's time to meet my oncologist.

I'm referred to Stewart, a young, smartly dressed physician with a gentle, soothing demeanour. My wife and I front up to my first appointment full of questions and trepidation, my reporter's notepad and pen at the ready. Stewart is calm and reassuring. Yes, advanced prostate cancer is considered incurable and ultimately fatal. Yes, mine is particularly aggressive and having it spread to the bones is not great. But it is reasonably manageable in the short to medium term.

'Men can live for years and years with this condition,' he offers comfortingly.

I find myself doing quick mental calculations. Years has to be at least two, right? So, years and years means at least four, surely?

'Years and year and years,' Stewart continues, for emphasis. Okay, so that has to be at least six, I reason, as if this is some sort of iron-clad guarantee.

Between Stewart and my Google searches, I'm soon receiving a crash course in prostate cancer. If you had to choose a cancer to get, this appears to be the one. It's generally slow growing and so my decline is likely to play out over years rather than months. It's one of the most common cancers in men, so it attracts lots of research and funding. In Australia, one in seven men will be diagnosed with prostate cancer in their lifetime. One study suggests that in autopsies of men who have died of other causes, over 30 per cent of them were found to have some trace of cancer in their prostate. Most men diagnosed with prostate cancer will die with it rather than from it. For many older men, where the cancer is contained within the prostate and deemed not so aggressive, a strategy of 'active surveillance' is considered prudent. In other cases, the prostate is surgically removed in a procedure known rather alarmingly as a 'radical prostatectomy'. This offers a good chance of a complete cure but usually results in a prolonged period of incontinence and impotence for a year or two, and sexual function might never return to normal.

Where the cancer has spread beyond the prostate, the picture alters dramatically. In cases like mine, where the cancer has already spread or metastasised to the bone, particularly in younger men, aggressive treatment is considered essential, though holds no promise of a cure. Prostate cancer feeds on testosterone, so the younger you are and the higher your natural levels of testosterone, the more aggressive the cancer tends to be. The recommended treatment, therefore, is to block or suppress your testosterone with what's politely termed hormone therapy, but in effect amounts to chemical castration. This news takes some time to sink in, as do the side effects – complete loss of libido and sexual function. Other likely side effects include lethargy, mood swings, depression, an increased risk of heart disease and diabetes, hot flushes, loss of muscle tone, bone density and body hair, weight gain, shrunken genitals and breast swelling. And that's just from the treatment.

Prostate cancer, particularly in its advanced form, has long been considered an old man's disease, and these side effects are regarded as less of an issue for men in their twilight years, whose natural testosterone levels are already in decline, and who are perhaps less likely to be shagging like rabbits every spare moment. In recent years there seems to have been an increase of cases in younger men for reasons no one has been able to identify. In 2014, a University of Michigan study suggested prostate cancer in younger men (generally defined as below sixty) had increased six-fold in the past twenty years, and that their cancer is generally more aggressive, their emotional distress greater and survival times shorter than older men. Yet treatment protocols haven't changed to recognise this younger subset of patients.

I think it's fair to say a lifetime of enforced celibacy is rather more daunting at fifty than at seventy or eighty. It seems a cruel and inhuman sentence: submit to chemical castration, effectively become a eunuch, and watch all that makes you a man slowly ebb away – sex drive, the ability to have an erection, that wellspring of inner energy that allows you to dig deep and push through difficult situations. To witness your body hair slowly recede while your genitals gradually shrivel and your breasts enlarge. Hormone therapy seems a polite euphemism for involuntary, slow-motion gender reassignment, rendering you neither fully man nor woman, but leaving you in some kind of neutered, non-binary state. Consent to all this or allow the cancer to spread throughout your body. Some choice. The particular androgen deprivation therapy (ADT) I'm prescribed is the same drug given to transgender teens transitioning from male to female to block puberty and prevent its masculinising effects.

The particularly cruel part is that no one can say how long this drastic and eviscerating treatment will even remain effective. Prostate cancer continues to mutate and eventually becomes hormone resistant and able to progress and spread even in the absence of testosterone. And then you will be in the unenviable position of being impotent, sexless, depressed and riddled with cancer. Is it any wonder that men with advanced prostate cancer are four times more likely to commit suicide than the general population? Despite this, I'm offered no emotional support services while being prescribed a treatment that amounts to medically induced depression.

Stewart explains that he has seen men – *enjoy* is not quite the right word here – *experience* ten years of efficacy from their hormone treatment before it fails to keep the cancer at bay. For others, it can last as little as three months. That is the level of uncertainty you live with as a man with advanced prostate cancer, atop its myriad other challenges to mind, body and spirit. When hormone therapy fails, modern medicine can offer only palliative chemotherapy and radiation to try to extend survival times, while quality of life steadily declines. A grim future to contemplate.

All this information never seems to be neatly laid out in one place – it is gathered in short grabs and snatches from oncologists' appointments, cancer council brochures, internet searches and online support groups or forums, and information sheets spelling out the range of possible side effects from each form of treatment.

For the younger man, this misery is compounded by the fact that almost all the literature on prostate cancer assumes you are an elderly retiree – full as they are of happy photos of beaming senior citizens walking on beaches, riding bikes or enjoying healthy meals with their smiling wives, as if they're advertising upmarket retirement villages. One pamphlet I'm given contains the helpful advice to 'get the most out of life by playing with your grandchildren'. My children are nine and thirteen. I hope grandchildren are still some way off, though I'd dearly love to be around to meet them whenever they do arrive.

Another section contains the comforting assurance that 'loss of body hair doesn't make you any less of a man'. The very next paragraph is headed, with no apparent irony, 'Breast swelling and sensitivity'. Just to complete the picture, you are also advised to expect hot flushes, like menopausal women. I can scarcely believe hormone therapy is considered a viable and humane treatment option. I'm shocked to learn from Stewart that this has been the accepted frontline treatment for prostate cancer for over fifty years.

In many developing countries, Stewart explains, as if I should consider myself lucky, men with prostate cancer are often physically rather than chemically castrated because the ongoing cost of hormone therapy is prohibitive. I imagine the medical fraternity would ask, *Well, would you rather die of cancer?* A question intended to be rhetorical, but one that is very real for the men who must wrestle with it. For a disturbingly large number of men, the answer is yes.

Not content with chemically castrating me, my oncologist is also inordinately excited by the prospect of early chemotherapy in combination with hormone therapy. Chemotherapy is traditionally saved as a last resort once hormone therapy fails because of its extreme toxicity. But a recent large clinical trial has found that early chemo combined with hormone therapy increases survival times for men with advanced metastatic prostate cancer by an average of fourteen months. I'm 'chemofit', Stewart explains keenly, and he strongly recommends the infusion of toxic chemotherapy drugs along with chemical castration, so I'll be bald, pale and listless as well as impotent.

I'm not so keen.

4

SALTWATER THERAPY

GROMMET FROTH IS A kind of surf-stoked state of grace all surfers aspire to. It's how we all start out as kids, when we first fall under surfing's spell, when the mere sight of a peeling wave can send us into raptures of pleasure, before work and family and responsibilities begin to encroach on the great wave-riding romance. It's a condition many of us spend the rest of our surfing lives hoping to recapture. My nine-year-old son Alex has developed a particularly acute case and his reputation for animated surf babble has already spread among my circle of friends.

My great pal and former workmate Gra Murdoch requests I surreptitiously turn on the voice recorder on my phone during one of my morning surf checks with Alex to capture this legendary grommet froth. Gra wants to use this as the soundtrack for a trailer for the beautiful surfing journal he publishes, *White Horses*, and asks me to write an article on these early morning father–son surf missions in a special 'conversations' edition of the magazine.

I have mixed feelings. Am I exploiting my son's innocence, commercialising his pure surf stoke? I figure it might be nice to have a record of this intergenerational surf banter for posterity and I can ask Alex how he feels about it being used for the magazine before I submit.

I could not have scripted the scene better if I tried: a grey winter morning with a small south swell running, as we swing past the enormous Kirra Surf shop, featuring a massive billboard of seven-time world champ Stephanie Gilmore gracefully bottom turning in black and white. Alex expresses his adoration of the image and, without any prompting from me, launches into a heartfelt oratory on the beauty of surfing.

'I love surfing,' he gushes.

'What do you love about it?' I ask.

'Everything,' he replies, then after a pause, 'except for the competitive part of it.'

'Why don't you like that?'

'Just because surfing shouldn't be that. Surfing is a nice feeling, not trying to beat people at it. Who cares if you're not as good as someone else? You're good in your own way, you've got your own style. I just reckon it shouldn't be all about the competitive side of it. It should be all calm, like good feelings, good vibe, anti-bad vibe shield,' he explains seriously, quoting a recent Volcom t-shirt slogan. We pull up at Kirra and his philosophical reflection dissolves into excited, almost indecipherable shrieking as tiny peelers run down the famous point.

This recording still exists online. (Google search: 'white horses issue 13 conversations' and press on the little video play button). When I re-watch the *White Horses* trailer, I realise with a pang of grief that it was posted only a couple of weeks before my diagnosis and captures a simpler, more carefree time, before our worlds were altered forever, when our biggest dilemmas were where to surf and which boards to ride, if we had any wax or sunscreen in the car, whether to hit the bakery on the way home. Listening back to it from the other side of a cancer diagnosis is an oddly poignant, joyful experience.

And yet surfing provides a wonderful thread that somehow stitches together these before and after worlds, offers some continuity of simple, playful, immersive pleasure, in the rapturous midst of which I can forget the oncology day unit and scans and blood tests and chemo infusions and doctors' waiting rooms and anxious waits for results. Just me and my boy and the sea.

I'm leading a seesawing double life – between the giddy highs of my ecstatic play in the ocean, cherishing every salty, sun-kissed moment with my child, and the endless tribulations of the world of oncology, where I exchange the happy jargon of surf banter for the brutal language of prostate cancer.

Oncologists have a morbid sense of humour. Men who become fixated on their PSA, recording it to the third decimal place, plotting it on graphs over time, are known among oncologists as 'PSA cripples'. When hormone therapy becomes ineffective it is said that the cancer has become castrate resistant. Long-term hormone therapy can lead to a condition known as 'hypergonadism', which is not a state I am looking forward to.

The newly diagnosed prostate cancer patient can become lost in this maze of alarming language. Even the names of the various pharmaceuticals are strangely dehumanising.

Oncologists refer to patients with an extreme fear of chemo-therapy as suffering from chemo-phobia. This seems unfair. Phobias usually refer to irrational fears of things that represent no real threat – foreigners, confined spaces, homosexuals. The fear of chemotherapy is entirely rational.

Chemotherapy was developed from mustard gas after doctors noted that bone marrow and lymph nodes were depleted in soldiers exposed during World War I. The thera-peutic potential of these chemicals to target cancer cells became the focus of serious study. Chemotherapy is essentially a poison that kills fast reproducing cells and impacts hair, fingernails, the inside of the mouth, as well as cancer cells. The list of side effects from chemotherapy treatment makes for chilling reading – hair loss, ulcers inside the mouth, loss of appetite, nausea, numbness or tingling in the feet and hands (periph-eral neuropathy), dizziness, elevated heart rate, fever or chills, lethargy and, in rare cases, death. I'd say *not* having a fear of chemotherapy is irrational.

Chemotherapy does, however, kill cancer cells and many people are alive today because it does this so effectively. Yet I'm filled with dread when it becomes clear chemotherapy seems to be the most prudent treatment option for me to extend life and hopefully buy me time to find less toxic ways to manage my health.

I want a second opinion and seek out one of the country's leading authorities on prostate cancer, who repeats the view

I'm a prime candidate for early chemo. At this point, I could reject conventional medicine and put my faith in any number of online webinars and self-proclaimed health gurus, but I'm not convinced any of them are entirely credible.

Some people do achieve lasting, unexplained remissions through their own discipline and devotion to a healthy lifestyle and diet, or plain good luck, but such cases are exceedingly rare. I come across more stories of those who've tried and failed than those who've succeeded. I watch one woman waste away to skeletal proportions on a hardcore fasting program at an Indian health retreat via her own heartbreaking Facebook posts. At one stage they have her sunbaking under banana leaves as a healing therapy, at which point I want to organise an emergency medical intervention. Eventually she is too sick to travel home and dies a sad and lonely death among strangers, clinging to hope until the bitter end, rather than at home surrounded by loved ones. An unspeakably awful way to go.

So, chemo it is. Welcome to the oncology day unit – rows of Jason recliner rockers line opposite walls of a large room, with a TV screen suspended from the ceiling in front of each to pass the time. Business is booming, with barely a spare seat in the house. Clear plastic bags of the toxic liquid hang from long metal stands, their contents slowly fed intravenously into each patient over an hour or so. The mood is sombre. Some patients are on their own and pass the time reading, staring at their phone or watching the TV screen. Others with company chat animatedly to distract them from the process. Women in head scarves, vibrant and stylish despite the ordeal; elderly patients who look bowed and defeated; worried partners or friends gamely trying to remain cheery.

The staff, the oncology nurses, are amazing – kind, patient, good humoured, compassionate, full of helpful tips and advice. The receptionist is studying reiki in her spare time and tells me she can see my guardian angels watching over me. Once I might have scoffed at such New Age bunkum, but I'm ready to accept all the goodwill and comfort anyone feels like offering me.

Kirst comes along to every one of my chemo sessions – six in all at three-week intervals. We play Scrabble and bring our own healthy snacks rather than succumb to the sugary treats on offer from the tea lady doing the rounds. Kirst's emotional support does not extend to showing any mercy on the Scrabble board and she delights in whipping my arse in my weakened and vulnerable state.

Only three months earlier, Kirst's mum Sharon was in the chemo ward of the same hospital with pancreatic cancer. Kirst and her sister staged a medical retrieval with a registered nurse to get Sharon home from Italy for treatment. In Dubai for a brief stopover, they almost weren't allowed to re-board the plane because of Sharon's fragile condition and risked being stranded there. They got their mum home but Sharon died a month later. Some of the oncology nurses recognise Kirst and ask her what she is doing back in here, as if she's developed some weird chemo fetish. Grief on top of grief.

On arrival, I get a little white wristband, weigh myself, then find a spare armchair while they take my blood pressure and pulse. When the oncology nurse dons the purple smock, you know shit's about to get real. This signifies they are handling toxic chemotherapy drugs and you'll soon be hooked up to your plastic bag of poison, a goon bag of misery. The best advice I read about having chemo is that if you're going to do it, embrace it. Visualise it killing cancer cells. Be grateful. Welcome it into your body. Bless it. Often easier said than done.

I'm given steroids before each chemo session to offset the worst of the side effects so for a day or two after each treatment I feel remarkably chipper and full of energy. Then, once the steroids wear off and the effects kick in, I feel tired and lethargic with a weird metallic taste in my mouth and odd tingling sensations throughout my body. I gargle baking soda in warm water to prevent mouth ulcers, and Kirst gives me acupuncture, which also helps with sleep, anxiety and the strange tingling.

A few days after the second treatment I run my fingers through my hair and come away with great chunks of it in my hand, an entirely expected side effect of chemo but the reality still prompts a stab of sadness. Rather than resemble a half-plucked chook I promptly shave the lot, involving the kids in the process to try to make light of this strange new development. Even so, I look in the mirror after the deed is done and I'm struck by a new level of awareness of my situation. I look like a cancer patient.

Friends are kind – I have a nice-shaped head, they reassure me. I give thanks to eleven-time world surfing champion Kelly Slater for making the chrome dome fashionable in surfing circles. I regard this strange new apparition in my bathroom mirror each morning running a hand over the peach fuzz, and ponder how it has come to this. People I know well pass me in the street or the surf and show no flicker of recognition. It's deeply disconcerting, as if I am becoming a different person altogether, or fading from existence, a ghost.

Far and away the best thing I can do for myself to offset these toxic effects is to get in the ocean, though it's often the last thing I feel like doing. My saviour is Alex with his hardcore, early-stage surf obsession. He coaxes me out of bed, insists on a thorough surf check of the southern Gold Coast beaches, shrieks with delight at the slightest hint of a rideable wave and goads me into the ocean even in the most marginal conditions.

I'd taken to wearing a surfing hat even before I knew I had cancer, wary of the accumulated effects of four decades of sun exposure. Alex wasn't too keen on the hat at first, a simple black nylon 'bucket hat' with a neoprene strap that fastens under the chin. 'Do you have to wear that thing?' he'd cringe, as if I was the most embarrassing father in the world. I, on the other hand, had come to see the surfing hat as a tool of spiritual growth. I've read that one of the stages on the path to enlightenment is the annihilation of the ego, and as any surfer knows, nothing annihilates ego faster and more comprehensively than a surfing hat. No one wears a surfing hat because it looks cool.

Once my hair starts falling out, Alex suddenly becomes inordinately keen on me wearing the hat. He watches me smearing my newly shorn dome with sunscreen and asks, 'Aren't you going to wear your surfing hat?'

These early morning excursions together are a high point of this strange, frightening, surreal period. Watching him scratch into a wave, scramble to his feet and trim joyfully across little peelers at Rainbow Bay or the Alley or Kirra, or hearing him hoot me into one, makes my heart sing and leaves me feeling profoundly fortunate at a time when I could easily wallow in self-pity. He hangs on to my legrope and begs me to tow him back out or goads me out into tiny waves that I would usually turn my nose up at. I paddle out with him one glorious spring morning at Rainbow Bay, miniature peelers running for hundreds of metres, sparkling as if they're encrusted with diamonds. As I wade into the water, feel its mild chill creep up my legs, then launch forward on to my board and start paddling out next to my young son, all seems right in the world. If this has been my life and it is to end prematurely, it has been a fucking cracker, way beyond anything I could have imagined as a surf-obsessed but landlocked kid growing up in suburban Blackburn.

When the surf is over 3 feet it's my time to go surfing for myself. Although, if it is over 5 feet it's questionable whether I should be surfing at all. I've been put on a bone-strengthening agent but the unwelcome side effects of that drug may be that if I were to have serious dental problems, rather than strengthening my bones, on my particular dosage it could cause lesions in my jaw bone (known as osteonecrosis of the jaw), requiring drastic medical intervention, the details of which I didn't even want to know. I have to carry a card in my wallet declaring I'm on this bone-strengthening agent in case of accident. Modern medicine seems to work like this. One treatment addresses one issue but then creates a whole other set of issues that require another treatment, which creates other issues. A stunning business model, perhaps inspired by the proverbial old lady who swallowed a fly.

So my surfing, never of a particularly expert level, grows tentative, risk averse, conservative, though wildly liberating and more cherished and precious than ever; my own ocean therapy that, if I'm careful, carries no side effects more serious than a saltwater nasal drip.

One late spring day during chemo, an unseasonal east swell lights up the Gold Coast points. I watch Greenmount from the beach, almost as good as it gets, 5 feet, sheet glass, metallic grey, ruler edged. Sets stand up as if they're destined to close-out for 500 metres from Greenmount to Kirra, but instead they zipper along in a perfect highspeed peel with a sharp cracking sound, just makeable at maximum speed. Weak and groggy, I'm not sure if I should paddle out at all. But the need for saltwater immersion overcomes the fear of injury. I paddle out timidly, weakly, like Matt Johnson after a big night out in the Hollywood surf film *Big Wednesday*. I might easily have muttered Jan-Michael Vincent's immortal line, 'I'm going to drown and all they're going to find is this shitty board.'

I've never been great with crowds, but now, amid the snarling, snapping Superbank line-up, I'm little more than a priority buoy for others to paddle around before picking off another perfect wave. A bloke I know named Al, one of those blokes I know from the surf and rarely sight on land (henceforth known as the best bloke in the world) recognises my pathetic state, must know something of my circumstances, and takes pity on me.

'If I get one, drop on me,' he offers charitably.

That small act of kindness is enough to boost my flagging spirits and, in the end, I don't even need to take him up on the generous offer. Miraculously, a set wave comes straight to me unmolested, with no one on the inside. I drag my arms feebly through the water, feel that familiar exhilarating surge as the wave lifts me up. I crawl to my feet by faint muscle memory, flail down the face, arms waving like a car yard windsock man, and somehow survive the drop, lean on my inside rail, and look up at that sublime view as water drains off the bank and the wall stands up and tapers towards Kirra.

From the beach I probably barely disappear from view. I stand in the mouth of the thing, flying, no longer a cancer victim or chemotherapy patient, but a surfer locked in the sweet spot. I drive high up the face, racing to make a feathering lip line ahead, then drop into the next section, again barely barrelled but mesmerised by that hypnotic view, before straightening out ahead of a final, dumping close-out and ride prone to the beach, a medicine far more powerful than any chemotherapy drug coursing through my veins.

As our boy gets older, there will be a narrow window when our tastes in waves and the size of the surf we are comfortable riding will coincide. On a graph, my surfing development is more or less a flat line, perhaps starting to slowly decline with the effects of the meds and simple ageing, while his is on a sharp upward trajectory, and at some yet to be determined point in the future his will intersect with and overtake mine. I want to stay fit and healthy for many reasons but one of the most compelling is to keep that window open as wide as possible for as long as possible, so by the time he's ready to tackle 6-foot reef waves I'm still up for it; that we might manage an Indo boat trip together, hoot each other into clean, spitting barrels, before he completely leaves me in the dust and my health will no longer allow even the mild acts of surfing competence I'm capable of in my best moments.

It's difficult to adequately convey the sheer joy of surfing with Alex, but a few moments stand out. On a busy day out at the Alley, I'm desperately scratching for waves amid the rabid crowd. I see a likely one swinging wide towards me and turn to paddle, catching a glimpse of someone already on it further up the point in my peripheral view but looking way too deep. As I start to dig in, I take a last glance inside and see the surfer locked in the tube racing towards me and I pull back in frustration. My mood soon lifts when I look again and realise it's my young bloke squatted coolly in the pocket, flying through a tight little tube towards me, the ridiculous grin on his face presumably reflecting the same idiotic smile on my own.

AB, as I call him, gives the best backhanded surfing compliments. On another day at the Alley, I manage to string a few turns together on a decent little right – nothing too spectacular, just three clean top turns in a row linked by reasonable bottom turns with minimal wobbling or flailing. AB just happens to be walking back around after a wave of his own and sees the whole thing. When he catches up to me, he's incredulous. 'I didn't think that was you, Dad. Is that the best wave you've ever ridden?' he asks, breathlessly.

On another little run down the coast, we luck into a magic beach break session with a few friends – inviting little peaky A-frames all to ourselves. I'm having a good day, the old body feels reasonably fit and loose, and I squeeze into a few tight backhand barrels, crouched low and grabbing the outside rail in a position bizarrely known in surfing circles as the pigdog. Alex is down the beach a bit having just ridden one of his own and starts screaming in a glorious high-pitched wail. By the time I kick out near him he's babbling. 'I didn't know you could do that,' he marvels.

On the way home, we stop for fish and chips, scoff them at a picnic table in the winter sun overlooking the Tweed River and the towering, ancient, volcanic peak of Wollumbin (Mount Warning), in the distance. I'm normally pretty strict with my diet but I swear deep fried salty potato and battered fish has never tasted so good or contained such healing properties.

I'm not above copping an ego stroke from my kid, but it's the sight of him flying along a wave in his casual, crouched style, or soul-arching it out on his favourite single fin, or neatly cross-stepping on a longboard that really elevates my spirit. I love the way he'll ride anything without self-consciousness, or the preconception that one type of surf craft is cooler than another. It's simply a question of the right board for the conditions. He'll happily ride a bodyboard if there's a thumping little shorebreak or mad backwash mutations off Elephant Rock to be braved or charge in for a good old-fashioned body whomp at the end of a session if the mood takes him.

I've made plenty of mistakes in my life, had cause to question my parenting style and major life choices on many occasions. But when I see my kid happily at play in the ocean, I know I've got one thing right.

5

CANCER IS NOT CONTAGIOUS

IN THE WEEKS AND months after my diagnosis I occupy a strange limbo world, suspended in time, life brought to a screeching halt. I'm the cartoon coyote who runs off a cliff, outsmarted by the road runner yet again, hanging for protracted seconds, the gravity of his fate sinking in before plummeting back to earth.

Except initially I defy gravity and rise to the challenge with a kind of missionary zeal, abruptly overhauling my diet, eliminating coffee, alcohol, red meat, wheat, sugar, dairy. 'What's left?' you might be wondering. Lots and lots of fresh fruit and vegies. And a great deal of green tea. I consult a nutritionist who guides my dietary regime, and, while it sounds drastic, I'm so determined it hardly feels like an effort.

I go hardcore vegetarian, then vegan, then someone recommends a ketogenic diet, avoiding carbs too – the idea being to reduce the production of glucose that might feed the cancer. I'm prepared to be disciplined but it's unclear if any of it's going to make a difference, and my oncologist is openly dismissive of my efforts. The strict diet feels extreme, even to me, and Kirst is concerned I'm going too hard and too fast. She has a point. I lose 15 kilograms in the first month after my diagnosis and she's understandably unnerved by my new, svelte physique.

But weirdly I feel great, lighter with more energy. I bottom out at 79 kilograms, and at 5 foot 9 or 175 centimetres it honestly feels like my healthy body weight. I've wanted to be 5 to 10 kilograms lighter for most of my adult life and haven't been below 80 kilos since my early twenties. But the transformation is so abrupt and dramatic, it's little wonder people around me are freaked out, particularly given the way cachexia, or wasting due to loss of appetite, is the haunting popular image of the cancer patient.

Cachexia is defined as losing more than 10 per cent of body mass, so I definitely qualify, but the sudden weight loss is due to the abrupt change of diet and a rigorous exercise regime rather than the cancer. At the gym my personal trainer mate Shiike gives me two 7-kilogram hand weights to lift. 'That's what you've been carrying around with you,' he points out. No wonder I have more energy. I also manage to re-establish relations with my abdominal muscles.

I'm meditating daily, juicing bushels of carrots, going to the gym and Pilates, doing a bit of yoga, still surfing regularly. I try to convince myself I enjoy my morning turmeric soy latte almost as much as coffee, and post photos of my plant-based meals on Instagram – rainbow-coloured salads, sautéed vegies and tofu, and quinoa bowls. It's just as well I have cancer, otherwise I'd be just another sanctimonious wellness wanker. Despite the onset of chemo side effects, some days I feel wonderful.

Other days my world comes crashing down and it's all I can do to get out of bed and put on a brave face for the kids. It's been tough to know how to talk to them about my diagnosis, and the parental instinct to protect and shield your offspring goes against the recommendation for complete candour. Kirst and I travel to Sydney a few months after my diagnosis to consult one of Australia's foremost authorities on prostate cancer, who tells me I can expect five years of reasonable health. 'I don't give prognoses anymore because I'm usually wrong,' she admits, with disarming honesty. 'So, we see how you're going in five years' time and make an assessment about the next five years.'

We've settled on a strategy of explaining as much about my condition as we feel the kids need to know, short of the incurable and fatal bits. I've made a pact with myself: I'll encourage and answer any questions they have, and I won't lie to them, but I don't think they need to go on my rollercoaster of fluctuating results or live with the same existential dread that stalks me. I'm still not sure if it's the right approach. But in five years' time they'll be fourteen and eighteen, so we figure it can be a different, more candid conversation then if need be. Somehow, I have this curious conviction I'm going to be all right despite the grim prognosis.

'I knew you were going to be okay because I googled it,' Alex tells me a few months after my diagnosis. The idea of a nine-year-old doing an internet search on prostate cancer to see if his dad's going to survive is heartbreaking. I can't bring myself to tell him that what he's been reading about is local-ised prostate cancer, which is curable, rather than the advanced variety his father has.

Many people around me don't seem to know how to respond to my diagnosis, but a few reactions stand out as particularly helpful. Angie is the mother of one of Vivi's school friends, whom I barely know beyond a few cursory greetings at drop-off or pickup, and lives out on acreage in beautiful Currumbin Valley. She starts leaving bouquets of her fresh, homegrown leafy greens – spinach, kale, parsley, rainbow chard – on our doorstep, wrapped in brown paper and tied up with string. Such a beautiful, simple act that never fails to buoy my spirits. A good friend of my wife's, Kirstin with an 'i', organises a meal roster of local women who deliver home-cooked dinners to our house, eliminating one domestic chore as we navigate our new reality.

Brett, a friend and massage therapist I've seen off and on for years, offers me a free weekly massage for the best part of a year. He's the most skilled, intuitive masseuse I've ever experienced and does a nice line in esoteric banter during treatment, which strikes the perfect tone in my current circumstances. 'Incur-able just means what it says, it's in-curable,' Brett announces one day, while kneading my stress-knotted shoulders. 'That is, the cure has to come from within.' Some sessions it feels like he's playing my spine like a keyboard. 'We're just curing cancer here, no big deal,' he comments flippantly, and some-thing about his lightness is oddly reassuring.

Suzanne, who runs the local yoga studio I've frequented with varying regularity over the past twenty years, tells me to come as often as I want and pay whatever I can afford. Mark, one of the yoga teachers, offers me one-on-one hybrid relaxation/meditation/counselling sessions at a substantial discount. He listens to my deepest fears, holds space for my messiest meltdowns, leads me through breathing exercises while he applies a firm pressure to my abdomen, which seems to squeeze the tension out of me, like toothpaste from a tube. One session he facilitates a three-way role-play/dialogue between myself, my cancer and death, like a relationship counsellor encouraging us to make our peace with each other. I leave the session feeling the lightest I have since my diagnosis.

Indie and Radd, the dynamic young couple who run the health studio where Kirst works as an acupuncturist and attends Pilates as a client, offer me mates' rates for Pilates classes and it quickly becomes my go-to physiotherapy. For years I've ribbed Kirst for favouring Pilates over yoga. Our first date was a yoga class, and while she's maintained her home practice, for structured classes she's been all about Pilates. I've teased her that she's gone to the dark side, in the mistaken belief that Pilates is like a modern-day, repackaged aerobics. I couldn't have been more wrong. Pilates' capacity to target and correct specific physical ailments proves a revelation, fixing nagging old lower back and neck and shoulder issues and giving my surfing a new spark.

My personal trainer mate Shiike sets me up with a program at the local gym, below the Currumbin Vikings surf club, an idyllic ocean-front location that costs me only the annual surf club membership fee of $130 for twelve months. A spartan set-up, with none of the fancy electronics of modern gyms because of the salt air and sea spray, Vikings has the significant bonus of affording a view of breaching whales while you're pumping iron. I've never been a gym guy but the intense workout followed by a bodysurf is the best antidote to chemo fog and fatigue.

Steve Snow, the renowned seafood chef of Fins restaurant, just over the Queensland/New South Wales border in Kingscliff, messages me out of the blue. I've known Steve for a while, and he generously hosted the launch of one of my books, *High Surf*, back in 2007, but I couldn't claim we've ever been particularly close. He's heard of my predicament and prescribes some 'enzyme-rich fish', offering to host my family and I for dinner, on the house. Steve's gesture is such an unexpected kindness, I find it difficult to adequately convey the emotional boost his warm hospitality and perfectly prepared fresh seafood provides us all.

Dr Dave Jenkins is the founder of a humanitarian not-for-profit SurfAid, which delivers health support for the locals in the remote, wave-rich Mentawai Islands in Indonesia, and an old friend. Dave starts sending relevant health info, studies and recommendations of dietary approaches and supplements supported by credible evidence.

Another David, a casual acquaintance, sends me an email assuring me I'm an exceptional person to whom the usual rules don't apply and if anyone can defy their prognosis I can. Something about this emphatic declaration is utterly convincing. My writer mate Jock Serong takes the time to check in via phone or text and always seems to strike the right tone – telling me he has no doubt I'll manage this new challenge with the kind of style and positivity he's long admired from afar. I'll be forever grateful. My mate Al takes me hat shopping to protect my newly naked scalp from the harsh Queensland sun. I repay his generosity by selecting the most expensive Panama hat in the joint and he doesn't flinch. Most of these people might never know how much their small gestures mean to me. Just to be remembered, to know others are thinking of you and care, is priceless at a time when it feels like I'm watching my old life recede in a rear-view mirror.

I've often thought it's a shame funerals and wakes deliver such glowing testimonials for the recently deceased that they'll never get to hear, that we should really do more of this while people are still around to appreciate the regard and affection they are held in. My experience feels a little like that – as if a kind of communal wake is being held while I'm still alive to enjoy it.

Less helpful is the acquaintance whom I briefly find myself standing next to at a barbecue, a bustling family affair with kids charging around on scooters and skateboards while their parents throw back craft beers and white wine. She's clearly made uncomfortable by my presence, as if she's lost out in the social game of musical chairs and been stuck with the least desirable company in the room. She stares at me helplessly, suddenly deprived of the power of speech, shrugs her shoulders and shakes her head before walking away as if my attendance is a breach of polite protocol. I'm left standing there looking about me wondering who I might talk to that won't find my company an uncomfortable reminder of their own mortality.

I've been a part of an informal men's group for a few years with a great bunch of mates, which helped sustain us all through new parenthood. It's no one's fault, but the standard fare of marital spats, unsatiated libidos, parenting and career conundrums feel of a different order of magnitude to my own mortal turmoil. One friend asks what they can do to help and at the peak of my carrot juicing binge I suggest they call by some time with a bag of carrots and have a juice with me. The loneliness of the long-term juicer is real, the interminable chopping, processing and cleaning of the cold-pressed juicer is a daily exercise in tedium that would be relieved by a bit of company.

A couple of mates take me up on this once or twice before losing interest, and the bloke who asked in the first place rings to say he is on his way one morning. I'm delighted by the prospect of company for my morning juice, but he never shows. He texts me later to say he'd bumped into a mutual friend and got sidetracked, oblivious to the emotional sting of his flippancy. He never makes it back.

The most welcome comment is simply that I'm looking well, even if it is a little white lie. But this kindness doesn't require the surprisingly frequent qualifier: 'because the last time I saw you, you looked like shit'. As if I need reminding of the ghostly visage I present in the grip of chemo. The bathroom mirror tells no fibs – I'm pale, gaunt, and bald, with a certain haunted look of desperation on bad days, perhaps something approaching a monk-like Zen clarity on good days.

I've heard pregnant women describe how their bodies and appearance become public property, that even casual acquaintances feel at liberty to comment on their weight, appearance, how they are 'carrying', and to even pat their bellies in public. Maybe I'm getting a little taste of this – that my condition and appearance is now up for public comment. I have a disconcerting sense that people are scrutinising me for signs of my decline or recovery. The reality that I will, in all likelihood, linger in a twilight state between health and illness for some years, neither fully recovered nor on the way out, is deeply uncomfortable for some.

The least helpful comment is the ubiquitous and glib 'You got this!' Always with an exclamation mark if delivered via text or social media. I most definitely do not 'got this'. The brightest medical minds in the world don't got this. If by *You got this!* they mean the cancer, well, yeah, I already knew that. It's understandable that some might not know what to say to a person with cancer or feel awkward, but what I crave most is simple connection and clear communication, friends who can ask *How are you?* and have the time and emotional reserves to listen to an honest answer.

A couple of dear friends always seem to know what to say. In my darkest hours it's difficult to reach out to anyone, to resist just going into the cave and wallowing. These fine, highly evolved folks explicitly and repeatedly reassure me they don't mind what kind of state I'm in, that I can call on them at any time. Steve suggests a text signal as a distress call if I ever need him and we settle on the little disco dancing man emoji with one hand held aloft like John Travolta in *Saturday*

Night Fever – not waving, drowning, as it were. Simply being able to hold space while I fall apart requires a rare courage and emotional intelligence. I don't know if I'll ever be able to adequately repay his kindness. If you have a handful of friends of this calibre, even if you have one or two, count yourself lucky.

It's impossible to predict who steps up and who doesn't. There are a whole lot of friends and old work colleagues I simply don't hear from. My condition is not a secret and news gets around the surfing community pretty quickly. Plenty of people who might write or utter kind words about me once I'm gone are nowhere to be found when their goodwill might have made a difference.

One who does step up is legendary surfboard shaper Maurice Cole, who's had his own experience with prostate cancer and has come out the other side in reasonable nick. Maurice is a ferocious presence with his bushranger beard and a stint in Pentridge Prison back in the seventies for a minor drug bust that has left lasting scars. He's generous to a fault, big-hearted and determined to help guide me through the minefield ahead.

Maurice wants me to jump on a plane to California to see the oncologist he credits with saving his life, Dr Duke Bahn. The fact he shares a first name with the father of modern surfing, Hawaiian legend Duke Kahanamoku, seems a curious coincidence. Maurice offers to pick me up from Los Angeles airport, book me an appointment, and drive me to Dr Bahn's grandly named Prostate Institute of America in Ventura, California. An incredibly generous offer. But there's no way

I am getting on a plane to California or anywhere else just now. All I want is to be at home with my family.

Maurice also introduces me to the most instructive text I find in these desperate early days, *Anticancer: A New Way of Life*, by Dr David Servan-Schreiber, a medical researcher who diagnosed his own brain tumour and kept himself alive for twenty years with a mixture of conventional and complementary therapies. The book is the most sensible middle path through the cancer treatment maze I've found and sets the trajectory of my own journey.

In other ways, Maurice's approach could not be more different from mine. 'You've got to wake up every morning and go to war with it,' he barks down the phone at me from California on one of his periodic surfboard-shaping stints. While this combative attitude appears to work for Maurice (he's in an unexpected remission six years on), I'm more inclined to make peace with my cancer, call a truce and see if cancer and I can settle our differences amicably. There's a lesson here – we're all different and our approach to cancer self-care will be similarly varied. My own philosophy has been to regard cancer as a teacher and to trust that when the student has fully learnt their lessons the teacher can move on. Naïve? Perhaps. Sanity preserving? Absolutely.

For all the kindness and good intentions, over time a sense of social isolation takes hold, a feeling that life is going on without me, that I am watching from the sidelines as others go about their exciting lives. In cases like mine, which will play out over years, where the disease is largely invisible after the obvious ravages of chemo have faded, people suffer a kind of compassion fatigue. It's almost as if people unconsciously want you to get completely better or shuffle offstage quietly without too much fuss. To linger in a kind of limbo, a slow decline with no hope of a complete cure, seems deeply uncomfortable for friends and family.

I'm often asked, 'Is that all behind you?' or 'Are you in the clear now?' Well, no, and no. It probably won't ever be completely behind me and I might never be 'in the clear'. This is not what people want to hear, with our basic human need for resolution, for a story to meet some kind of tidy conclusion, for a chapter to close. To endure, but with an open-ended death sentence hanging over you, means others must confront their own mortality, an uncomfortable reminder we are all here temporarily.

People have seen me lose my hair, turn a frightful, pale, grey pallor, and dramatically drop weight, and then seen my hair grow back thicker than before (a strange quirk of chemo), my naturally olive complexion return, and my weight normalise, and they assume I am better. Explaining the true nature of my prognosis can get exhausting. I've become comfortable with the language of cancer, with discussions of mortality, but I sense it is a confronting conversation for others. 'Incurable', 'stage four', 'advanced', 'metastatic' and the dreaded 'terminal' are terms that can arouse our deepest fears of death. People are uncertain how to respond. When people ask how I am, I've learnt to say I'm doing well or feeling great. If they press me for more information, I might explain that my situation is ongoing, that I'm still having treatment, regular blood tests and scans.

Cancer, it might not need saying (but I'm going to anyway), is not contagious. Social isolation is one of the worst and most insidious side effects of a cancer diagnosis. If you know someone living with cancer, please don't keep your distance. And don't reach out as an act of sympathy. People living with cancer often experience profound insights about their lives and relationships, have confronted their mortality in a way that can offer deep life lessons. They're not victims or casualties to be pitied but can be seen as potent social assets who may have glimpsed the great beyond. Often, all we require from friends is company. You don't have to know what to say, or how to fix things, or pass on every whacky folk remedy you come across. Sit with us. Listen. Making soothing noises. Juice some fucking carrots if that's what your cancer buddy wants. A few errant cells that do not know when to stop dividing and spreading do not diminish our humanity.

6

HOW TO MAKE BROWNIES
(with apologies to Paul Kelly)

Just add cacao, almond meal, a little coconut cream, don't forget a dollop of buds for sweetness and that extra tang.

SOON AFTER MY DIAGNOSIS, I get a call from a mate Alan in Tassie. He's heard the grim news and wants to send me some cannabis oil made from his own homegrown buds. He's not making any wild claims for its medicinal properties but thinks it might at least help take the edge off chemo and allow for a good night's sleep.

He does this as a covert good Samaritan for a few friends and acquaintances dealing with chronic illness, purely as a community service, for no payment. Alan's no slacker stoner. He has a tertiary education and a good job as an environmental scientist and a young family, but happens to believe in the therapeutic properties of cannabis.

He's even sourced a special kind of plastic container that emits no odour, so the oil can pass through the postal service undetected. I happily accept the kindness. A few days later an Express Post satchel arrives in the mail. I'm as excited as a pothead at Nimbin's annual Mardi Grass festival. I tear open the packaging, liberate the small screw-top container from its cocoon of bubble wrap and admire the dark, jade green oil curiously.

It's tempting to ascribe this potion some magical property – the kind, unsolicited service, the impressive odour-suppressing vessel, the fact the care package made it through the post at all. I'm desperate for some relief from my broken sleeps – lying awake in that grim, 3 am twilight zone, where every worry and challenge seems highlighted, like the scans that light up the cancer in my body. Chemo has added a new edge to these long dark nights of the soul – strange phantom sensations buzzing up and down my body, electrical pulses, a metallic taste in my mouth, headaches. The promise of a good night's sleep that the oil offers is compelling enough, the rumoured anti-cancer properties of cannabinoids, a new frontier of medical research, a tantalising bonus.

Half an hour before bed, I take a teaspoon of the thick green liquid – homegrown bush buds slow-cooked in avocado oil, so I am getting my Omega 3s too! The effect is subtle, gradual, to the point where I begin to suspect there's no effect at all. Then slowly, after about half an hour, I realise I'm feeling pleasantly relaxed – very different from the sometimes disorienting head stone of smoking, more of a body stone, mild and soothing. Every cell in my body gently hums in unison and I soon drift off to a deep sleep. I wake once or twice during the night to pee but fall back to sleep quickly.

My friend sends me three or four such care packages over the subsequent months, but I figure I can't rely on his charity indefinitely. He imparts his recipe and I soon procure some bush buds locally from another mate, grown organically in the glorious New South Wales north coast hinterland, and begin production. Give a man some oil and he sleeps well for a day, teach him to make oil and he can sleep well indefinitely. Half an ounce of buds in 250 millilitres of oil, slow cooked for two hours between 70 and 90 degrees Celsius. I use a meat thermometer to diligently check the temperature of my brew every fifteen or twenty minutes, as if I'm Walter White in his desert trailer ice lab – *Breaking Bad* lite. The temperature needs to be just right, like Goldilocks and her porridge. Too hot and the THC (the psycho-active component of cannabis) will burn off and lose its potency. Not hot enough and the herb will fail to infuse the oil.

I seem to get the mix right and my own homemade oil does the trick nicely. The comfort offered in this challenging time cannot be overstated. I sleep soundly, free of worry. If I take the oil before meditating, I can drop into a deeply meditative state easily. The whole process reminds me of a phrase a stoner friend used in our twenties, the cosy green cardigan, and that's how it feels, a soft comforting cloak gently descending and insulating me from the troubles of the world.

Once the oil is cooked, I let it stand for twenty-four hours then strain it through a muslin cloth. I'd been in the habit of tossing out the leftover cooked herb, but one day I look at this dark lump of oily weed before tossing it in the compost and wonder whether it might not still contain some THC and what impact it might be having on our worms. As an experiment I decide to make some vegan brownies using the cooked buds and my own self-styled recipe, adding almond meal, raw cacao, baking powder, coconut cream, olive oil, and a little honey to make them palatable, but not too much, just in case the kids stumble upon them. I keep them well hidden, but our son has an uncanny ability to sniff out any sweet treats in the house, like a labrador hunting for truffles, so my hope is if he does discover them and is tempted to nibble, he'll spit it out.

The brownies imbue the house with a pungent and unmistakable aroma. I undertake all this while the kids are at school, and I open all the windows, so they don't suspect their dad's dark descent, turning the family home into a suburban drug facility. Around midday I sample my first brownie, still warm from the oven. This seems like an oddly clandestine operation for a middle-aged family man to be engaged in on a workday, and I quite enjoy the sense of naughtiness when I've become such a clean-living freak.

I take a nibble. They have a rich, nutty flavour from the almond meal that combines nicely with the cacao and just a hint of sweetness from the honey, with subtle undertones of weed on the back palate. Delicious. I have one and wait. Half an hour later, no discernible effect. But, damn, they're good brownies. I have another and wait, remembering the golden rule. Start low and go slow. Another half an hour passes and still no effect. I guess all the THC has leached into the oil. But one more brownie can't hurt, right?

Wrong. Suddenly, as if some critical tipping point has been reached, they kick in. It's a wild ride. My head swimming, my body numb, I find myself starfished on the matrimonial bed trying my best to regain some semblance of composure. It's 1.30 now. I haven't had bed spins like this since sculling a bottle of spumante outside a blue light disco when I was fourteen.

The kids will be home in two hours. I have to get it together. This seems a preposterous position for an adult cancer patient to be in. How old am I anyway? The minutes tick by, I try to focus on my breath and slowly the effects moderate. I have a shower, a cup of tea, go outside for some fresh air and begin to feel something approaching normal. Once, we tried to disguise our pot use from anxious parents reared on *Reefer Madness* propaganda. Now, I'm trying to hide it from my kids. Peter Pan syndrome gone rogue, but I may just pull this off.

The kids come home complaining of homework and school-yard politics and I think I manage to appear like a regular suburban parent greeting their children cheerily, offering afternoon tea, discussing homework and plans for dinner. But it's been a close scrape. 'What's that smell?' Vivi asks.

In Kirst's work as an acupuncturist she sometimes uses the Chinese herb moxa that smells uncannily like weed, offering the perfect cover. 'Mum's been burning moxa,' I lie. She seems to buy it. I think I've gotten away with it.

An ounce of weed goes for around $250, the avocado oil about $15 for 250 millilitres. I can get two batches out of an ounce and between the oil and the brownies, each batch lasts me about a month. So $280 for two batches, or $140 a month.

It's not cheap and fairly labour intensive but well worth the cost and effort for a good night's sleep. If I'd mapped out my life journey before my diagnosis, middle-aged stoner is not a fate I would have had on my bingo card. But here we are.

7

THE REEF

CHEMOTHERAPY DOES NOT GENERALLY put one in a mood to plan a holiday.

Sometimes, it's all you can do to get through the night, the day, the week, the next infusion, the broken sleep, the phantom sensations dancing about the body taunting you with fears of cancer's spread, the daily sight of your freshly shaven dome and pallid complexion staring back at you in the mirror like a death mask.

Fortunately, others have done the planning for me.

Lizard Island is a small mound of granite, 10 square kilometres in area that sits about 25 kilometres off the coast of Cape Melville, north of Cooktown, in Far North Queensland. A sacred place for the traditional owners, the Dingaal people, who know it as Jiigurru, a site for initiations into manhood and for collecting seafood. The island is seen as the body of a giant stingray, a string of small neighbouring islands forming the tail.

These days, Lizard Island is the site of an upmarket holiday resort, recently reopened after being hammered by Cyclone Ita in 2014 and a $45 million rebuild. I'm unaware of its existence until a family holiday to the Great Barrier Reef is proposed by my father-in-law, Ken. We will fly to Cairns and take a light plane from there to the tiny airstrip on Lizard Island, where we'll board a charter boat for a week cruising the reef. Our trip's been timed neatly between chemo treatments, in the last week of my three-week chemo cycle when I am, hopefully, at my best, the toxicity gradually leaching from my system before it's poisoned again.

During chemo it's easy to feel vulnerable and reclusive – immuno-compromised, weakened, tired, self-conscious. But the idea of casting aside the identity of a cancer patient, the sterile environs of the oncology day unit and doctors' waiting rooms, to snorkel and cruise through one of the great wonders of the natural world and gorge on fresh fish and stunning ocean vistas while I still can, before the reef or I succumb to our grim prognoses, proves irresistible. I can empathise with the coral bleaching of the reef – a morbid metaphor for the metastases in my own bones.

It is November 2015, four months after my diagnosis, and I'm four infusions into my scheduled six cycles of chemo. I'm bald, pale, about 80 kilograms – down 15 – and still adjusting to my dramatically altered circumstances. Bucket lists aren't really my thing. I'm uncomfortable conceding my time here is likely to be significantly abridged and that I must urgently tick off my life ambitions. But I've never been to the reef, which seems like a heinous oversight even if I was fit and well.

We fly into Cairns airport on a warm and sunny spring day, with directions to catch a cab to East Air, a small, light plane service just around the corner from the main airport that will transport us out to Lizard Island and our floating home for the next week. We have time to kill, so first we head into the wonderful Cairns markets to stock up on fresh produce to help cater for my new dietary requirements.

Far North Queensland feels like another country, more South Pacific island vibes than mainland Australia – lush greenery, towering peaks, thick humidity, palm trees and sugar cane. The markets are a teeming, multicultural melange of fresh tropical produce, Asian influences, satays and laksas alongside fresh coconuts and pawpaws and mudcrabs. We arrive at the small East Air terminal loaded up with our luggage and several foam boxes of produce, which cheery staff are happy to accommodate.

It is a one-hour flight to Lizard Island, and our ten-seater Cessna buzzes its way north-east out over the Coral Sea, the vast expanse of aqua blue punctuated with fringing reefs and tiny atolls. Alex, about to turn ten, suffers terribly with ear pain on the flight, howling in agony while his mother cradles him. An inauspicious beginning.

My in-laws have already been out on the boat for a week in the midst of a month-long immersion in this aquatic play-ground and greet us at the island's tiny airstrip, tanned and relaxed – the tropic's sedative effects already have taken hold.

A golf buggy transports us and our baggage in two shifts down to the wharf to board our charter boat.

We've been forewarned: she's a simple, utilitarian old dive boat, with few concessions to luxury or comfort. Three sets of bunk beds in a rear cabin for the four of us and my wife's sister, Shan; a master suite for the in-laws; a pleasantly open and sunny kitchen and dining area, and space to lounge on day beds at the rear. She's nothing fancy but she'll do nicely, like a road trip in an old Landcruiser rather than an Instagram-worthy #vanlife fantasy.

Our skipper Greg's a typically sun-damaged, old North Queensland sea salt, a bit worse for wear from a recent fall on a wharf that nearly curtailed this whole mission, with nasty scrapes and bruises up and down his legs, but he's pressing on valiantly, despite being in considerable pain and prone to the odd bout of ill-temper. The in-laws, Ken and Jude, have already bulk-bought kilos of frozen blueberries and fresh turmeric, bless them, to cater for my diet.

Ken is the lifestyle king, a former lawyer turned property developer turned bon vivant in semi-retirement, variously known as KO, Grand Kenny (not to be confused with Grant Kenny the ex-ironman, though that risk is minimal), or the Teenager for his youthful embrace of pleasure seeking. Ken will pull stunts like this on a whim but I can't help thinking he's orchestrated this one to buoy the spirits of our little family since my diagnosis and as a salve to the rigours of chemo.

We climb aboard, find our bunks and dump bags; the kids and I are soon snorkelling in a garden of seagrass and free-range aquarium of tropical marine life close to our mooring. The oncology day unit seems a world away. I drift with the tide, luxuriating in my new environs, kids close at hand, wide-eyed at this marine wonderland, pointing and marvelling at every fish and mollusc and colourful outcrop of coral like the clueless reef debutantes we are. For perhaps the first time in four months, my existential dread dissipates in the tepid, crystal waters. Only later do I learn of recent shark and croc-odile attacks in the area.

Back on board, ham and salad sandwiches have been prepared for lunch, which breaks at least three of my strict dietary guidelines. But I'm hungry, there are few alterna-tives at the ready and, to be honest, the sandwiches on fresh brown bread look amazing. I toss out the rulebook and tuck in and, in the circumstances, they're the best sandwiches I've ever eaten.

This experience leads to an enduring policy change to my nutritional regime – while I'm on holidays I'll give myself a little holiday from the strict diet as well. The stress of trying to stick to it while I am away from home, unable to source and prepare my own food, is probably worse for me than the occa-sional transgression, the odd bit of cheese or ham or glass of wine or slice of bread.

Our little tug drifts about the Coral Sea without schedule or agenda. We fish, snorkel, nap, play Scrabble, read, take the tinny in to explore islands and mangroves and beaches. At one deep-water fishing spot called the Hole, thick with giant trevally just inside the reef, the water drops off spectacularly, turning a dark purple colour pierced by spectacular shafts of sunlight. We jump overboard and snorkel and it's as if we're diving in outer space.

We find an anchorage inside the reef on dusk completely out of sight of land and I take a moment to stand at the bow of the boat and slowly turn 360 degrees, gazing at the unbroken line of the horizon in all directions and then up at a clear, navy blue, twilight sky, the first few stars popping on like street-lights. I have the powerful sense, for the first time I can recall, of being in a giant dome – *The Truman Show* writ large. I can discern not just the curvature of the earth but the curvature of its atmosphere. I call my boy over to see if he'll share in my sense of wonder, but the only wonder he's experiencing is what the hell his babbling dad is on about.

Below sea level, things are less wondrous, the scourge of coral bleaching well in evidence, but even this environmental travesty can't spoil my mood. To be out in the world, feeling fully alive, surrounded by ocean and family, with time and space to fully decompress after the trauma of the past four months is precious beyond words. If there's an ideal way to process a cancer diagnosis, this must be close to it.

Kirst has fond memories of snorkelling the reef as a kid and is dismayed by its denuded state. I don't know any differ-ent, but I have to admit it's still disheartening to see the large expanses of ghostly white, dead coral. In his book *Anticancer*, David Servan-Schreiber poses the confronting question: 'How can we be healthy on a sick planet?' Are my own bones – infested by cancer cells, weakened by the double whammy of hormone therapy and chemotherapy – and the blighted, bleached reef all signs of the same planetary malady?

Our skipper suggests a spot of drift snorkelling down one side of Eagle Island, a tiny teardrop of reef-fringed sand and mangroves not far from Lizard Island, where he assures us coral bleaching hasn't yet wrought such devastation. The kids and I don masks, snorkels and flippers and are dropped just offshore on one end of the island and float languidly with the current, taking in the technicolour, pristine reef and teeming sea life on display – brightly striped and coloured like miniature jockeys in their silks – angel fish, butterfly fish, clown fish, the electric blue of damsel fish. And I'm happy to report we find Nemo, the ubiquitous clown fish, whose own survival has been threatened by poachers drawn to the market created for them by their animated avatar. The three of us are within arm's length of each other and we regularly resurface to exchange expressions of awe and wonder.

I've spent plenty of time in the ocean with Alex, but shared marine experiences with Vivi are particularly precious. She's always been a bookish child with a pronounced poetic streak. When we travelled round Australia, the first order of business in any little town we hit was to find a second hand book store to keep her stocked up with reading material. Viv took up surfing for a time but I think was deterred by the oppressive machismo of the lineup and the relentless lure of another literary gem to consume or produce. So it's particularly gratifying to see her immersed in the natural world, eyes sparkling, discovering that some stories can be found beyond the printed page in vivid, 3D technicolour.

We cruise back to Lizard Island on Alex's tenth birthday in order to catch the return flight to Cairns. Without the ingredients for a cake, his grandma has made him a giant cornflake cookie with chocolate icing for our last day on the boat. The rule about never eating anything bigger than your head goes out the window. When we squeeze into the little Cessna for the return journey and the pilot hears he has a birthday boy onboard, Alex is invited up into the cockpit for part of the flight. Our boy, like his dad, flies back to Cairns in significantly better spirits than when he left.

We've booked a couple of nights at a mid-range resort at Palm Cove before flying back to the Gold Coast, and we luxuriate in its pleasures after the spartan confines of the boat – the buffet breakfast, comfortable beds with crisp, high-thread count cotton, hot baths and a large circular pool occupying the centre of the resort, complete with bar, poolside dining and landscaped tropical gardens, forest of cabbage palms, melaleucas and bamboo. The kids lap up the luxury, reclining on sunlounges, ordering baskets of hot chips and mocktails in tall glasses and whacking it on the room bill like little monarchs. My confrontation with mortality is relegated to the back of my mind.

On our final night, the kids are sleeping soundly, Kirst is about to go to bed, and I step onto the balcony of our second-floor apartment and gaze out over the pool and the night sky, wanting to savour the experience before it ends. I'm feeling rested and at peace; I've regained some colour and optimism, and the future doesn't feel quite so scary.

Something causes me to look down, and there laid out on the tiled patio of the apartment below me is the dead body of a young Asian man, pale, wet, dressed only in brief swimming shorts. I'm dumbstruck. I can hear voices and sobbing from inside the downstairs apartment. I have no idea what to do. I walk back inside, circle on the spot and Kirst looks at me inquiringly. Still in shock, I let her know there's a dead body downstairs. We walk back out again to double-check what I've seen wasn't some troppo-induced hallucination. Already, a sheet has been draped over the corpse. I tiptoe downstairs and encounter two ambulance officers going into the apartment with grim expressions. I ask what has happened and they tell me they can't discuss details, but a guest appears to have drowned in the hotel pool.

What could have happened? The pool laps right up to the back patio of the downstairs apartments, separated only by a glass balustrade. Could he have fallen and hit his head getting in or out and rolled into the pool unconscious? Or had he been drinking at the pool bar and got into trouble swimming back to his apartment?

A man has lost his life, his partner bereaved during what should have been a happy holiday. Selfishly, I find myself ruminating that, even after the most sublime week imaginable, I can't escape the looming spectre of death stalking me.

The next morning, an extended Asian family huddle together in the foyer, red-eyed, clearly grieving, being consoled by staff. I'm approached by a staff member and asked if I require counselling over the incident. I assure her I'm fine.

I'm normally a big fan of the hotel buffet breakfast, but I seem to have lost my appetite.

8

THE GAWLER EXPERIENCE

KIRST IS BUSY ON Google, searching for support for me, respite for her. It is clearly unsustainable for Kirst to be my only source of support. I reach out to mates, but few can truly empathise. In the weeks and months following my diagnosis, people rally. But as time passes, there are other crises to attend to, the myriad challenges of modern life, and mine doesn't take centre stage for long. No one can really know what this is like. Ultimately, Kirst and I feel like we are on our own.

Hormone therapy has begun to sink its claws into me; a slow, cumulative creep but after six months of low testosterone the side effects have well and truly kicked in – a miserable, hollowed-out feeling, like the day after a bout of food poisoning but without end. I lie awake at night gently sobbing and crumple into my wife's arms. 'I feel like I'll never be whole again,' I moan.

Some days I manage a kind of Zen calm and acceptance. I've lived an incredible life, full of more joy and adventure and wonder than I could have imagined as a kid growing up in suburban Melbourne. Up until very recently in human history, fifty would be considered a ripe old age. To be granted a life at all is a miracle. What are the odds of that little tadpole fertilising that particular egg, and for it to go full term into a viable human life with parents prepared to raise and nurture it? I've already hit the jackpot of existence. Who am I to rail against its duration?

Other times, I'm gripped by a steely determination. I will do whatever it takes to remain healthy, juice carrots by the truckload, swill herbs and supplements and train like a triathlete, meditate like a monk, flood my body with white light and breath and awareness and undefined healing energy. I'm going to be the miraculous cancer survivor defying the medical orthodoxy, stunning my oncologist, writing a book (hah!), helping and inspiring others, ushering in a new era of integrative cancer care that treats the whole person, acknowledges the roles of diet, exercise, meditation, emotional support. In time I will come to regard my diagnosis as a blessing that has redesigned my life, infinitely for the better.

Then, out of the blue, the reality of my situation sends all that hope and idealism crashing down in a landslide, burying me alive, leaving me desperately groping for light. How can this be happening? An echoing question, a panicked static drowning out all rational thought.

Kirst sits on our bed cross-legged nursing her laptop, with a look of earnest intent, and calls me over to see what she has found – a website for something called the Gawler Foundation and its Yarra Valley Living Centre in Victoria. I've heard of Ian Gawler, the celebrated cancer survivor, recall hearing him interviewed on the radio and being impressed by his adoption of meditation as a healing tool. Many in mainstream medicine have been damning of Gawler's conviction that cancer can be healed without the debilitating treatments mainstream oncology offers, through a patient's own disciplined efforts.

Both Gawler and his critics seem to have softened their positions over the years. Meditation and mindfulness classes are now promoted by the Cancer Council. The Gawler Foundation is at pains to point out that it does not try to dissuade anyone from following conventional treatments as recommended by their oncologist but offers lifestyle strategies to support patients through treatment and improve their prognosis. Even my risk-averse, conservative oncologist is supportive of the idea of me attending a Gawler retreat.

Ian Gawler was just twenty-four when he was diagnosed with osteogenic sarcoma, a type of bone cancer in his right leg, and told he had a 5 per cent chance of survival beyond five years. A veterinarian by trade and a champion runner, he had his right leg amputated at the hip soon after, but the cancer recurred in his chest and lungs, and he was given only a few months to live. Ian claims to have healed himself with a combination of meditation, nutrition and esoteric healing techniques, such as 'psychic surgery' practised by shamanistic healers in the Philippines, and an audience with Indian mystic Sai Baba (who pronounced him cured). His is a far-fetched tale and yet that hasn't stopped a steady stream of cancer patients seeking counsel and guidance from Ian, attempting to emulate his remarkable recovery.

Ian started the Melbourne Cancer Support Group in 1981, the first of its kind, promoting the program of nutrition, meditation and emotional healing he claims to have used to heal himself. This led to the launch of the Gawler Foundation in 1984 and a roster of wellness retreats at its Yarra Valley base. Thousands of people have been through its programs since, not just to manage cancer but to learn to face their mortality, tackle multiple sclerosis and for general wellness coaching. In 1987 Ian Gawler received an Order of Australia medal for his services to the community.

Gawler's approach is not without its critics. When he first put forward these ideas in the early eighties, there was widespread derision and hostility from the medical mainstream. The notion that meditation, sitting on a cushion focused on our nostrils, could improve our health was seen as the stuff of voodoo. Old TV news clips show Ian debating medical oncologists who brand his ideas dangerous and reckless. Today, few oncologists would dispute the role diet, exercise and meditation can play in improving quality of life and patient outcomes, and it has certainly helped me. Yet most cancer patients are still left to seek out these evidence-based, supportive therapies on their own, rather than as a part of standard care. And there are still those who seek to discredit Gawler's story.

In 2011, two prominent oncologists, Associate Professor Ian Haines from Cabrini Hospital in Melbourne and Professor Ray Lowenthal from the Royal Hobart Hospital, studied Gawler's case and, without consulting Gawler or any of his treating physicians, concluded that he had never suffered from secondary cancer as he claimed. Instead, they offered a theory he had contracted tuberculosis, which was successfully treated by conventional medicine – they argued the secondary cancer was a misdiagnosis.

Gawler and his doctors stood by their original diagnosis but, crucially, no biopsy had been performed on the secondary cancer back in 1978 so it was impossible to conclusively prove the matter either way. But the controversy cast a shadow over Gawler's work and severely impacted the business of the foundation. Having read both sides of the debate, I'm inclined to accept Ian's version of events. Though I won't be booking an appointment any time soon for psychic surgery – wherein faith healers claim to be able to reach into the body without making an incision, using only their fingers, and remove the unnamed dark matter causing their patients' ailments.

I attend my first retreat in January 2016, six months after my diagnosis, soon after finishing chemo. I fly to Melbourne, and spend a night with my mum before she drives me out to the Yarra Valley, past opulent wineries and quaint country towns. How must she feel delivering her child to a cancer retreat? We hug and say our goodbyes; she'll be back in five days to pick me up. Mum has been stoic ever since my diagnosis – only later do I reflect on how that drive home alone must have been brutal.

Mum and I have always been close. She's largely the reason I became a writer. An English teacher by trade and a library assistant before that, she read to us diligently as kids, imparted a love of story and language. She's kept a file of my published works, will go into bookstores and ensure my titles are displayed prominently, and still cuts out articles she thinks might be of interest and posts them to me. In retirement, she's been a big wheel in the University of the Third Age (a national education program for seniors), organising conferences, lobbying various levels of government for funding, running book clubs. She's my biggest fan, and I try and remain upbeat and positive in front of her.

It comes as a relief to arrive at the forested environs of the retreat, to be surrounded by people who are facing a similar challenge to mine, who can empathise, among whom I can drop the façade of bravely coping with my diagnosis and allow my emotions to spill out.

I hope they get a good bulk deal on tissues at the Gawler Foundation. Boxes of them are positioned everywhere, and for good reason. Plenty of tears are shed here, enough to swell the humble flow of the Little Yarra River that winds through the property into a wide brown torrent by the time it reaches Melbourne.

Ian, now semiretired, does not personally facilitate the program these days. Instead it's delivered by those who have studied under him and according to his principles. In Ian's absence, we are greeted by the foundation's current director, Siegfried Gutbrod, a gregarious German of indeterminate age with a mane of wild white hair that brings to mind a modern-day Einstein. Siegfried fled the corporate world and a career in IT twenty years ago, pursued an interest in holistic health and healing and took to dressing as a clown in the manner of his friend and mentor Patch Adams (the real-life clown doctor played by Robin Williams in the film). He volunteered in Africa, then came to the Gawler Foundation as a business manager before training as a therapist and counsellor and eventually replacing Ian when he retired in 2008.

Siegfried still likes to get about in a red clown's nose and dresses up as a clown at least once during each retreat to lead a session on the therapeutic value of laughter. He tells a story of he and Ian going to see the local bank manager about a loan, he in clown costume, Ian in his trademark kaftan and on crutches. They must have been quite a sight but were ultimately successful in securing the necessary funding.

Siegfried stresses that this is not a medical facility, and they make no recommendations about any patient's treatment options but strive to empower people to make informed decisions and to be the drivers of their own 'recovery bus'. Who we take aboard and where they sit is up to us. Oncologists, nutritionists, naturopaths, exercise physiologists, even shamanic healers can all come aboard our recovery bus, but we are at the wheel, being proactive and taking responsibility for our own health, using our team of health consultants as required. Not everyone who attends the retreat will miraculously heal themselves of cancer, in fact they are upfront about the fact that most won't. Facing and accepting one's mortality is a large part of the program.

The retreat is based on a healthy vegetarian diet – much of it grown on site in the centre's own organic vegetable garden – three daily meditation sessions, information sessions on diet and nutrition, emotional healing, and gentle exercise classes. We are given plenty of free time to take in the towering eucalypts, meandering creek and abundant wildlife – kookaburras, wallabies, wombats, koalas, even platypuses. We can navigate a small stone labyrinth set in the forest, book a massage or do some reading from the centre's extensive library. Accommodation is offered in simple, motel-style single or twin rooms or school camp–style dormitories for those on a budget. Places are offered in each retreat for anyone in need who cannot afford the centre's regular fees.

For me, Gawler's philosophy, deified and decried in equal measure by his legions of admirers and a sceptical medical fraternity respectively, comes as a blast of fresh air. He's not advocating alternative, complementary or traditional medicine, he says, which he characterises as therapies others do to or for us. Instead, he promotes what he calls 'lifestyle medicine', defined as what you can do for yourself – diet, exercise, meditation, emotional healing, building a support team – in tandem with whatever forms of conventional treatment you make informed decisions about.

'Believe the diagnosis but not the prognosis' is one of the first principles we're introduced to, as nineteen of us take our place in a central hall for a busy roster of daily information sessions. A prognosis is based on statistical averages, and as unique individuals those statistical averages need not apply to our specific circumstances, we are told.

For the next five days we follow this gentle routine – starting the day with qi gong (a form of tai chi utilising posture, breathing and balance) and meditation, as we're encouraged to look within and find a spiritual dimension to our healing journeys. Our group quickly bonds, and a safe space is created for deep emotional revelation and release, accompanied by lots of tears and hugging. We form pairs and spend long minutes staring into each other's eyes, or scrawling our old emotional wounds on sheets of paper, which we then release by tossing them into a fire. We nominate others in the group to represent figures from our past we need to forgive, and role-play these emotional reconciliations. I find myself in the role of one woman's estranged father and hold space for her emotional outpouring of childhood grievances. I might have once thought this was all profoundly weird, but cancer seems to have cracked me open.

A reverent silence is observed whenever we enter the meditation sanctuary, an octagonal building of bare timber beams that resembles a large and well-appointed yurt, with windows offering stunning 360-degree views of the surrounding forest, a living wallpaper of mature stringy barks. 'The word LISTEN contains the same letters as the word SILENT', a small plaque reminds us. We are being encouraged to listen to ourselves, tune in to our inner voice. I resolve to spend as much time as possible in this space, where thousands have meditated and conjured their own healing energy over the past thirty or more years. I soak up its silent ambience alone early in the mornings and late at night before bed, outside of the regular meditation sessions, as if I might be able to imbibe its residual healing powers.

When Ian Gawler himself makes a short guest appearance one afternoon, his presence and gravitas is immediately striking. Getting about with the aid of crutches and dressed in his trademark sky blue kaftan over a turtleneck top, he looks like a cast member from *Star Trek*. He delivers a short pep talk and leads a meditation session that leaves me wanting to spend more time in his company, to unpack his secrets. His primary message is one of hope. 'It only needs to be done once to prove it is possible,' he says. Their most successful clients are the '100 percenters', those who follow his protocols to the letter.

We are a diverse group in age, gender and ethnicity. Some have brought support people to share the retreat – friends, partners, parents, even adult children. We are bonded by a common knowledge of the dread and disbelief that comes with a cancer diagnosis and what's required to climb out of that dark hole and find cause for hope.

I form some particular bonds with several of my cancer comrades. There's Eddie, also known as Shreddie, a young surfer/skater whose skin is covered in small, angry, red pock-marks from a particularly aggressive chemotherapy for his stomach cancer. I can recognise the surfer's lithe physique even in his chemo-ravaged state and fitted with a colostomy bag. Eddie is the most Zen meditator I have ever come across, as still as a buddha until well after each guided meditation finishes and everyone else files out, off in another dimension. 'I reckon death's going to be really interesting,' he enthuses over lunch one day. 'I'm super curious about it.'

Ben is a lovely young bloke in his early thirties, dealing with an aggressive brain tumour. He's also a musician who runs community choirs and speaks frankly about his journey coming out as gay. I assume his male companion is his partner, but it turns out he's an old childhood friend accompanying Ben to offer support.

On our final night, Ben and I convene a bit of a jam session in the communal lounge area, where there's an upright piano, a pair of old nylon string guitars and a few assorted percussion instruments. For a sublime couple of hours, we're no longer cancer patients attending a retreat, desperate for guidance through the maze of cancer care, but a happy group of humans bonded not by our diagnoses but the universal power of music. Ben's a far more accomplished musician than me but no one seems to care. I've never been a big Billy Joel fan but when Ben busts out a pitch perfect rendition of 'Piano Man' and poignantly declares we're all in the mood for a melody, he's definitely got us feeling all right, and there's barely a dry eye in the place.

We're snapped out of our communal musical revelry by the sobering news from a staff member that one of our number has just been whisked to hospital by ambulance after suffering severe abdominal pain associated with her stomach cancer. The news is a chilling reminder of why we're here and brings a swift end to the merriment. The suspended reality was nice while it lasted.

By week's end I think most of us would agree the experience has more than met its three KPIs — to provide hope we can influence our prognosis through our own actions, to empower us to make informed decisions about our treatment options, and to help us achieve inner peace whatever the future might hold.

I gain so much from the experience I return for a second five-day retreat in April, this time facilitated by the man himself, Ian Gawler, and his wife Grace, a qualified medical doctor. They make an impressive double act. This will be one of Ian's final retreats as a facilitator before he retires, and I feel privileged to study at the feet of the master. 'When I got well the thing that surprised me most was the lack of curiosity from the medical profession,' he tells us. 'What I hadn't anticipated was that it would become a turf war.'

While much of the outright hostility to his teachings has past, some of his views remain controversial. Ian's mentor, Dr Ainslie Meares, was one of the first Western doctors to promote the health benefits of meditation. Meares once famously declared that for some people, cancer represented a 'socially sanctioned form of suicide' and Gawler encourages us to consider if this might apply to us, as confronting as this is, that we somehow invited cancer into our lives in response to some insurmountable psychic pain.

When he says this, I think about my own struggles with new parenthood and provider responsibilities with a young family as a work-from-home freelance writer. I remember at one of our men's group gatherings a couple of years before my diagnosis, complaining it was all starting to feel like too much. While my world became more demanding, with work, co-parenting, sleep deprivation and financial stress, my sources of succour – free time to surf, play music, see friends – were more limited than ever. I felt like a diver having his oxygen supply cut off. 'It's not just a little bit too hard, it's way, way too hard,' I'd moaned to my mates. Did I unconsciously wish this upon myself as a way out? The thought is deeply uncom-fortable and I'm not at all convinced it applies, but in my quest for healing I'm willing to consider all options.

I'm left intrigued by Dr Meares, a psychiatrist and trained hypnotist who advocated for the use of hypnotism rather than drugs to relieve pain and believed meditation could help slow the progression of cancer by reducing levels of the stress hormone, cortisol. Wanting to know more, I later purchase a copy of his book *Cancer: Another Way?* online. When it arrives, I'm alarmed to find it's a book of his fairly awful poetry, unless his words contain some deep wisdom I'm missing. In a long meandering collection of freeform verse, Dr Meares makes the case that meditation and mind power can indeed cure cancer, though I'm not sure his means of delivery really strengthens his case.

Throughout my time at Gawler, I oscillate between hope and doubt. Can a vegetarian diet, meditation and emotional healing really cure cancer? Gawler is also big on the distinction between curing and healing. Modern medicine aims to cure, with big, dramatic, often expensive interventions imposed on the patient, requiring nothing of them but their consent, with serious side effects but quick and reliable results. Healing, Gawler posits, is a slower, gentler, less predictable process, requiring the patient to be proactive in managing their own health, reversing the slow gradual development of the disease over time. There seems to be a lack of exemplary case studies, apart from Gawler himself, to support his claims and he expresses regret that they have always lacked the financial resources to keep meticulous records of the results their clients have achieved. But he maintains that innumerable people have dramatically improved their own prognoses with his protocols, while conceding spectacular long-term remissions are relatively rare.

In many ways, I'm probably a fairly typical Gawler client – my advanced prostate cancer has not disappeared from all the hours of meditation, the vegetarian diet, the daily juicing, the array of supplements, the yoga, the wholesale lifestyle renovation, but it has not progressed either. Whether all these lifestyle interventions have made the slightest difference I am unqualified to say. But I do feel fitter and healthier leading an altogether more meaningful and enriching life than I did before my diagnosis. And I thank Ian Gawler for that, as do thousands of other cancer patients he has helped over the past thirty-plus years.

On the final day, Ian asks us to go outside and commune with a tree, to sit under it, walk around it, hug it, talk to it, or just admire it, as we choose, then to come in and write something poetic about the experience. I find a large stringy-bark and soon find myself on unusually intimate terms with this majestic eucalypt. At one stage I remove my shirt and press myself against its smooth trunk as if it might impart some mysterious healing energy. Ants scurry from the tree trunk to my bare torso. A cynical inner voice runs a mocking commentary. *What are you doing you weirdo? Are you really buying this stuff?* But I pay it little attention – I figure I'm not going to heal myself with cynicism.

I have kept in touch with Ben after the first retreat, watch the periodic YouTube videos he posts to update friends and family on his health. He's somehow managing to complete a PhD on the role of community choirs, always upbeat and full of optimism even when facing another surgery, his third, to try to remove the growing tumour. Ben's work with community choirs and his PhD focuses particularly on young LGBTIQ+ people and the power of song to support them and foster mental health.

Then there's a break in transmission and no new videos for several months. Soon after, I receive a message from Ben's husband, Khang, a young Vietnamese Australian. Ben had lived just long enough to see the passing of the Marriage Equality Bill, for them to be legally wed, and for Ben to complete his PhD and graduate as a doctor of philosophy from Melbourne University. Ben died a month after they married, after a short stay in hospice care. I've only spent five days with the guy, but I'm deeply rocked.

Fatefully, I happen to be in Melbourne visiting family on the day Ben's funeral is held in the grandeur of St Paul's Cathedral, the imposing gothic Anglican church opposite Flinders Street station. It's cutting it fine, but I just have time to attend the service and jump a taxi to the airport for my flight home. I don't know a soul but greet his parents and explain our connection and what an impact their son made on me in such a short time. I sit by myself up the back of the cathedral for a quick getaway, as friends and family make a series of moving speeches about a man who clearly touched many lives and was greatly loved. Khang asks everyone to honour Ben's legacy by doing one selfless and good thing for the next person they meet.

I'm holding it together until the familiar strains of 'Piano Man' are echoing through the cathedral at the end of the service. Suddenly I'm bawling uncontrollably, transported back to that joyous window in time at the Gawler retreat when it felt like music alone was enough to stave off the ravages of cancer.

I stay for as long as I can with one eye on the time, until I have no choice but to bolt for the door and flag down a taxi to the airport, still weeping in the back of the cab all the way to Tullamarine. The cabbie cops a generous tip in Ben's honour, and for putting up with my bawling.

I speak to Khang later and apologise for my abrupt departure. Other mourners must have wondered who this bloke was who turned up alone, sat up the back by himself, cried his eyes out and then bolted, like some weird funeral fetishist.

In a sad footnote, the COVID-19 pandemic proves too much for the already fragile finances of the Gawler Foundation, which relies largely on philanthropy to make its services as affordable as possible to as many people as possible. In February 2021, I receive an email informing me the board has made the reluctant decision to close the doors indefinitely. This news passes with surprisingly little fanfare or media attention, given the thousands of lives Ian Gawler and the foundation and retreat he started must have touched.

9

ESCAPE FROM TWEED CITY

A FRAUGHT YOUNG MOTHER drags her preschool son by the arm through a busy suburban shopping centre – a common scene around the world every day.

Except this young mother looks especially fraught – her hollow cheeks and gaunt frame belie the cracking pace she sets. Her pale, whippet-thin son clings to her hand as if he might float away in her wake like a balloon.

Maybe 10 metres behind them, two burly security guards stride purposefully after the pair, protesting their hurried passage towards the exit. Past the nail salon. Past the building society. Past the optometrist, the Telstra centre, the donut joint.

Other shoppers pause to regard the grim tableau, shaking heads, exchanging mournful glances. Tweed has its share of social problems – crime, drugs, generational welfare dependency, though their combined effects are rarely on public display so graphically.

'What chance does that young fella have in life?' a sun-spotted pensioner asks me, a question to which there is no adequate response.

I can't tell whether the poor little bloke is trying to impede or assist his mother's escape. More than anything, he looks like he wants to cry, make himself invisible, transport himself to some harmless childhood scene – a playground swing, a jumping castle, a footy field, anywhere but here.

'LEAVE ME ALONE!' the mother howls, as if to the entire shopping centre.

'Ma'am, if you could just stop and let us inspect your bag, this can all be over,' a security guard calls after her with a certain soothing yet emphatic tone.

My heart lurches. Intervene? Console? Play peacemaker?

I opt for none of the above. I have enough troubles of my own, as, it seems, does everyone else on this otherwise unre-markable spring midmorning at the Tweed City shopping mall, a location already imbued with industrial-strength doses of fear, dread and resignation, even without the public exposi-tion of a sad addict's petty thievery.

I'm attending my first prostate cancer support group at the reassuringly branded 'community room' in the bowels of this cavernous concrete monument to discount consumerism, a fluoro-lit bunker within a bunker, as if doubly fortified against the scourge of natural light.

My sympathies are with the mum. I, too, feel like I'm being stalked, want to turn around and get the hell out of here before my dignity, my survival, my tenuous hold on a bearable existence and everything, everyone I hold dear is ripped from me.

For the first year or so after my diagnosis, I resisted the idea of attending a support group. I had my friends and family and my meditation and surfing and thought that was enough emotional scaffolding. I felt reluctant to find myself sitting in a circle with a group of grim seniors on folding chairs under fluoro lights sipping International Roast out of foam cups and earnestly discussing the state of their prostates and PSA scores.

But when I start getting the wobbles emotionally, when it feels like the hormone therapy and its nasty side effects are really getting to me, I figure it's time to swallow my pride and find some companions who can truly empathise with my predicament. I'm conscious, too, of leaning too heavily on Kirst. She's the only one who sees me at my lowest ebb, who's privy to my deepest fears, witness to my most desperate freak-outs, hears me quietly sobbing at night when sleep eludes me and a dark dread takes hold. I know I need to spread the load.

I discover there's a prostate cancer support group that meets monthly only a ten-minute drive from home. I fire off an email to the two addresses given and receive prompt and cheery replies from both, urging me to attend their next meeting.

'I too have advanced metastasised prostate cancer PSA 540 Gleason 8/9 in 12 of 12 biopsies. Prognosis 6 months,' writes one of the convenors. 'Now at 4 years and counting. I am also an ambassador for PCFA (Prostate Cancer Foundation of Australia) so can give you the clear facts of this journey. I welcome your call.'

That sounds encouraging so I head down to the designated venue. One of those roll-out banners that pulls upwards and latches on to a vertical pole like a projector screen confirms my approach to the monthly meeting of the Tweed Heads chapter of the Prostate Cancer Foundation of Australia support group.

Inside the community room's bare, whitewashed, besser-brick walls, a dozen or so elderly men sit in a circle, several with sad-eyed wives by their sides. In a troubling portent, they are indeed holding styrofoam cups of instant coffee under fluoro lights. I step inside cautiously, the youngest by fifteen years or more, apart from the convenor Dave, an upbeat chap in his late fifties. He welcomes me warmly and a place is made for me in the circle.

Dave introduces himself with a snapshot of his diagnosis and condition in a shorthand familiar to men with prostate cancer – PSA on diagnosis, Gleason score, site of metastases. In these sorts of medical introductions, I always feel like I have some weird, unwelcome bragging rights. Usually my stats – PSA 120, Gleason score 9, with bone metastases in my leg and rib – trump most other men, who look at me with an odd mix of sympathy and respect. But Dave adds his own dose of dark humour to his clinical profile that I find more than a little unsettling: 'and a penis the size of a press-stud'.

This nasty side effect of hormone therapy is something most men don't like to talk about, and dragging it out into the open is both admirable and deeply confronting. But Dave has been schooled by a Cancer Council convenors' course and he's big on this kind of chirpy banter, making light of grave circumstances.

'Hair is something that grows on the outside of our bodies, I think we can all agree on that,' Dave begins cryptically. 'You get up in the morning, take a look in the mirror, give it a comb and get on with your day. You go to the barber every couple of months to get it tidied up. You don't spend all day fussing over it.'

Where is he going with this, I ponder?

'And cancer is something that grows on the inside of our bodies. Can we agree on that?' Aha! 'You wake up in the morning, see how you're feeling, take your meds, and get on with your day. You see your oncologist every couple of months, but you don't dwell on it all day every day.' Simple!

Murmurs of agreement ripple around the circle. There's an appealing simplicity to this imperfect metaphor but something about it leaves me unconvinced. Like, your hair's not going to kill you if you leave it unattended, is it? No one dies from bed head.

As the new and junior member of the group, I'm invited to share my story early on and quickly find myself tearing up as I tell my tale of woe. My age, my young family, the cataclysmic shock of diagnosis, my grim prognosis elicit nods of empathy from the circle. These men are mainly retirees with grown-up children and no compulsion to work, for whom the fatigue and impotence of hormone therapy is likely less of a blow than for a man at my stage of life, with young kids, mid-career, still providing for a family. Several of the wives in the group appear moist-eyed as I speak.

'I get close to a kind of Zen acceptance of all this,' I offer shakily, 'but then I think about my kids, and it just breaks me.'

Someone offers me a box of tissues.

'It's only a bit of water, nothing to be embarrassed about,' Dave offers comfortingly as I wipe my tears away.

'I've tried to take a holistic approach to my diagnosis,' I press on, but this is a term that clearly triggers some alarm bells for several of the men.

'Oh, that holistic stuff doesn't work. Stay away from that,' one old bloke counsels sternly. *Do you even know what the word holistic means?* I want to yell at him.

'Who was that other bloke who reckoned he'd heal himself with pumpkin seeds? What was his name again?' he asks.

The stark reality of this kind of group is that most only leave it one way – though there's no shortage of new recruits; an endless conveyor belt of despair.

The convenor attempts to get the discussion back on track, as he's been trained. And no one can accuse him of gilding the lily or peddling false hope. 'You've been given your use-by date. You might have five or six years. Draw up your bucket list, ask the kids what they'd like to do with you before you're gone and get on with it,' he prescribes almost flippantly. 'Your oncologist's job is to keep you alive for as long as possible.'

I almost physically recoil in my chair. These are not my people, I quickly surmise.

I don't wish to sound ageist, and it's not fair or rational, but I feel a bit resentful of the older members of the group. They've had a good innings. Many have been diagnosed with localised prostate cancer, had the thing ripped out and are now freaked out that their PSA is gradually rising again. Some track the progress of their PSA to the third decimal place, terrified that the cancer may have escaped the prostate before its removal.

'Last month my PSA was 0.015 and now it's 0.021,' one complains, and I find I have 0.000 sympathy. I'm their worst fears made manifest.

They'll get another four or five years with conventional treatment, perhaps longer (prostate cancer tends to be less aggressive in older men), are unlikely to have been humping like porn stars prior to their diagnosis, and from where I sit it doesn't seem such a wretched fate to see out your twilight years in such a fashion. If someone offered me reasonable health until age seventy or eighty and then a slow decline, I'd take it in a heartbeat. Something's going to take you out sooner or later, right? Half of us will be diagnosed with some form of cancer in our lifetimes. They seem to have little in common with my own desperate circumstances.

But then one of these older gents takes his turn sharing how he's worked his whole life to look forward to retirement, how he and his wife had planned the great grey nomads' round-Australia road trip. Now he's spending his retirement in medical appointments, battling fatigue and anxiety. His wife nods sadly in agreement. And I realise this isn't a competition to see who's been dealt the toughest hand, that the goal here is shared empathy.

As well intentioned as it all is, I find the experience as deeply depressing as I'd feared. But Dave the convenor asks me if

I want to get a coffee after the meeting and I figure, why not? We sit at a table in the middle of the busy shopping centre after the group disperses and he grabs a takeaway coffee, tipping several sachets of sugar into it. He notices my look of surprise. 'It's nonsense that sugar feeds cancer, you know,' he declares emphatically. I've ducked into an adjacent health food shop and grabbed myself a turmeric and ginger kombucha, which he regards with similar suspicion. 'And there's no evidence that turmeric suppresses cancer either.'

Despite our different approaches to our diagnoses, we chat amiably enough for half an hour or so. Outside the support group, he seems to have dropped his cheery, sunny, look-on-the-bright-side, cup-half-full demeanour. He tells me that when he'd done the training to become a support group convenor, he'd been asked to think of some positives that had come out of his diagnosis. 'I thought about it, and I couldn't come up with a single thing,' he reckons solemnly. Off the top of my head, I silently list: an established meditation practice, reduced workload, reduced stress, healthier diet, more surfing time, heightened appreciation of a myriad of life's simple pleasures, improved overall health, a fuller head of hair after the initial ravages of chemo, and learning to acutely cherish all of my familial relationships and close friendships.

I beat a hasty retreat to the car park and vow never to return.

Yet I'm still beset with feelings of loneliness, a sense no one really understands what I'm going through and how I feel. Mine is a largely invisible disease. People often default to a positive, optimistic assessment of my circumstances even without any prior knowledge. 'How long have you been in remission?' they ask. *Ah, I'm not.* Or, 'Lucky they got it early?' *No, they didn't.* Or, 'My Uncle Arthur had prostate cancer and he's still kicking twenty years later.' *Your Uncle Arthur had localised prostate cancer, they ripped it out and, for all intents and purposes, he is cured.*

So I still feel a nagging desire to connect with other men facing the same health challenges; ideally other younger men with advanced prostate cancer and an interest in an integrative approach to managing their disease. But as far as I can tell, no such forum exists.

What I do find is an online forum for men with advanced prostate cancer that provides a space where members can post questions or share experiences and have other men dealing with a similar diagnosis respond. If you want to, you can post your own case study and update it periodically to keep others abreast of your health and any developments. Longstanding members can flag themselves as potential mentors for men recently diagnosed. The website proves an invaluable resource and I often take advantage of it to get other men's perspectives on treatment options or how they are dealing with the side effects and challenges. They do, however, have a policy that any discussion of 'alternative' therapies is strictly off limits. The founder and moderator of the site uses the title 'Jim (not a doctor)' at the start of all his posts.

They also hold regular 'put a face to a name' days where members in a particular city or region can catch up in person, so I decide to go along to one in Brisbane. The venue is a cavernous RSL club on the city's southern outskirts, about as depressing an environment as the Tweed City community room, with a large gaming room extracting the pensions of its elderly clientele. Again, I seem to be the youngest man present by a good ten or fifteen years, except for one other bloke who might be only a few years my senior. One of the many side effects of prolonged hormone treatment is premature ageing, so I could be way off the mark here, but I comment to Jim the convenor, 'I guess I'm the junior member of the group.'

Jim, a silver-haired, bearded gent who I'd pick as around seventy, seems puzzled. 'Why? Do we look old?' he asks.

I've long gotten used to following a strict, plant-based diet as an essential element of my self-care. So I'm a little surprised to see the assembled old boys merrily tucking into the club's staple fare of spaghetti bol, chicken parma, and deep-fried fish and chips. There isn't much on the menu that meets my dietary requirements, but I eventually settle on a salad, which I pick at while I listen to the buzz of conversation around me, names of pharmaceuticals bandied around and scribbled down by dutiful wives. Most of these blokes seem to know each other so it's a little hard to get a word in.

I've booked myself a flight to Melbourne to attend a conference devoted to holistic cancer care at an organisation called the National Institute for Integrative Medicine (NIIM). At one stage, I find myself sitting next to Jim, and mention my upcoming trip as I figure it might yield some information useful to others. He seems deeply taken aback.

'Oh, I'd be careful of that,' he cautions.

'Why?' I ask.

Several others have taken an interest in this conversation now, as if this is perhaps a semi-regular event, the wise elder taking to task the uppity youngster with spurious ideas on alternative medicine.

'Integrative is one of those weasel words like "alternative" or "complementary" for things that are unproven,' Jim claims.

My understanding of the term integrative medicine is that it is practised by qualified medical doctors who integrate elements of natural or complementary therapies where there is compelling evidence of their efficacy. But Jim is having none of it.

'Basically, there is medicine over here that is evidence-based,' he indicates with his left hand. 'And everything else is over here, alternative, complementary, integrative, call it what you like,' he gestures with his right hand, 'until it is proven and then it comes over here and can be called medicine.' He brings his right hand over to his left to demonstrate.

'But it takes a long time to get from there to here,' I suggest.

'No, it doesn't,' he declares with an air of finality that suggests he wants the matter closed.

All this is said in front of half a dozen others, and I feel both shut down and shamed. I leave soon after. I won't be returning to the 'put a face to a name' gathering.

I understand the need for medical and scientific rigour, especially when it comes to cancer treatments. It's all too easy to exploit the vulnerability and desperation of cancer patients, and there's no shortage of shameless grifters happy to do just that. But anyone dismissive of the value of an integrative approach should read David Servan-Schreiber's

Anti-Cancer: A New Way Of Life. After his own cancer diagnosis, Dr Servan-Schreiber became co-founder and director of the Center for Integrative Medicine at the University of Pittsburgh Medical Centre and was a strong advocate for an integrative approach to cancer care.

In 2010, he defined integrative medicine as a comprehensive treatment plan that addressed the physical, psychological-spiritual and social dimensions of a cancer diagnosis, to improve quality of life, manage symptoms and improve efficacy of conventional treatments. He wrote:

> It is time to provide our patients the education and clinical tools necessary to support an anti-cancer lifestyle to help them remain cancer free and to improve clinical outcomes, quality of life, and symptom control for those with cancer and cancer survivors. We need to empower people to become active participants in their own health. We need to show them how to best care for themselves; not only because they will feel better if they get involved, but because it's good science and good medicine.

This is what I would have told Jim if I had thought of it at the time, rather than stewing on my humiliation all through the long drive home to the Gold Coast.

10

MOVING HOUSE

THE LAST THING I feel like doing twelve months into a cancer diagnosis, six months after finishing chemo, is move house.

Midwinter 2016, we've been granted a month's guest residency in my father-in-law Ken's classic old beachfront home while he and his wife Jude are away. This is a rare treat, falling asleep to the restless murmur of the ocean, rising with the sun and trotting across the back lawn straight onto the beach, watching our son paddle out in the tiny waves, ablaze with the pink and orange sunrise, while I sit on the sand with our poodle, Lucky.

In moments like these, I manage to feel profoundly at peace, grateful even, still disoriented by my dire circumstances, but beginning to learn to drop into these golden moments as they appear and soak them up, to imbibe them like a tonic to fortify me against the cyclical descents into despair and dread.

But the move I'm referring to is a bigger, more permanent one than house-sitting my in-laws' dream beach home. A text pops up on my phone from Kirst one day out of the blue. 'I've found our new home,' she's typed, with a photo of a for sale sign attached. Oh, I didn't even know we were looking. The sign depicts a low-set, blond brick, late sixties beach house in the neighbouring suburb of Tugun, in a street Kirst reveals she has been driving up and down just waiting for something to come on the market.

I guess we'd better sell the old one then, I think.

Our current home is a timber pole house on a steep block surrounded by towering gum trees. I've lived here for twenty-five of my fifty-one years, the longest I've lived anywhere. My old dog Boo Boo, an eccentric kelpie–red cattle dog cross who resembled a dingo, is buried in the backyard. The house has hosted many fine parties, jam sessions, late-night shenanigans and has moved through several discrete eras – from grubby surfer share house to cosy love nest to a warm and tasteful family home. Kirst has overseen these dramatic makeovers, with renovations and soft furnishings and decorative touches – what I refer to fondly as lifestyle improvements. But she's keen to make a fresh start.

This has been a live issue for a while, and I've been the reluctant party. I have so much history here: have written five books, created a lifestyle around surfing and writing about it, evolved from a young hedonist to a responsible family man. After the many moves of my childhood, this is the most stable home I've known.

I bought it as a single, unencumbered 26-year-old who had

never previously even considered home ownership, because it seemed ridiculously cheap after moving north from Sydney's inflated real estate prices. In 1991 I earnt $45,000 gross as editor of *Surfing Life* and bought the place for $135,000, the last time any surf journalist anywhere in the world would buy a house that was walking distance to quality waves for the equivalent of three years' salary.

Ever the pragmatist, Kirst is thinking of the future, of a time when we might require a more low-maintenance home, not surrounded by tall trees, where the gutters don't require regular clearing, where heavy branches don't fall on the roof in high winds, where the wild jungle of a garden doesn't require constant taming and bush turkeys don't run amok digging everything up. The unspoken subtext to this is to prepare for a time when my health deteriorates and these domestic duties are beyond me, or I'm no longer around to perform them.

This is a confronting topic but, in the end, I can't deny Kirst. She may well have to fashion a life for herself and the kids without me and I figure it's the least I can do to assist her in that process while I'm still here. Plus, there is the small matter of the neighbours from hell.

We've had a bad run with neighbours in what is otherwise an idyllic, leafy cul-de-sac, high on a hill that catches the breeze and affords what real estate agents are fond of calling filtered ocean views through the trees. First there was the old biker Vietnam vet and his family with a crop of hydro growing in a small room under the house and a V8 Charger he liked to rev loudly at 5 am when he left for work as a butcher. Our requests to try to minimise the pre-dawn cacophony only encouraged him to rev the throaty beast more loudly. Karma caught up with him when I woke one morning to find their place crawling with police in hazmat suits busting him for his crop. They sold up and were gone within a month.

But the greater threat to neighbourly peace comes from a childless Boomer couple at the end of our cul-de-sac, your classic Karen and Darren, who take exception to children playing in the street. Our road winds up the ridge of a hill, with steep blocks falling away on either side, and the turning circle at the end is the only flat area available. The neighbourhood kids will often kick a ball or ride bikes here, but the couple, both schoolteachers, wage a campaign of terror and intimidation to try to discourage this innocent play. Things came to a head years ago when I was kicking a footy with a then five-year-old Alex, long before my diagnosis, and the lady of the house emerged to spray a high-pressure hose in my face.

Another neighbour told me later she'd been gazing out her window at the time, thinking what a heartwarming sight it was watching a father and son kick a ball back and forth, when Karen shattered the happy scene. Things only deteriorated from there. They hurled abuse, ran over my kid's ball, got in a fist fight with another neighbour, and five other households eventually sold up and moved out of the street because of their hostilities.

After my diagnosis and during chemo, once my hair had fallen out, they had taken to driving past me pointing, laughing and yelling, 'Aren't you dead yet?' I kid you not. I'm not normally one to wish ill on others, but in a just world it wouldn't be me with the cancer diagnosis. Kirst turns full lioness protecting her brood, takes them to court and gets a restraining order against them, and that shuts them up for a while but it's clearly time to go. Even so, the idea of buying and selling houses, particularly in that order, while managing my health feels overwhelming.

This otherwise fraught process is assisted by a dream real estate agent, Paul, who takes charge of both the purchase of our new home and the sale of our old one with a cheery efficiency. It's an anxious few months just the same. The sale of our old place is complicated by torrential rain that floods our downstairs office and guestroom, requiring some hasty repairs. My mates help out with a working bee to clean up our wild garden for inspection.

In the end, we find a lovely young family who fall in the love with the place and the deal is done, for slightly less than we'd hoped. And Coral and Graham, the old couple selling the place my wife has fallen in love with, eventually accept an offer slightly above what we'd hoped to pay, after some delicate negotiations by Paul. We're moving. Coral and Graham have lived in this cute hilltop home for forty years, raised a family and are now moving into a retirement village. It's an emotional departure and they invite us over to pass the baton. Graham shows me how to operate the pool filter and they introduce us to all the idiosyncrasies of windows and keys and locks and stoves.

Paul comes along to witness the signing of contracts but before we get to that formality Coral asks if she can pray for me. Tugun is a small town. Turns out Coral is Kirst's old primary school music teacher. She's heard about my diagnosis and invites Kirst, Graham and I into a huddle as Paul watches on bemused, perplexed by this unexpected segue from contract signing to faith healing.

'Oh Lord, heal this man,' she thunders like a preacher. 'The cancer will leave his body and the doctors will be amazed at this miracle.' Coral has her arms around our shoulders, pulling us into a tight circle with surprising strength, so we are suddenly on more intimate terms with our vendors than we might have expected. I'm not a religious man but I'm touched by her sincerity.

We're only moving about a kilometre as the crow flies, but it feels like a monumental event in our family's life, leaving the only home we've collectively known. The sheer volume of stuff we've accumulated and the prospect of relocating it all is frightening. Family and friends chip in, moving furniture and packing boxes. In the midst of the madness, I slide my son's bed out from the wall to sweep behind it and find a hand-written note from his sister in red texta: 'Dear Alex, I promise everything will be okay. Love, Vivi.' Oh, my heart. When did she write this? Was it in response to my diagnosis? I stare at her neat handwriting and try to imagine the emotional state it was written in and how it was received.

Viv has always had a way with words, and a knowing presence beyond her years. There's a potency to her use of language, from astute casual remarks (at age five, she flummoxed her grandma by asking 'What genre of literature do you enjoy?') to a flare for poetry that will no doubt bloom in the years ahead. Those few words in texta on a scrap of paper only strengthen my resolve to somehow defy my prognosis, to make good on her promise to her little brother.

The gods and Paul smile on us and miraculously we're able to orchestrate settlement for both properties on the same day. The removalist truck arrives in the morning, and I watch the contents of our home get carried out piece by piece. A few friends help with the smaller and more fragile stuff – crockery, guitars, surfboards, pot plants. Back and forth we go all day relocating our lives all the way to the next postcode.

How far we've strayed from our nomadic roots. How easily humans once moved across this landscape, relocating according to the seasons and food sources, finding everything they needed in their environment. Now it requires a small army, a large truck and all day to move a family of four a mere kilometre. And it's considered one of the most stressful events in our lives. At the end of our exertions, we'll be living among piles of boxes for days or weeks and freaking out about what to have for dinner. We're a strange species.

But the new place is a joy and Kirst's longed-for fresh start delivers a welcome sense of renewal and excitement after our annus horribilis. The place isn't big but Kirst has a vision to convert the garage into the master bedroom and parental retreat; it is already fully lined, and has its own bathroom – it was a deluxe garage where Graham restored vintage cars. As we begin to set it up with our furniture it feels like some cool inner-city warehouse apartment. We have a pool, a big front lawn and a view of the Pacific Ocean that takes in Coolangatta Bay and its triumvirate of point breaks – Snapper, Greenmount, Kirra.

For now, this feels like a good place to heal, where I can sit and watch the ocean's changing moods from my bed, the lounge or the front porch, away from the neighbours from hell. The kids can walk to the beach and the shops, Alex can ride to the skate park, Vivi's school bus leaves from the bottom of our street. The hospital I visit monthly is just down the road, about a three-minute drive. We are, more than at any time since my diagnosis, sorted.

I feel like declaring they'll carry me out of here in a box, but that particular chestnut cuts a bit close to the bone.

11

SIT DOWN AND
SHUT UP

I AM HYPERVENTILATING. My arms are waving about wildly, involuntarily, in what must appear like a reasonable impersonation of the *Lost In Space* robot warning Will Robinson of some impending danger. My fingers have stiffened into contorted claws.

Strictly speaking, my spontaneous piece of performance art does not adhere to the traditional practice of Vipassana meditation, which aims to cultivate stillness and equanimity. Instead, in my case, it appears to have triggered some sort of spontaneous exorcism.

If you were a fly on the wall at a typical Vipassana retreat, you would see a group of up to eighty people sitting cross-legged on cushions in a large hall, eyes closed, hands folded in their laps or resting gently on their knees, in silence. For ten hours a day. For ten days. A wonderful slow TV documentary is just waiting to be made.

I had an interest in meditation long before my diagnosis, and when I began plotting my cancer self-care regime I knew instantly meditation had to be a part of it. I was initially drawn to Vipassana when Kirst was first pregnant and I was wracked with anxiety at the prospect of supporting a family as a free-lance writer. We'd honeymooned in Italy, where Kirst's mum Sharon lived, and where that first child was conceived in the golden glow of a warm Tuscan afternoon. A few weeks later, on the beautiful island of Elba, where Napoleon was once exiled, my beloved emerged from the bathroom of our enig-matically named guesthouse Casa Lupi (House of Wolves), waving a little pregnancy test strip with telltale pink lines.

We stopped over in Thailand on the way home and happened to visit a Buddhist monastery set around a series of natural caves, where the resident monks had been meditating for centuries. I will never forget stepping into one cave to the sight of rows of young monks meditating silently, and being overwhelmed by a sense of peace and palpable calm. Some-thing was going on here and I wanted to know more.

A couple of days later, we were briefly in Bangkok before flying home and I wandered into a Buddhist bookstore in Khao San Road where rows upon rows of weighty texts offered various paths to enlightenment. I picked out one at random, *The Art of Living: Vipassana meditation as taught by S.N. Goenka*, by William Hart, with its gold-embossed lettering and the simple yet captivating image of an old-style wagon wheel on the cover. I began reading and found something immediately convincing in the central premise – an encouragement to see the world 'as it is, not as we would like it to be'.

I've never been a card-carrying Buddhist but it has always seemed the most pragmatic and plausible of the major religions, inviting followers to first and foremost trust their own experiences rather than blindly swallowing some ancient dogma. I read on, enthralled, sensing this practice, to calmly observe one's inner reality, might hold the key to taming my rapidly mounting provider anxiety.

We all live in two realities, Goenka posits, our inner reality and our outer reality, but most of us have the relationship between the two back-to-front. We think if we can just engineer our outer reality to suit us, to make the things we want happen and to avoid the things we don't want, then we will experience happiness. But this strategy is doomed to fail, he argues. There will always be things we want but do not have and things we have but do not want. If our focus is, instead, on our inner reality, cultivating peace and acceptance and equanimity, then our outer reality will begin to reflect our internal state – the world around us reflects our inner condition.

Back home, I discovered a Vipassana retreat a couple of hours' drive north, in the picturesque Sunshine Coast hinterland village of Pomona. I signed up as a meditation novice, witless to the reality that I was hurling myself in the deep end as rashly as a beginner surfer paddling out in huge Hawaiian waves for their first lesson.

The setting was sublime – a central dining room, a series of small one-, two- and four-bed cottages and a large meditation hall set along the flank of a gentle slope, surrounded by towering gum trees and populated by a lazy herd of lolling kangaroos and abundant bird life – kookaburras and whipbirds and lorikeets. The towering, pyramid-like Mount Cooroora to the west dominated the view as a timeless example of how to sit in stillness. In between hour-long meditation sessions, I'd stand and stare at the mountain, willing myself to become it.

My main obstacle to achieving this was not just a restless mind but also a rotating roster of bodily aches and pains that beset me every time I plonked my arse on the meditation cushion. I was clearly not alone. Large boxes of cushions of various shapes and sizes and wooden backrests and kneeling stools were on hand to allow meditators to try and fashion the most comfortable seating arrangement possible. Some seemed intent on building their own Jason recliner rockers, constructing enormous piles of cushions into which they would insinuate their posteriors, and wriggle and squirm until they had achieved the desired state of comfort, wedging yet more cushions under knees, hips, buttocks. All they needed was an esky and they might have been settling in for the Boxing Day Test.

For some reason (perhaps a deep, abiding self-loathing?), I was intent on a more purist approach, sitting on a simple arrangement of two cushions for optimal height, with rolls under each knee to try to minimise their nagging aches, spine erect, head slightly bowed, hands folded in my lap. For the first three days our only instruction was to focus on the breath moving in and out of our nostrils. For ten hours a day – an absurdity I nevertheless applied myself to diligently, intent on cultivating the desired equanimity that would allow me to embrace my new provider role free of panic.

Each session, I'd begin with a steadfast determination, find a comfortable sitting position and focus on my nostrils. When thoughts inevitably arose, we were to simply return to the breath, not reacting, not admonishing ourselves, making no judgements. 'No cravings or aversions' is the Vipassana mantra. Soon aches would start up – a searing burn in my lower back, wild jabs of pain in my hips, cramps in the arch of my feet, electric shocks up and down my spine.

I came to believe this ancient art, when transposed to the West, failed to take into account that dastardly Western invention, the chair. For those of us brought up sitting in them six hours a day at school, and eight hours a day in a workplace, not to mention while driving, eating, watching TV or movies or concerts or lectures or in places of worship, the reality of sitting cross-legged on a cushion for extended periods was a journey into heretofore unknown levels of pain.

I'd attempt to stretch my spine from either end by pushing down into my sit bones and pushing up through the crown of my head, as if lifted by a string. For brief, euphoric moments I would be pain free until holding the position became too much and I'd be wriggling and squirming again to find a more comfortable position. Each hour-long session seemed interminable. During short breaks, I'd stride through the forest – the only exercise permitted – around the perimeter of the property like an Olympic walker, desperately trying to free tight muscles and joints, then traipse back into the hall grimly to face the next round of torture. Each morning when we returned to the meditation hall there would be one or two more empty cushions as some traumatised novice meditator had gone AWOL during the night. I nearly bolted several times myself but was gripped by a desperate determination to last the distance.

On day four, we received Vipassana which, without wishing to spoil the plot, involved spreading the acute awareness of sensation we'd cultivated around our nostrils to the rest of our body. The object was to repeatedly scan the body from head to toe and back again, observing sensations as they arose and passed away according to the universal law of impermanence. Respiration and sensation were to be our only focus. We also now had three one-hour 'sittings of strong determination' each day, in which the goal was not to adjust your position at all. At first, this seemed like madness. Over time, however, I came to see it as sadism and developed an odd love–hate relationship with Goenka, as his recorded voice encouraged us at the start of each session. 'Work patiently and persistently. Patiently and persistently. You are bound to be successful.'

Somehow, I persevered through the pain, but by day eight I'd developed serious reservations about this whole deal and was wondering if this was the night I would crack and make my escape. In our evening sitting of strong determination, I resolved to give it my best shot and not move a muscle, desperate for some kind of breakthrough. Five minutes in, the pain started, and I figured I was toast, despite my good intentions. I went through my pain aversion routine, pressing down through the sit bones, lifting up through the crown of the head, and found a posture where the agony eased. But how the hell was I going to maintain this for another fifty-five minutes? I felt like I was walking a tightrope with gnashing crocodiles waiting beneath me if I stumbled. My breathing grew laboured. I tried to go into the pain as instructed, to explore it, drop into it, abandon all resistance. Then . . . something snapped.

Maybe it was long clenched muscles finally surrendering and releasing, or kundalini (a kind of awakened spiritual energy) spontaneously arising. I wouldn't have been any more surprised if I'd started speaking in tongues. I lost all control of my arms, as they flailed about me like high-pressure hoses let loose. I tried to focus on my breath, but I was panting like a dog on a hot day. I have no idea if this went on for three minutes or thirty, as waves of energy jolted through my body.

Gradually, the energy began to subside, my breathing slowed and my arms flopped weakly by my sides. What the fuck just happened? Before I knew it, Goenka's deep, guttural chanting started up to signal the end of the meditation session, and the start of a short break before the evening's discourse. I tested my limbs and they all seemed to be operating normally as I gingerly arose from my cushion and stepped outside into a star-filled night.

Gazing up into the cosmos, a powerful sense of peace and well-being cascaded through me. I felt oddly, deeply blissful for no apparent reason. With no opportunity to debrief or discuss this strange phenomenon, I was left to try to make sense of it by myself. Perhaps I was enlightened? Yes, that had to be it. Only eight days into my first Vipassana retreat I had achieved the ultimate goal and reached nirvana. Some meditators practised for years and never reached this exalted state. I must be a remarkably, highly evolved individual to have been fast-tracked to the Buddha mind so rapidly, I congratulated myself. I'd write a book. There'd be lecture tours. I was the next Eckhart Tolle!

But this euphoria was short-lived, quickly followed by another, more sobering thought. *Oh. That sounds like my ego talking. I guess I'm not actually enlightened after all, just another narcissistic Westerner window-shopping at the marketplace of Eastern mysticism.*

Even so, the next couple of days were blissful. Instead of grimly marching to the mediation hall like a prisoner sent to solitary, I couldn't wait to get back on my cushion to see how much deeper I could go, how much more blissful I could become, welcoming that delicious descent of stillness and emptiness.

On day ten, after the morning mediation, we were allowed to start speaking again as we prepared for the transition back into the outside world. I was almost sorry to break the spell. We'd no sooner walked out of the meditation hall than the bloke who'd been sitting next to me for the past ten days looked at me curiously and asked, 'What the fuck was going on for you on day eight?' I wasn't sure how to explain what had happened to him or to myself, but I came to understand it as a kind of spontaneous release, a rebirthing if you like. I did feel unfathomably light and happy and full of love for my fellow humans.

Vipassana prescribes two hours of meditation daily for the householder and I did my best to maintain my practice, but once that first child arrived, sleep deprivation and the relentless, grinding demands of new parenthood and provider duties wore me down and it fell by the wayside. It has taken me fifteen years and a cancer diagnosis to return for my second Vipassana retreat, this time intent not just on peace and stillness but on halting or even reversing the creeping advance of the disease.

After the obligatory three days focusing on our nostrils, when we receive Vipassana on day four and spread our awareness throughout our body, the dull ache I sometimes experience in my right thigh suddenly goes haywire. I've become hypersensitive to this site of metastases, where the cancer has colonised the bone, paranoid about any sensations as a signal of the cancer's progression. Now I feel as if there's a python writhing in there and I'm terrified that this is not the right thing for a person with stage four cancer to be doing. Sure, spreading awareness throughout the body sounds fine for a healthy person, but the last thing I want to do is somehow spread the cancer.

I make an appointment to see the teacher during lunchbreak (when students are permitted to ask questions) and explain my anxiety. Is he sure this practice is safe for someone with my medical condition, I ask. The teacher, a soft-spoken, bespectacled fellow in his fifties, with the trace of a Scandinavian accent, very calmly reassures me. 'It's perfectly safe and, in fact, very beneficial,' he says, gazing deep into my eyes. Something in his quiet manner puts my mind at rest and for the rest of the retreat I have no pain in the leg at all. Walking through the forest during a break the next day, I stop to contemplate my surroundings and am suddenly overwhelmed by a surge of emotion and a powerful thought ringing as clear as a bell through my consciousness. *You will get to meet your grand-children.* Tears stream down my face, and for the first time since my diagnosis I feel a warm surge of reassurance I might yet navigate a way through my dire prognosis.

As a returning, or 'old', student, even after a fifteen-year absence, I'm entitled to use a private meditation cell, a small chamber about the size of a phone booth, with just enough room to sit up and meditate. Pitch dark and almost completely silent, I find it remarkably easy to quickly drop into a deep meditative state. By day six I feel like a vibrating field of energy and not solid matter at all, a state known as *bunga* in the Vipassana tradition, a condition that seems to allow no room for disease – my cells humming harmoniously.

At home, I meditate morning and night, usually from thirty to sixty minutes each time, around ninety minutes a day on average, some way short of the prescribed two hours. Even so, the benefits are profound and long-lasting. I usually sleep well, even the night before scan and blood test results, free of anxiety thanks to the inner peace I've been so diligently cultivating. Sure, I still go up and down and some days are better than others, and the spectre of this thing hanging over me sometimes feels unendurable. But when I sit and drop into a meditative state, there is just the present moment and this quiet, blissful vibration and emptiness in which all thought drops away.

I'm not claiming meditation cures cancer. But I know there's a place of stillness and quiet I can access, where light and breath and awareness flood my body, and I can conduct an inventory of every cell and reassure myself I am strong and whole and healthy.

12

FEAR AND LOATHING IN THE RADIOLOGY DEPARTMENT

Is THE RADIOLOGY ROOM a sneak peek of what life will be like when our AI overlords mercilessly seize power? I'm sliding in and out of the giant donut of the PET machine again for my six-monthly scan to see if my cancer has spread.

'Hold your breath,' the robotic, disembodied voice commands. And I obey, unquestioningly.

Perhaps ten long seconds later, 'Breathe normally,' it eventually relents.

Scan day is never fun. Rising at 6 am, drinking a litre of water, driving for forty-five minutes to Southport on the northern Gold Coast past the inevitably pumping surf at Currumbin Alley, bladder bursting. Fasting until the two-hour ordeal is over. Being shunted in and out of the big donut while my insides are scrutinised. But this one has gotten off to an especially inauspicious beginning.

Sitting in the waiting room, I'd received an email from Centrelink asking me to check my Centrelink app. As any welfare recipient knows, such notifications are enough to send a chill through your body, particularly in the age of Robodebt, an automated Centrelink debt recovery scheme to reclaim alleged overpayment of welfare benefits. Under this delightful government initiative, another form of artificial intelligence stalks and traumatises our most vulnerable with demands for the repayment of dubious debts, with a cruel (and, as it turns out, illegal) reversal of the presumption of innocence.

I open the app, click on the notification and squint to read the tiny text in the official decree. My disability support pension and concession card have been abruptly cancelled without warning because I've failed to fill in a particular form on time. Amid the tide of paperwork Centrelink demands, I have no idea what this particular form is or when it was due. The scan I've just paid for equates to roughly a fortnight's worth of the part–disability pension I've been on.

I'm eventually shown through the big sliding doors and taken to my changing room where I'm monitored by CCTV as I undress and change into a hospital gown, then sit and wait some more. I've come to despise these sad little rooms. Every six months or so, I find myself here, alone, undressing, putting on the unflattering, pale blue surgical gown, fumbling around the back to try to tie the thing up. The adjustable armchair. The wall-mounted TV beaming the unremitting misery or inanity of breakfast news – climate chaos and guffawing hosts and sporting and political scandals. Other men in surgical gowns shuffle in and out of their rooms, to and from the radiology suite, like a middle-aged zombie apocalypse, the morning of the walking dead.

The male radiology nurse reappears, threads a clear plastic tube through a purpose-built hole in the wall, jabs me in the arm with a small needle and attaches the tube to the end of the needle to infuse me with the radioactive dye, or tracer, which will cause any cancer cells in my body to light up like fairy lights. We must wait another forty minutes for the tracer to circulate through my system before I'm ready for the scanner.

I've already signed a waiver declaring I understand that this process entails certain risks and side effects, not least of which is a one in 200,000 chance of death. If I live another ten years and have a scan every six months, does that mean I have a one in 10,000 chance of being killed by the scan to detect my cancer, rather than the cancer itself? Or the side effects of chemo? Or the side effects of hormone therapy? My heightened risk of suicide, depression, diabetes, cardiovascular disease? I'm no statistician but I sense the odds are mounting up against me. At least Centrelink are alert to the possibility of me being a welfare cheat.

When my time comes, I'm led to the scan room, where I lie on a narrow mattress, have my legs strapped together to assist me to keep perfectly still and am instructed to hold my arms above my head in a position that quickly becomes painful five minutes in.

The PET scan machine is a lonely place. The technician works from outside the room to avoid daily exposure to radiation. The disembodied voice issues commands to regulate my breathing and the narrow bed slides in and out. The scan captures cross-sections of my interior for examination, as if I'm being cut into thin slices like a terrine. PET stands for positron emission tomography, an imaging technique that uses a radioactive tracer injected or swallowed, which then accumulates in areas of the body with higher levels of chemical activity, neatly corresponding to areas of disease. This variety is a PSMA PET scan, a more sophisticated and more expensive type of scan than a standard PET. PSMA stands for prostate-specific membrane antigen, a protein found on the surface of normal prostate cells, but occurs in higher concentrations on prostate cancer cells, which the tracer attaches to.

The integrative doctor in the United States I've been consulting with by phone occasionally has recommended this scan because since my diagnosis I've only ever had two metastases, in my right femur and left seventh rib. He refers to this condition as oligometastatic, from the Greek word *oligos*, meaning few. He's suggested there's mounting evidence that oligometastatic prostate cancer may be treated successfully with targeted, or stereotactic, radiation. The more sophisticated PSMA PET scan is necessary to establish if this targeted radiation is likely to be effective.

He has explained to me the abscopal effect, a fairly recently recognised and quite rare phenomenon, by which targeted radiation of tumours appears to have a knock-on effect, a little like immunisation, eliminating not just the targeted tumours but other, more distant, cancer cells. The precise molecular mechanisms that cause this are not yet well understood, but it appears to help the immune system recognise these distant cancer cells, especially when combined with immunotherapy.

My US doc has sent me half a dozen studies to support his thesis, but my oncologist was unimpressed and appeared to regard all this as far-fetched straw-grasping. He advised against the PSMA PET scan because its greater sensitivity can often detect many smaller micro-metastases, which some patients might find confronting. 'Some men light up like a Christmas tree,' he warned me earnestly.

I dug in my heels. I'd rather know exactly what I'm dealing with.

The integrative doc openly admitted he practised what he called optimistic medicine. 'If you were in the US, we'd be trying to cure you,' he contended.

My oncologist is more of a pragmatic, glass-half-empty guy, and regards all this as wishful thinking, an expensive waste of time and energy. I'm caught in the cultural chasm between their differing philosophies. I understand the abscopal effect is by no means a sure thing, even a long shot, maybe even a Hail Mary, but it is something. Why wouldn't I give it a crack?

My shoulders are burning in pain in their extended position and I've no idea if I'm five minutes or twenty-five minutes into my scan. Those surfers who say that time stands still in the tube really ought to try a PET scan, where a minute feels like an hour. I attempt to breathe through the pain, as I've learnt in Vipassana meditation, to surrender to it, not name or react to it, but to merely observe sensation with equanimity. But in the unnatural setting of the scan room, this proves difficult.

Eventually, I ask the technician how long I've got to go, and he assures me through a little speaker that it's only a matter of minutes, though they seem exceedingly long. Alone in the scanner, listening to the constant hum and whirr of machinery, the circular surface inches from my face, my shoulders screaming in pain, something in me breaks. Tears stream down my face and I'm unable even to wipe my eyes.

I've had these scans before without a meltdown, but suddenly I'm fed up with the whole thing. The scans. The blood tests. The anxious wait for results. The hours sitting in my oncologist's waiting room. The sad little change rooms. The emasculating effects of hormone therapy. I want my life back. But no amount of sulking will change a thing. Even in this wretched state, I'm still trying to be a good patient, to keep perfectly still, not let my chest rise and fall too dramatically, to cry silently so the technician doesn't hear me.

Finally, it's over and I wipe my eyes with my forearms quickly before he re-enters the room. I return to my little change room, where a cup of green tea and a plastic package of sandwich triangles awaits me to break my fast. Another sad little ritual, changing out of my hospital gown and back into my street clothes, nibbling on my sandwiches and sipping my tea, ready to escape my confinement and step back out into the world. And all this for the bargain price of $450 for repeat customers, with no Medicare rebate.

I have to wait a week to get the results from my oncologist, the same oncologist who warned against said scans because I might 'light up like a Christmas tree'. They show the tumour in my right femur is completely gone. Only the small metastases in my left seventh rib remains. No other signs of cancer show up in my body, beyond the prostate. This seems like good news, but I'm unsure how to take it. I think of the writhing snake in my thigh during Vipassana, and then the delicious state of *bunga*. Is it preposterous to believe I could meditate a tumour away? My oncologist senses my excitement. 'This doesn't mean you're cured you know,' he scolds me.

He won't even allow me a brief moment of celebration. *Fuck off*, I want to tell him, but don't. He suggests I've just had a particularly good response to chemotherapy, which I finished eighteen months ago, and hormone therapy, which I'm currently enjoying a six-month break from. *Okay. Whatever you reckon.* There's no entertaining of the possibility that two years of a dedicated plant-based diet, high intensity interval training, Vipassana meditation, cannabis oil and a variety of herbs and supplements might have contributed to my result in any way. Not even the vague encouragement that whatever I'm doing appears to be helping and I should stick to it. With his immaculate, navy blue suit and long slender fingers that he folds and unfolds as he speaks, and his impassive, inscrutable facial expressions, he gives off a kind of impenetrable aura that deters any dissent.

I'm not an oncologist. I'm not qualified to argue with his professional, expert assessment. I can, however, allow myself a totally immature, irrational, emotive response to all this.

My oncologist can go eat a dick.

13

THE TOUR DE CURE

THE TOUR DE CURE is a ten-day charity cycling event to raise money for cancer research, like a Variety Club Bash on bikes instead of in clapped-out old cars.

I've been invited to be the after-dinner speaker on the penultimate night of the 2018 Tour de Cure through Far North Queensland. I'm flying to Cairns with a mate who works for Optus, an event sponsor, and I'm quietly shitting myself.

Since its inception in 2007, brainstormed by three friends over a cup of coffee, the Tour de Cure has raised over $66 million for cancer research, funding 554 cancer projects and forty-five significant cancer breakthroughs. A total of 4500 people have ridden in the Tour de Cure, supported by 2500 volunteers. It's attained that corpo, big end of town support that sees business execs taking ten days out of their busy schedules to don the lyrcra. Big corporate sponsors are all throwing their weight behind the Tour. *Sunrise* presenter Mark Beretta has been doing live crosses throughout the Tour and is MC for the night. You don't get much more mainstream than that.

As we touch down in Cairns, the Tour's 180 riders are gathering at a hotel in the CBD to strip off the lycra, shower, douse themselves in deodorant, change into their party clothes and enthusiastically celebrate the near completion of their arduous journey. The Tour has wound its way along a 1110-kilometre circuit through tropical North Queensland, from Mackay to Cape Tribulation and on to Cairns, through cane-fields and rainforests, and up and down mountains, raising $2.2 million along the way.

When we arrive at the hotel, the plush foyer is crowded with cyclists checking in, comparing injuries and near-accidents on the road, the scent of sweat and Tiger Balm thick in the air. I'm introduced to the event organisers and taken to the vast dining room where I'm to speak, for a tech run-through. This does little to settle my nerves. Endless circular tables fill the vast room with seating for around 300. I'll be on a raised stage, at a lectern, with my hastily assembled PowerPoint and a little handheld clicker, to wow the crowd with my profound insights and candid account of living with cancer, to inspire the weary riders on the final leg of their journey.

Most of the cyclists are doing the Tour de Cure because they or someone they love has had an experience of cancer, so I'm playing to a sympathetic crowd. But they're also keen to blow off steam after spending up to ten hours a day in the saddle for ten days straight. They're mainly middle-aged executive types who know how to have a good time, the work hard/play hard crowd. I'm not sure I can make my presentation entertaining enough to delay the commencement of post-dinner conga lines and tequila shots.

I check in and find my room, which has sweeping views of the Cairns foreshore and out to the Coral Sea. I shower, change and do some deep breathing exercises before heading back to the dining room. My clean-living, alcohol-free, plant-based lifestyle always feels like an awkward fit at such events, where booze flows freely, and steak and chicken dinner options are dropped at alternating places. My Optus buddy Sam is sticking tight, making sure I feel supported. It's the first time I've spoken publicly about my diagnosis. I'm not entirely sure what's expected, but I've decided to use the occasion to bang on about my pet topic – the need for a more integrative approach to cancer care, treating the whole patient and not just the tumour. At a function devoted to raising money for mainstream cancer research I'm not too sure how this will go down. Maybe I'll be decried as a Pete Evans–style whacko.

I pick at my vegetarian option, an uninspiring 'risotto' which more closely resembles steamed rice decorated with a few diced vegies, resist the urge for a little medicinal red wine nerve settler, figuring it might be a bad look for the holistic cancer self-care advocate, and review my notes. I've got twenty minutes and I don't want to go over time, but I also want to make it count.

After a series of short speeches, it's my turn. Suddenly I'm mounting the stairs, gripping the lectern, launching my

PowerPoint and staring out at a sea of expectant faces. Most are a few drinks deep into their evening and there's a restless buzz of chatter before quiet eventually descends. Is this the point at which you imagine them all naked to calm the nerves? Honestly, the masses of lycra in the hotel lobby earlier were confronting enough. I'm not sure I can go there.

Deep breaths. Empty mind. They want you to be good. They're on your side. I launch into a quick precis of my writing career, the dream life of the surf writer, the books, the far-flung travels, then . . . I press the clicker and it brings up an image of my first bone scan, showing the large tumour in my right femur. The mood has shifted. I have their attention now.

I detail some of my experiences with the world of mainstream oncology and what I regard as some of its shortcomings. The lack of bedside manner, the disregard for nutrition or complementary and supportive therapies, the cavalier dismissal of the often devastating side effects of treatment. Then, with no qualifications other than my experience living with cancer, I lay out my vision for integrative cancer care. My self-care mantra: take your MEDS – medication, exercise, diet, sleep. My list of lifestyle approaches and supportive therapies that have helped: a plant-based diet, Vipassana, high intensity interval training, massage, naturopathy, emotional support, time in nature, acupuncture, surfing, yoga, Pilates.

To wrap up, I outline the team of health professionals I wish every cancer patient had access to from the time of diagnosis – from an oncologist to a counsellor or psychologist, a nutritionist to exercise physiologist, massage therapist to herbalist or naturopath – who could all work in concert to address the multi-layered needs of the patient. The danger in talking about this kind of stuff is that you can easily be portrayed as an anti-science quack spruiking dangerous and unproven therapies, a Belle Gibson–style charlatan, even if all you are doing is pleading for a wider embrace of evidence-based supportive therapies to make life more bearable during conventional cancer treatments.

I end my presentation with that old personal development mantra I first heard while lying in Shavasana (the corpse pose) in a yoga class nearly three years ago: 'What's in the way is the way'. A cancer diagnosis isn't a hurdle to be climbed over in order to resume our old lives, but a portal to a whole new way of life, if you are willing to jump through.

I thank everyone for listening, place the handheld microphone back on the lectern, and look up at the crowd. My twenty minutes has gone in the blink of an eye, but the audience seems to have grown restless as the noise in the dining room suddenly builds. Perhaps they can contain their conga line kink no longer. But as I look out over the crowd I'm struck by an odd and entirely unexpected sight – 300 people on their feet loudly and enthusiastically applauding. I did *not* see that coming.

It turns out the Tour de Cure is making a sizeable donation to a local cancer charity, the Cairns Organisation United for Cancer Health (or COUCH). Its chairman Ron Holden, a stately silver-haired gent, joins me on stage to accept the oversized cheque the Tour de Cure has to present him with. He tells us COUCH was launched in 2006 by husband and wife Charles and Pip Woodward, after Charles was diagnosed with cancer, to make oncology services more readily available to the people of Cairns and its surrounds. Charles succumbed to his cancer in 2017 and since then Pip, a former nurse, has carried on their work, successfully fundraising for the purchase of vital medical equipment and a shuttle bus to help patients attend their medical appointments; lobbying for the opening of the Liz Plummer Cancer Care Centre; and establishing the COUCH Wellness Centre.

'I don't have a speech to make because Tim just made mine,' Ron says humbly. I am among kindred souls. The integrative approach I've just outlined is precisely what the COUCH Wellness Centre aims to provide, Ron tells the crowd – oncology massage, meditation, yoga, Pilates, acupuncture, and reflexology to mitigate side effects and enhance quality of life for cancer patients; offering support services through every stage of cancer treatment and post-treatment. It is the most inspiring, holistic model of cancer care I have encountered in Australia.

This is not Byron Bay. These are not long-haired anti-vaxxers or self-appointed New Age gurus extolling spurious miracle cures, sitting cross-legged in yurts in the NSW North Coast hinterland. These are grey-haired senior citizens living in regional Far North Queensland advocating for a better quality of life and some level of agency during cancer treatment for themselves and their loved ones. I'm heartened to discover there's a groundswell of community demand for this kind of holistic cancer care – that I'm not alone in my quest for a sensible middle path through the maze of mainstream and alternative treatments, that it needn't be an either/ or deal. That the answer, as the Buddha reminds us, is in the middle way.

There shouldn't be anything controversial about this. Requesting the tools to manage the devastating side effects of conventional cancer treatment is not radical or anti-science. Accepting the evidence that diet, exercise, emotional support, meditation and other complementary therapies can improve outcomes for cancer patients should not see you labelled a dangerous quack or treated with a patronising disdain by your oncologist. We are not delivery systems for our tumours. We are people, with dreams and vulnerabilities and hopes and fears, like anyone else.

Cancer care should not be divorced from basic principles of general health and well-being. The noble quest to find ever more effective ways to kill cancer cells should not be at the expense of the patient's sense of self and quality of life and a respect for how they would choose to navigate their cancer treatment journey.

As I return to my table and the formal dinner winds down and the partying livens up, I'm introduced to a string of people living with cancer, as well as the founders of COUCH. I hadn't come to Cairns expecting to find allies, but I leave feeling part of a community growing and demanding to be heard.

If a group of Cairns seniors can create and secure funding for this model of supportive cancer care, why can't it be rolled out across the country and around the world? Future generations in more enlightened times, I am willing to bet, will scratch their heads and wonder why it took so long to see cancer patients as people.

14

USE IT OR LOSE IT

IMAGINE IF THERE WAS a single treatment that improved bone density, cardiovascular health, mental health, muscle tone, helped suppress cancer and might even improve sexual function? Surely oncologists would be heralding this stunning break-through, spreading the good news to their patients, making it an essential element of prostate cancer care to offset the awful side effects of treatment. What is this miracle therapy?

Well, you won't find it in any pharmacy and few oncologists will write you a script for this game-changing treatment, even though (or perhaps because) it is essentially free. It is called exercise and its benefits are so spectacular and far-reaching, a growing chorus of medical researchers are calling for it to be prescribed as medicine for cancer patients.

In 2018 the Clinical Oncology Society of Australia released a position statement on exercise and cancer care stating:

'Clinical research has established exercise as a safe and effective intervention to counteract the adverse physical and psychological effects of cancer and its treatment.' Its recommendations include:

- exercise to be embedded as part of standard practice in cancer care and to be viewed as an adjunct therapy that helps counteract the adverse effects of cancer and its treatment
- all members of the multidisciplinary cancer team to promote physical activity and recommend that people with cancer adhere to exercise guidelines
- best practice cancer care to include referral to an accredited exercise physiologist or physiotherapist with experience in cancer care.

While this is encouraging news, I'd like to know more about this interdisciplinary cancer team of which they speak, because in seven years of being a cancer patient I've never encountered such a thing. And I've never had an oncologist refer me to any kind of exercise therapist.

In my own case, the only person who alerted me to the key role of exercise, and high intensity interval training (HIIT) specifically, in my cancer care was my naturopath. And yet every medical doctor I've spoken to is also entirely dismissive of the role and expertise of naturopaths in cancer care.

As a relatively young, relatively fit prostate cancer patient, encouragement is all I need. Give me something to do that holds even the slightest promise of improving my prognosis or quality of life, and I'll do it. It makes no sense that I'm powerless to do anything to support my own health, which is the overwhelming message from mainstream oncology. My workouts at the surf club gym quickly become an essential and joyous part of my self-care, as whales spout and waves explode against the rocks, and where I can go for a quick surf after a session.

It doesn't take me long to get the attraction of this sort of carry on. I'd once regarded those who pump iron as narcissists, admiring their own images in gym mirrors, getting about in muscle shirts, and scoffing protein supplements and steroids like Russian weightlifters. But once I get a taste for it, the endorphins of sustained effort, the growing sense of strength and empowerment, the visible signs of increased fitness, I'm hooked. I imagine cancer cells shrivelling up and dying as I use the weight machines, balance on the Bosu (an exercise tool kind of like a fitball cut in half), sprint the steep stairs leading to the top of Elephant Rock, perform chin-ups and burpees, tackle sprints on the exercise bike. Like my meditation practice, in the midst of a good workout I'm convinced there is no place in my body for disease.

I get back into my yoga, become a regular at Pilates and vow to never again drive past good waves because of work. In a good week I do some sort of intense exercise every day and honestly feel the fittest and healthiest I have in years. There's an indefinable energy humming throughout my body, a new spring to my step, a lightness and vitality, which I'm determined to maintain. I'm reminded of the words of legendary surfing medico Dorian 'Doc' Paskowitz, founder of one of the world's first surf schools, from my 2007 book *High Surf*: 'Health is more than the mere absence of disease. It's the presence of a state of vigour, vitality, pizzazz, that can be purposely come by, by working on it day after day.'

And so that's what I do. My old mate, 1978 world champ Rabbit Bartholomew, is another regular at the surf club gym, he knows what I'm going through and is an enthusiastic cheer-leader of my efforts. 'Geez, you've got a six pack,' he marvels one day. 'That's the hardest thing to achieve at our age.' He's ten years older than me but I don't quibble.

After a brisk thirty-minute workout, a quicky bodysurf and a freshly squeezed carrot juice at home, I feel bulletproof. Throw in a few surfs a week and I'm probably fitter than I was ten or even twenty years ago, when the sedentary life of a deskbound writer began to take its toll. A regular weekly Pilates session with a qualified physiotherapist is another reve-lation. My instructor Indianna seems to know what my body needs better than I do, and she's not averse to kicking her client's arses when required, which she does to mine on a regular basis. Indie sees her job as pushing me to my edge, to prevent the gradual physical decline brought on by hormone therapy. The worst thing she can do, she says, is underload me, and so every exercise routine is designed to take me to that edge. I bitch and moan, am frequently unable to complete the prescribed number of repetitions for a particular exercise, but know it's what I need.

Like a newly converted religious zealot, I sign up to an exercise clinic for cancer patients at the University of Queensland, working with their fourth-year exercise physi-ology students to explore the role of exercise in cancer care. Participants are given a thorough fitness assessment and then have a personalised exercise plan prescribed. This is both hands-on training for the students and valuable physical therapy for the subjects. The train ride from the Gold Coast to UQ takes over an hour and we attend one morning a week for six weeks, but the sense of empowerment I enjoy is well worth the long commute.

Being back on a university campus after a 35-year absence hits me with a powerful dose of nostalgia; all these bright-eyed youngsters filing into a place of learning, their whole lives in front of them, full of hopes and dreams. UQ is a classic Queensland campus, an ongoing stoush between the resident bush turkeys and ibis a running gag, with students holding a poll to ask if you are on Team Ibis or Team Turkey. Tales of lunches swiped by predatory birds are legend.

I find my way to the school of human movement, a middle-aged man resplendent in my gym gear, Adidas shorts and New Balance sneakers. A few fellow cancer patients are assembled in the foyer and we're each assigned two students who'll put us through our paces. My trainers Zoe and Charlotte are delightful – young, enthusiastic, fit as triathletes themselves. If you want to inspire a middle-aged man to challenge his physical limits in a series of fitness tests, I recommend having two attractive young women cheering him on as an effective strategy. Please remember, I have no libido so there's nothing particularly creepy about my enthusiasm for this arrangement, but I can't recall the last time I had anyone cheering me on this keenly in any capacity. The effect is intoxicating and, I suspect, wildly performance enhancing.

Zoe and Charlotte push me to the limits of my physical endurance in a variety of tests – a series of sprints on the exercise bike, weights, balance, fast walking – measuring blood pressure and heart rate before and after exercise. My resting heart rate and blood pressure are very low, which is regarded as a good thing, and my maximum heart rate when exercising is very high, which Zoe and Charlotte become quite excited about. All very encouraging, particularly as cardiovascular health is one of the many things compromised by hormone therapy.

My cheer squad really come into their own on the bike sprints. For the purposes of this test, I cruise for four minutes then sprint for four minutes, repeated three times. Sprint is defined as over 80 rpm (revolutions per minute), and Charlotte and Zoe's job is to ensure I don't fall below this pace. I haven't heard such impassioned cheering since the upstart Hawks surprised the all-conquering Cats to win the 2008 AFL Grand Final. It must make quite a spectacle, fifty-something-year-old me sweating and panting and trundling away gamely while these two impassioned young women egg me on mercilessly as if I'm in the final moments of a *Masterchef* challenge, with only a few minutes left to plate up.

'Come on, Tim, keep going. You're doing great. You got this,' they chorus. My heart rate gets up to 170 beats per minute at the height of my exertions, which pleases Zoe and Charlotte no end, and I beam with pride, like a toddler who's just tied his own shoes for the first time. Flogging myself to this level of exhaustion on my own would be near impossible. The difference their encouragement makes is stunning.

Zoe and Charlotte then draw up a prescribed exercise plan for me, which I come in and perform weekly for the next four weeks. Each week I leave feeling stronger and more energised than the last. In the final session, I'm given another fitness test and a customised and detailed exercise plan to continue with on my own. It won't be the same without Zoe and Charlotte in my corner, but they've kickstarted an enthusiasm I'm determined to maintain. My surfing buddy Marty is so enthralled by my tales of being urged on to ever-greater feats of physical performance by my personal cheer squad, he calls his two new surfboards Zoe and Charlotte in their honour.

A year on, I get an email about a clinical trial called the GAP4 Interval study, to determine if 'supervised high intensity aerobic and resistance training increases overall survival compared to self-directed exercise in patients with metastatic prostate cancer'. Numerous universities through the United States, United Kingdom, Canada and Australia are overseeing nearly 1000 participants over several years, funded by Movember, the annual men's health fundraiser. Quite the commitment but I figure I need to walk the talk. If I want to advocate for a more integrative approach to cancer care I'd better be prepared to support research in the field. I sign up and I'm soon back at UQ being cheered on by another young, attractive exercise physiologist. There appears to be a deliberate strategy at work here.

Gisela is a fully qualified exercise physiologist who oversees my fitness testing for the study and she's a gem, perhaps not reaching quite the decibel levels of the dynamic duo Charlotte and Zoe, but with a certain understated gravitas that snaps me into action.

'I wish all my men were as motivated as you,' she tells me, which leaves me feeling like the favourite slave of an Egyptian queen.

A little pathetic, I know, but I'd do anything to impress my queen. I just about max out the weight machines and smash the exercise bike sprints.

Once the initial testing is completed, we are randomised into two groups – those who'll follow a supervised weekly exercise program, and a control group who will not, but are free to do their own self-directed exercise. Both groups will be offered psychosocial support that takes the underwhelming form of a monthly email newsletter with lifestyle tips. Gisela and I are both strongly barracking for my inclusion in the exercise group, but my fate is in the lap of the gods and I draw the short straw. I'm in the control group and Gisela seems genuinely saddened by the news.

But, honestly, I could save everyone a lot of time, effort and money – supervised training will definitely, 100 per cent produce better results than self-directed exercise. The cruel catch-22 of hormone therapy is the very thing that would best offset its insidious side effects is often the thing we feel least capable of, because of its attendant fatigue and lethargy. And the psychosocial support of an email newsletter feels as good as useless, as well-intentioned as it may be, with its monthly declarations of the bleeding obvious – eat well, get enough sleep, seek out emotional support. One handy tip is to watch TV 'walking around the room or marching on the spot'. Yep, right, I can totally foresee myself adopting this ludicrous strategy. Even the most erudite email newsletter in the world is never going to feel like effective psychosocial support or substitute for real human connection. My idea of psychosocial support involves a living, breathing human listening, empathising, and making soothing clucking noises while I vent my darkest fears, not a notification and a link turning up in my inbox once a month.

I'm still free to exercise as much as I like, because no one wants to discourage men with prostate cancer from exercising, so I do my best to skew their results by exercising like a mad man and hopefully surviving for longer than anyone in the exercise group.

I purchase a second-hand weight set off Gumtree, borrow an exercise bike from friends and Kirst purchases a Pilates 'slider', her favourite bit of exercise equipment and one I take quite a shine to. We're lucky enough to have a pool and live walking distance to the beach. I surf most days there are decent waves and swim laps in the warmer months. I try to roll out my trusty old yoga mat at least once a week. But many days I look at all these options for physical exertion and just . . . have nothing. The very idea of strenuous exercise makes me exhausted and all too often I walk past the weight set and the slider, the pool and the exercise bike and the yoga mat, straight for the couch and Netflix. It seems cruel that just possessing all these means of exercising doesn't assist my campaign to maintain physical fitness and quality of life.

As part of the control group, I still come in for a six-monthly fitness assessment and, despite my disappointment at not being in the exercise group, it proves a valuable way to monitor how I'm tracking, and if my physical powers are in decline. This time, I'm under the care of two smart, young male exercise physiologists, Brent and Alex, and I'm pleased to report I'm just as motivated by their enthusiasm as my previous female trainers. I'm not just a sad, middle-aged bloke supping on the ego stroke of young female attention. What I'm getting off on, I realise, is the illusion I am some kind of elite athlete in the expert hands of highly trained sports scientists. I'm not a cancer patient, I'm an Olympian determined to register PBs and push my physical limits in a gruelling decathlon of athletic endeavours.

The testing is rigorous. My waist and hip measurements are taken, and my heart rate and blood pressure are recorded before and after exertion. A series of exercises on the weight machines establish my maximum capacity for the leg press, chest press, leg extension and the seated row. My favourite is the exercise bike test, which feeds my fantasy of elite athletic testing. I'm hooked up to electrodes all over my body, registering my vital signs on an adjacent computer screen. A long plastic hose connects to this hi-tech arrangement at one end and a mouthpiece I stick in my gob at the other, supported by a strap arrangement across my head. In this test I have to keep my cycling speed between 70 and 80 rpm as the resistance of the exercise bike is steadily increased at one-minute intervals. If I drop below 70 rpm for more than ten seconds, the test is over.

This is called a cardiopulmonary exercise test and as Brent explains to me in a subsequent email:

It objectively measures the gases exchanged through progressively harder exercise intensity. It's measuring how much oxygen you're breathing in and how much carbon dioxide you're breathing out in response to the exercise.

This helps us determine your peak or max oxygen consumption at the muscular level and we can also determine when you switch from predominantly aerobic metabolism (using oxygen to burn fat for energy) to anaerobic metabolism (using sugar stores for cellular energy, which starts to produce lactic acid).

Over time, this helps illustrate how my cardiopulmonary fitness is changing, measuring my 'VO2 max' or 'peak value' – that is, the millilitres of oxygen per kilogram of bodyweight consumed per minute of exercise. The challenge is to maintain or better my result at each six-monthy visit.

The exercise bike is programmed to automatically ramp up the resistance through fifteen one-minute intervals. I make it through thirteen one-minute stages, which Brent regards as a good result. But the crucial element is whether this result changes over time, whether I'm doing enough training by myself to offset the effects of hormone therapy and prevent a steady decline. When I return for my second test six months later, I'm intent on equalling or bettering my previous effort.

I'm quite anxious getting back on the bike. Amid the furious peddling and the eager barracking of Brent and Alex I lose track of how many one-minute intervals I've cycled through, until Alex informs me we've passed the pre-programmed fifteen-minute mark and he's going to have to override the program and continue the test manually. I've broken their system. By now I'm in a delirium of flashing pedals and hyperventila-tion and elevated heart rate like a runaway train I'm not sure how to stop. But fatigue, when it suddenly arrives, hits hard.

At the twenty-two-minute mark the resistance becomes too much, and I hit the wall. I can't maintain the required 70 rpm and collapse panting and sweating while Brent and Alex cheer like I've won Olympic gold. I'm almost embarrassed by how much I get off on the feeling of accomplishment when life, and cancer treatment, has stripped away many of my claims to physical prowess.

As if some kind of tipping point has been reached, or the evidence has become unignorable, exercise suddenly seems to be at the forefront of cancer research. I get another phone call about a study examining the role of exercise in improving sexual function for men on hormone therapy. Would I like to enrol? *Fuck yeah*, is my immediate response. I have to complete a highly personal questionnaire about my current level of sexual function (effectively nil) and when I submit my questionnaire, I'm told bluntly that I'm ineligible, in other words, that I'm too far gone to help. This is deeply depressing, particularly for a man on hormone therapy already prone to bouts of depression and even occasional descents into suicidal ideation. I provide this feedback to the researchers, and they seem to take it very seriously. These sorts of ethical considerations are critical in clinical research. A study designed to help men with prostate cancer that risks demoralising many of them needs to re-examine its methodology.

A couple of years into this manic exercise blitz, I discover the sweaty, masochistic delights of boxing training – a sentence I never thought I'd write. A friend recommends a woman named Nadine, a tall, frighteningly fit trainer who seems to derive great pleasure from driving her students to the point of exhaustion. She runs a day-time session at a local exercise centre, and it's just me and the yummy mummies of the southern Gold Coast hitting the pads, skipping rope, and knocking out short sharp sprints in between. Nadine's interested to hear I have a teenage daughter and suggests I invite her along to one of her evening classes, I suspect because none of the yummy mummies want to team up with the hyperventilating middle-aged bloke drowning in his own sweat. Viv's never been the sporty type but to my delight she's entirely keen on the idea.

There's a particular joy in seeing Viv discover her physical powers at close quarters. I've seen her do it with words, as she explores the power of slam poetry in her high school writer's club. But holding the pads while she unleashes a lightning fast combo of jabs, upper cuts and crosses, quite literally sets me back on my heels. What happened to that bookish little girl of ours? Warning to the world: Vivi Baker is NOT copping any of your bullshit. Weekly boxing training has the added benefit of giving me a shared activity with my daughter, when I spend so much time surfing with Alex. That is until Viv decides she would much rather pair up with one of her new gal pals a little closer to her age.

But for all these exertions, the studies and personalised programs and loudly barracking trainers, for all the sports science and data and machines that go 'ping', when it comes to exercise and cancer care, it appears I've hit the jackpot with surfing. Among the things recommended for my condition are: high intensity interval training, meditation, a sense of a spiritual connection, pursuing one's passion, getting out into nature, a sense of being part of something greater than the self. Surfing neatly provides all this and more.

Paddling out and duck diving waves delivers an intense aerobic workout and maintains upper body strength. Sitting out the back waiting for waves, scanning the horizon for subtle signs of an approaching set, can be deeply meditative (on a busy day on the Gold Coast points, not so much).

The riding of waves is a unique, gymnastic exercise, requiring balance, a certain flow to fit in with the motion of the breaking wave, a kind of intuitive reading of the constantly shifting energy of the ocean. Just paddling out is to give yourself over to a higher power, to get lost in something greater than yourself.

'A man trying to find god is like a wave trying to find the ocean,' philosopher Alan Watts once wrote.

I'm not sure I find god in the ocean, but I definitely lose myself, cease to be a cancer patient, a holder of a disability support pension concession card. Old instincts and muscle memory kick in. I watch the way the water is moving to discern where to paddle out, the signs of an accommodating current and a break in the waves to assist my passage out to the take-off area. I pull my arms through the water strongly, engage my core, treat it like a workout, breathing heavily, heart pumping. I've read that the action of breaking waves generates negative ions, which make us feel good via a biochemical process I can't begin to articulate but experience profoundly.

I've always veered towards a more spiritual understanding of surfing's restorative powers. You can get as cosmic as you like about the act of wave riding, which was very cosmic indeed for the first generation of counterculture surfers in the late sixties. The arrival of psychoactive drugs coincided with the development of modern, more manoeuvrable shortboards and intense new surfing experiences, like riding deep inside the hollow curl or tube of the wave. Attempts to articulate these profound aquatic experiences ranged from the sublime to the ridiculous, but as a sixties baby, I just caught the tail end of this so-called soul surfing era and it made a deep impression.

Surf movies of the times had gloriously quasi-spiritual names like *Morning of the Earth, Pacific Vibrations, Children of the Sun, Evolution, Sea of Joy*. Surfing very nearly gave rise to its own form of spiritualism during this mind-expanding era. A group of Californian surfers calling themselves the Brotherhood of Eternal Love borrowed heavily from Eastern mysticism before drifting into the dark realm of drug trafficking. When Hawaiian Pipeline Master Gerry Lopez was asked by a mainstream TV reporter if he was religious, he replied deadpan that he was a devout follower of the Church of the Open Sky, his own spur-of-the-moment invention, but one duly reported as a real religion. It has since been immortalised in an evocative surf film by Nathan Oldfield and a memoir by 1966 world champ Nat Young of the same name, surfing's own spiritual in-joke.

My time in the ocean elevates the spirit more than my limited exposure to organised religion ever has. I can recall peak moments from my surfing life in vivid detail decades after the fact. I emerge from a memorable session renewed, recharged. It enables me to go on in a way nothing else does, with the possible exception of meditation.

When I was growing up in the seventies, surfing was seen as a sure-fire path to delinquency, drug addiction and unemployment, a scourge on the nation's youth. Today surfing is used as therapy to ease the suffering of everyone from war veterans to disadvantaged youth, the disabled to refugees. Surfing's healing powers have been recognised by multiple organisations – The Disabled Surfers Association, Surfers Healing (which takes autistic kids surfing), Waves of Wellness (which helps treat mental illness), Life Rolls On, One Wave, and myriad other not-for-profits in Australia and around the world.

Surfing is being used to treat depression, anxiety, PTSD. In my book *High Surf*, author Tim Winton told me in an interview:

> Surfing and the sea got me through the grimmer parts of adolescence. When life gets overwhelming, it's incredible what a few hours in the brine will do for you. It's as though the ocean is this vast salty poultice that sucks the poison out of your system.

This is never truer than for the cancer patient, particularly when going through chemotherapy or radiation.

In that same book, sub-titled 'The world's most inspiring surfers, wave-riding as a way of life, the ocean as teacher', I quoted a Waikiki surfer Jeri Edwards:

> I'm 54, and just started surfing three years ago, but I surf almost every day. I was diagnosed with cancer seven years

ago, and I believe surfing heals me and makes me strong (physically and spiritually) so I can bounce back from all the constant chemo. I believe in the mana of the ocean. As many of the beach boys will tell you, it heals. Blue (well-known Waikiki beach boy) often tells me that that is what is keeping me alive: I believe it is. Less than 20% with my particular cancer are alive after five years, and I'm still kicking after seven. Many days after chemo, I go surfing weak and with a terrible headache, but I come in clear-headed, refreshed and stronger. I don't know why it works, but I know it works. Physically, surfing keeps my muscles strong so I can bounce back after treatments. I will never lose 'my fight with cancer'. No matter what happens in the end, every day I go out surfing is a day I have beaten cancer – I have already won.

When I quoted Jeri fifteen years ago, I could never have imagined her words would one day speak so eloquently for me. There are days I've dragged myself to the ocean almost too weak to paddle out, but the moment I hit the brine I'm renewed and everything else drops away. Surfing has become a yardstick for my wellness and sense of self. If I can paddle out through the breakers, get in position for an oncoming wave, paddle into it, scramble to my feet and ride it with some semblance of coordination, I feel whole, connected to my old self as well as the natural world. One sweet ride, one well-executed manoeuvre is all I need to convince myself I am holding ground, maintaining a sense of physical and spiritual wholeness, that I am not in terminal decline.

I've volunteered at the Disabled Surfers Association's 'hands-on' days, in which dozens of surfers assist people with profound disabilities experience the glorious flight and freedom of surfing, even for a few moments. I've watched the parents of children who are otherwise confined to wheelchairs cry tears of joy just to see their offspring being propelled shoreward by one foot of whitewater, washing up on the sand giggling and screaming with joy.

On one of these hands-on days, I had the job of standing on the shore and intercepting the incoming surfers before they came to grief in the shorebreak, faces beaming with euphoria. One large, non-verbal fellow with a wild mane of dark hair and heavy beard washed up at my feet as I caught the nose of his board and guided him safely to the shore. He looked up at me, wide-eyed, panting and released a kind of animal roar, the purest expression of surf stoke I've ever encountered.

I think about that moment a lot, and what the experience might have meant to him and his elderly parents watching on from the beach. Mum and Dad then wrestled their adult son back into a special beach wheelchair, laboured up the sand with him and towelled him dry, dressed him, helped him into his regular wheelchair and then back into their car. So much effort for those few seconds of flight.

I hope it is some time yet before I am on the other side of the DSA's services, assisted into tiny waves by selfless volunteers as my physical powers decline. But if it ever comes to that, I plan on roaring like an animal every wave I catch.

15

THE INCREDIBLE
SHRINKING PHALLUS

I miss my cock.

The size and appearance of my old fella was nothing remarkable. Circumcised, a tad over the average six inches when hard (I'll admit to measuring my erection as an insecure teenager to confirm its normality), it nevertheless possessed what I'd like to consider a certain sleek elegance. A no-nonsense, dependable appendage that stood reliably erect when needed without leading its owner into too much trouble with its appetites.

A cancer diagnosis tends to lend itself to nostalgia. I'm trawling through old photos, marvelling at my carefree former existence, when I stumble upon an image of myself in my late twenties, getting changed out of a wetsuit during an extended surf trip through South America. I'm posing brazenly for the camera, naked but for the black neoprene rolled down around my ankles, arms joyfully aloft like a Vegas showgirl, my phallus boldly swinging in the chilly morning north Peruvian desert breeze. Even accounting for the frigid Humboldt Current, my manhood is of modest dimensions, yet to my middle-aged eye it now appears enormous, impressive in both its girth and length, dangling proudly from a thick, dark thatch of pubic hair like a swollen bratwurst.

Today, both the hair and phallus have been dramatically abridged. Hormone therapy is presumably called hormone therapy because if it went by its more accurate descriptor, chemical castration, many of the one in seven Australian men diagnosed with prostate cancer might baulk at it as a recommended treatment.

If you had told me before my diagnosis that millions of men around the world were chemically castrated as a routine medical treatment for one of the most common types of cancer, my response would have been a gormless, *You're shitting me?!*

While men with prostate cancer are living longer, modern medicine concedes its ability to keep men alive has outstripped its ability to manage the often devastating side effects of treatment. It's like going to the proverbial restaurant where the food is terrible but the helpings are huge. The Prostate Cancer Foundation of Australia released a new psychosocial care model to address these urgent challenges in September 2019.

'The experience of diagnosis and treatment(s) of prostate cancer is for most men a major life stress,' it reads. I'd like to meet those men for whom this isn't a major life stress, shake their hands and learn the secrets to their superpower.

'A (prostate) cancer diagnosis represents a threat to a man's future, not only with regards to survival, but also in terms of physical wellness and bodily integrity; social, family and intimate relationships; lifestyle; and his financial and occupational security.' Check, check, check, check and check, I mentally tick off these familiar stressors. 'While men often demonstrate great resilience to this experience, a substantive subgroup report high levels of psychological distress and many have high unmet psychological support needs.'

Clearly, what I was lacking was a bit of good old-fashioned resilience, a big serving of harden the fuck up, even if an important part of me is now incapable of hardening up at all.

We are accustomed to the stark, harrowing realities of conventional cancer therapies, their brutal nature, the devasting toll they can take — the perils of toxic chemotherapy drugs, disfiguring surgery, the ravages of radiation. Almost every family has been touched by cancer and many of us have witnessed the eviscerating effects of treatment. Women with breast cancer can be heroically blunt about having their breasts lopped off. Hollywood star Angelina Jolie, the modern embodiment of desirable femininity, famously had hers surgically removed as a purely preventative measure because of a genetic predisposition to breast cancer.

So, hands up who knew chemical castration was the frontline treatment for the most common form of cancer among men? Why are we so coy on the subject? Is it that men are embarrassed to discuss its emasculating effects? Or are doctors afraid of scaring men off? Is it because prostate cancer, particularly the incurable advanced variety, is considered an old man's disease, and ageism allows us to castrate old men without too much outcry or squeamishness?

Statistics show a pronounced increase in the prevalence of younger men (generally defined as under sixty) being diagnosed with prostate cancer, for reasons no one has been able to divine. These men (and, where relevant, their partners) suffer more acutely from the effects of hormone therapy and are perhaps less likely to passively accept this treatment as inevitable, unavoidable and without outcry. It seems to me barbaric, inhuman, cruel, presenting men with an impossible choice – to cease to be men or to cease to be?

And yet, many men like me are alive today because of hormone therapy's ability to halt the spread of prostate cancer, which feeds on testosterone. Life without testosterone is a . . . *peculiar* experience. I sometimes feel like I am being hollowed out from the inside, emptied, that some vital essence or core is being siphoned away. 'Men are basically machines that run on testosterone,' one doctor tells me helpfully.

I am not who I was. I tire more easily. I can't push past fatigue. It's difficult to summon the drive to get things done. My nervous system seems more easily rattled. I find I need more time on my own, quiet, still, at peace, preferably in a natural setting. Nature is my balm.

My time in the ocean was always precious, now surfing is therapy. Absorbed in something greater than the self, the intellectual mind and its barrage of cycling anxieties is quietened by the other-worldly magic of riding waves, the enormity of the ocean – vast, undulating, indifferent. At the same time, I struggle in crowded surf, lacking that killer instinct to hustle for waves. I now understand what female surfers mean when they complain of line-ups being heavy on testosterone, a condition New Zealand's 'fourth most popular folk duo', Flight of the Conchords, refer to as 'too many dicks on the dance floor'.

I still don't know whether to be grateful I'm alive or angry at what's been done to me. Perhaps it's possible, indeed natural, to feel both. I'm reminded of Samuel Beckett's poetic exhortation for endurance: 'You must go on. I can't go on. I'll go on.'

It's not all bad. My skin is smoother, my hair thicker than it once was. Minus a libido, I can relate to women as fellow human beings without fixating on their physical appearance or the particular contours of their bodies. A friend whose teenage daughter is beginning to attract the attention of young men tells me, 'I wish they would see her as a person, not an assemblage of body parts.' I now understand that statement on a different level. In the age of the #MeToo movement, there is some relief in representing no threat to anyone, neutral, the Switzerland of the gender wars.

The absence of testosterone reveals itself at odd occasions. I'm inching through a beach car park at the height of summer, with impatient kids desperate to hit the surf, trawling for a free parking spot, when I see a car reversing out and quickly put on my indicator. When the car pulls out a bearded bloke in a van is facing me with *his* indicator on also waiting for the spot. He puffs up, begins remonstrating and mouthing inaudible expletives. He looks ridiculous, a grown man throwing a toddler tantrum over a parking spot. Once, I might have responded in kind. Instead, I smile, wave, leave it to him and continue on my way. I find a free spot about twenty metres further along.

My brother-in-law Tom and I take our young children indoor rock climbing, holding their ropes, lest they fall, with unwarranted vigilance as they effortlessly scale the vertical walls. Towards the end of the session, Tom suggests we have a crack ourselves. I get no more than a couple of metres off the ground and am paralysed with fear, unable to heave myself from one handhold to the next. When I try to dig deep and push through my paralysis, I find I have nothing in reserve, no emergency fuel tank to draw on. It's deeply disconcerting.

What, in this state, am I fit for? The life of a monk? Celibacy would be no problem. A servant or slave to a royal court, like the eunuchs of antiquity? A poet, quietly observing life's curious machinations? In an era of gender fluidity, in middle-age perhaps I am finally on trend. When filling in forms and confronted with the gender question, I've begun considering the non-binary option. Perhaps my preferred pronouns should be they/them. The younger generation's nuanced understanding of gender provides genuine comfort. If a three-monthly injection can gradually erase my gender, then perhaps it is a more fluid condition than most of us acknowledge. Though the implications for my marriage and sexuality are obvious and devastating.

And yet somehow, much of the time, I seem to be living a thoroughly worthwhile, meaningful, even joyful existence. Prostate cancer has redesigned my life in ways few other things could have, much of it for the better. I work when and if I feel like it. I don't do stress. If the surf is good, I surf. After a morning surf, a friend asks me if I'm working today. I have to stop and think about it. 'If it fits into my lifestyle,' I eventually answer, with a grin.

I have a sensation of wanting to pour myself into my children, to prioritise time with them above all else and savour the small things. I recognise I am in a privileged position and can't imagine how much harder it must be for men without supportive family and a decent income, those from marginalised minorities or rural and remote areas for whom services may be harder to access.

A cancer diagnosis is not an aphrodisiac for the diagnosed or their partner, if they have one. In the weeks and months post-diagnosis, sex is the last thing on my or my wife's mind as we struggle with our new reality. During chemotherapy, even my bodily fluids are considered toxic. I'm told to flush the toilet twice with the lid down and avoid allowing my semen to come into contact with anyone, though there's little danger of that. Even before my libido completely evaporates it is dealt some serious blows.

Little to no advice is offered on the importance of maintaining intimacy and closeness in a relationship, or recommendations for therapies to maintain sexual function. I'm still angry about this. In all the various forums, support groups and newsletters I've joined I've heard precious little discussion about this from other men and how they deal with these myriad side effects – the loss of libido, the challenge to their identity and relationships, the breast swelling, the hot flushes, the loss of body hair and muscle mass. Men, it hardly needs saying, are not good at talking about this stuff. If it were groups of women dealing with this, I suspect the conversations would be much more frank, open and supportive.

Oncologists and urologists routinely prescribe this treatment knowing full well the awful side effects, hand you a cursory information sheet listing them all, offering only the consolation that not all men suffer all of them. Mercifully, I seem to have been spared the hot flushes that leave some men awash in sweat at random moments, having to change sheets in the middle of the night, carrying spare clothes to change into when required. Or the incontinence that forces some men to wear nappies, to plot their every move according to the proximity of a toilet at short notice.

Kirst and I make a few fumbling attempts at sexual intimacy, but I find it fairly humiliating, and it leaves us both unsatisfied and awkward and uncomfortable about trying again. Author Nikki Gemmell once wrote that sex after childbirth was like throwing a sausage down the Sydney Harbour Tunnel. Obviously that's, um, a stretch . . . I'd suggest our predicament is more akin to putting a baby to bed in an adult-sized sleeping bag. It will flop around unhelpfully and not stay in its warm cocoon. We need help, but in the midst of my existential turmoil – navigating treatments, blood tests, and scans, overhauling diet and lifestyle, exercising to retain muscle mass and bone strength, trying to maintain some sort of income – finding a sexual therapist never seems to come to the top of the to-do list.

When I finally do make an appointment with a men's sexual health specialist, at the recommendation of my GP, it is four years since my diagnosis and my libido and sexual function are effectively non-existent. I am shocked to discover that something as simple as Viagra may have allowed me to maintain sexual function from the outset. Why wasn't I told? The specialist tells me this is a common story, that men are so focused on simple survival in the first few years after diagnosis that they fail to address their sexual challenges early on, by which time the chances of recovery are greatly reduced. This would seem a fairly simple oversight in the system to correct, to encourage every man on hormone therapy to consult with a sexual health therapist at the outset, or at least offer some basic information on the topic.

Kirst and I have had our challenges, but we're a happy couple who've enjoyed a rich, loving and warm relationship, producing two adorable kids, both pursuing work we find fulfilling, living in a beautiful home close to the beach. We have much to be grateful for, but the absence of sex is an insidious force that has a corrosive effect over time. How many times has make-up sex soothed a minor domestic spat? That physical closeness, the expression of passion, the sweaty animal outlet of surrendering to our desires, can be a glue that binds, a buttress against the many challenges of married life. Without it, even small resentments can linger and fester.

Gradually, over time, a space opens up between us that is difficult to bridge. There are no longer just the two of us in this relationship, but a third, dark and sinister presence. 'Cancer is a selfish bastard,' Kirst observes ruefully.

We're not the same people and our relationship, inevitably, is profoundly altered. We love each other but we are both dealing with our own grief, which can leave us feeling marooned on separate islands of despair. I can't say I miss sex because I don't have a libido, but I miss the closeness, our old life, and I envy other couples their simple domestic normalities. Sex scenes on TV and in movies make me uncomfortable, a fun park I can no longer enter. Kirst is upfront about how difficult celibacy is for her. 'It's hard to accept that I'll never be looked at in that way again,' she tells me, and my heart breaks a little.

I'm sure there must be some sort of tantric workshop in northern New South Wales we could sign up for but, to be honest, I don't know if that's really our jam. Various pumps, injections and implants promise some relief, but I find it hard to imagine these devices offering much in the way of spontaneity.

And, honestly, without a libido, sex seems like a slightly odd activity to engage in. It reminds me of sitting through sex education classes at school, well before any stirring in the loins might have helped explain this strange behaviour. *When two people love each other very much they do what? And you claim my parents did this? Eeww! What on earth for?*

Can you miss something you no longer have the desire for? Absolutely. This might sound like an odd analogy, but I imagine it might be similar to how retired elite athletes feel. The physical body may no longer be capable of the athletic peaks they once drove it to, intellectually they may understand this part of their lives is behind them, but it can still leave a great emptiness.

I wish I had more to offer other men and their partners here, but this is an area where we have been acutely let down by the medical system. My best advice would be to seek help from a qualified men's sexual health specialist early on, even though it might not seem like a high priority when you are fixated on survival.

I dream of a time when we can successfully treat advanced prostate cancer without the horror show of chemical castration, and not treat patients in the way pedophiles or rapists are punished in some jurisdictions. I seize upon news of new treatment options or research breakthroughs, only to discover they are some new combination of existing hormone therapies and chemotherapy that extend life by just a limited number of months, with little consideration of quality of life.

I'm happy to be alive and, given a choice of dying with a libido and sexual function or surviving without it, I'd still choose survival. I just wish I didn't have to choose.

16

PHYSICIAN,
HEAL THYSELF

MY ONCOLOGIST HAS ONE of those little motivational prints hanging on his waiting room wall with the simple statement: Trust Your Instincts. One day, bored with the long purgatory of the waiting room, I tweet this news to the world with the observation: 'If I trusted my instincts, I'd run screaming from this place and never come back.'

I'm only half-joking. I don't wish to appear ungrateful for the miracles of modern medicine, without which I very probably would not be alive. The scores of dedicated cancer researchers around the world searching for better treatments, the privilege of a functioning First World healthcare system that doesn't plunge me into bankruptcy, the long years of study and gruelling work regime of oncologists.

Yet the routine of the oncologist's visit feels deeply dispiriting. I sit and wait for anywhere up to an hour in an atmosphere thick with dread and stress and anxiety, wiling away the time on my phone or with a trashy magazine until my name is called. My oncologist takes a cursory glance at my latest blood test results, usually tells me to continue the medication I'm on, writes me a script for another blood test and tells me to come back in four to six weeks.

I head over to the oncology day unit for a shot of my bone-strengthening agent, to fortify my skeleton against the loss of bone density due to hormone therapy. Depending on my PSA I may or may not have another shot of that very hormone therapy, having won my campaign for an intermittent regime to try to escape the worst of its brutal side effects.

I have no reason to doubt my oncologist's professional expertise and deep knowledge of his chosen field. But I've become frustrated by his uninterest in anything I might be doing to support my own health, or any research or suggestions I've come across for credible supportive or adjuvant treatments, all of which are swiftly dismissed. But more than anything, I'd like a bit more evidence that he cares, which must be hard to deliver when he's seeing dozens of patients every day at roughly ten-minute intervals, many with conditions far more dire than mine, most of whom he won't be able to cure.

The final straw comes about four years after my diagnosis, as I stand up to leave another perfunctory ten-minute consultation after an hour's wait. Something just doesn't sit right about all this. It's my life hanging in the balance. The lack of opportunity for a more wide-ranging conversation about treatment options, how I'm holding up emotionally, and strategies to mitigate the life-sapping side effects of treatment just feels wrong. Like the old TV detective Columbo, whom I share a similarly dishevelled fashion sense with, I walk towards the door, pause, turn and announce, 'Oh, one more thing'.

My oncologist does not appear pleased by this development. He has a waiting room full of patients and is already running an hour behind schedule.

'It's been four years now. I work really hard at this,' I begin tentatively. We're entering unchartered territory. I'm talking about my feelings and expecting him to respond, a betrayal of our unspoken doctor–patient contract up to this point. I press on regardless. 'I follow a strict diet, exercise and meditate daily, do everything I can to support my health. How do you think I'm going?' I pose, opening the way for him to offer some soothing words of encouragement.

He briefly ponders this unscripted moment, as if I've just told a joke he doesn't quite get.

'About average,' he eventually declares, coolly. 'Some of my patients are doing better than you, some worse. You're about average.' His response seems designed to ensure I never again have the impertinence to ask such a question, or to attribute any therapeutic powers to my own lifestyle interventions.

Even if this was his sincerely held professional view, would it have killed him to say something vaguely positive like, 'It's great that you are being so proactive about supporting your health'? Or a kind-hearted white lie, even if he didn't actually believe it: 'You're doing great. Keep it up.'

I nod, thank him, turn on my heels and finally take the

advice of that wall-mounted print. I walk out of his office never to return. I sack my oncologist. I experience a delicious sense of empowerment striding out of his office, perhaps because the power dynamic in the typical oncologist–patient relationship feels to me a little, well, out of balance.

Oncologists have studied long and hard over many years to gain their qualifications and undertake ongoing professional development to ensure they remain abreast of new developments. They must make life-and-death decisions every day and deal with the grief and anxiety of patients and relatives when the news is grim. They could be forgiven for a certain arrogance in the face of the endless questions from patients about spurious alternative treatments or resistance to proven conventional therapies.

Oncologists like to appear all-knowing, and to bat away questions on topics they don't have the answers to. Try asking your average oncologist for nutritional advice, for instance. I was told at the outset to eat whatever I want. 'Organic vegetables, Hungry Jack's, cardboard – your body turns it all into glucose anyway so it makes no difference', my oncologist told me at one of our first appointments.

But the cancer patient need not treat their oncologist as an authority on high, above reproach, unquestionable in their omniscient wisdom. Oncology is full of unknowns. Advanced cancer is effectively incurable. The cause of most cancers will never be explained. One meta-analysis of cancer studies concluded that 66 per cent of cancers were due to 'bad luck', random genetic mutations during cell division that could not be attributed to environmental or genetic factors.

Particular chemotherapy drugs may or may not work for a specific cancer. I was told the hormone therapy drug I was first prescribed was effective for some men for ten years or more, and for others it worked for only three months, and no one could explain why. Perhaps no other medical specialist is so inadequately equipped to deal with the multitudinous and devastating health conditions they are called upon to treat. Given the paucity of treatment options for many, if not most, cancers and their toxic side effects, the emotional element of cancer care becomes even more critical. The cancer patient should feel empowered to switch oncologists as many times as they feel necessary until they find one who better meets their needs.

Australian politics has been awash with discussions about the need for empathy training for our elected representatives, but politicians are not the only ones who need a bit of guidance on reading the emotional cues of their constituents, and how best to respond. A 2011 US randomised clinical trial offered oncologists a lecture on good patient communication, while half the group were also offered a tailored CD-ROM presentation to improve their communication styles, recording and critiquing their patient interactions. The researchers noted the distress and mental health challenges of many cancer patients and observed: 'Oncologists frequently miss opportunities to respond to patient emotion and may instead exhibit behaviours that block feelings and create emotional distance.'

To which I would respond, *Fuck yeah, they do.*

Existing interventions to improve oncologists' communication styles, in the form of empathy training courses, were considered too time-consuming and inconvenient for busy oncologists, so the researchers came up with a computerised, interactive, tailored intervention that showed good results in a more acceptable format. This allowed oncologists to listen back to their own audio-recorded consultations as they were offered suggestions on how better to respond to their patients' negative emotions.

Report author Dr James A. Tulsky observed: 'So often patients aren't satisfied with the communication they have with their doctor, yet I know physicians care so much about their patients and really want to express that. Physicians may wish to communicate what they are feeling but may not always use the proper words.'

You could be excused for thinking this sounds a bit like toddler training, encouraging children to use their words, yet this is no laughing matter.

'One of the things we taught the doctors in this program was how to recognise an empathetic opportunity in a conversation; that is, a moment when the patient expresses negative emotion that really deserves a response. Sometimes doctors don't even see that,' Dr Tulsky explains.

Does this stuff really need to be taught? Isn't offering comfort a basic human instinct when someone is visibly in distress? And isn't someone drawn to a caring profession like oncology specifically because they want to reduce human suffering?

The problem here appears to be twofold. Oncologists generally fit a particular psychological profile – disciplined high achievers, able to process and retain vast amounts of highly specialised and technical information and make cool-headed decisions in what are often the most trying circumstances. People with the skill set to perform these demanding functions might not be naturally inclined towards obvious displays of emotion and empathy. And even if they were, it would be almost impossible to be deeply emotionally invested in every patient. Compassion fatigue is real.

But oncologists also suffer from a terrible physical and mental health profile. Numerous studies have shown they have higher incidence of anxiety, depression and suicide than the general population, and are worse at seeking assistance. It's difficult to offer emotional support when you're experiencing psychological distress yourself. According to one US study at the Mayo Clinic titled 'Oncologist burnout: Causes, consequences and responses', published in the *Journal of Clinical Oncology*, up to 35 per cent of oncologists suffer burnout.

> Although the practice of oncology can be extremely rewarding, it is also one of the most demanding and stressful areas of medicine. Oncologists are faced with life and death decisions on a daily basis, administer incredibly toxic therapies with narrow therapeutic windows, must keep up with the rapid pace of scientific and treatment advances, and continually walk a fine line between providing palliation and administering treatments that lead to excess toxicity. Personal distress precipitated by such work-related stress may manifest in a variety of ways including depression, anxiety, fatigue, and low mental quality of life . . . Substantial evidence suggests that burnout can impact quality of

care in a variety of ways and has potentially profound personal implications for physicians including suicidal ideation.

Another study, 'Addressing depression, burnout, and suicide in oncology physicians', found that over 300 physicians die of suicide in the United States every year.

> The stigma of depression runs deep in the helping professions and in medicine in particular. Although burnout in oncology is acknowledged, the other stigmatized mental health aspects of medical practice— depression and suicide—are rarely recorded or talked about. If this were another highly prevalent disease affecting one in four of the physician population and leading to mortality from suicide at a rate of 1 out of 1,500, it would be well described with an array of available treatments.

The study found the major contributors to stress and burnout in oncologists included:

(1) working with distressed or blaming relatives,
(2) coping with patients suffering during treatment,
(3) feeling disappointed about cancer treatment options,
(4) coping with unrealistic expectations about cancer treatment,
(5) delivering bad news,
(6) worrying about patients outside of work,

(7) worrying about withdrawal or inappropriate
continuation of cancer treatment, and

(8) communicating with crying or distressed patients.

The average oncology appointment varies in duration from seven to eight minutes in Korea, to 22.9 minutes in the United States. From my own experience, in Australia the average duration would fall somewhere in between, around the ten- to fifteen-minute mark, though I have been unable to locate any specific data. Given all these issues, it's little wonder oncologists suffer such high incidence of burnout and poor mental health. Wouldn't oncologists as well as patients benefit from an embrace of supportive therapies to address the unmet emotional needs and quality-of-life issues of patients and reduce the burden on oncologists to perform a counselling role they have little or no training in? Who knows? Oncologists might benefit from the application of some of those supportive therapies themselves.

To compound the problem, oncologists are often reluctant to report mental health issues, considering it a potential blot on their career record. 'Physicians have been trained to be perfectionists. They've been trained not to ever show any weakness, and they think of mental health issues as weakness,' Anthony L. Back, MD, professor of medical oncology at University of Washington Medical Center and co-director of the UW Center for Excellence in Palliative Care told *HemOnc Today*, an online journal of oncology and hematology.

Another US study, 'Doctor, are you healthy? A cross-sectional investigation of oncologist burnout, depression and anxiety and an investigation of their associated factors', found 30 per cent of oncologists 'drink alcohol in a problematic way', and up to 20 per cent of junior oncologists use hypnotic drugs or sleeping pills.

Fay J. Hlubocky, PhD, MA, clinical health psychologist in the department of medicine at University of Chicago, told *HemOnc Today* that senior oncologists need to lead the way in de-stigmatising mental illness. 'The oncology community, led by cancer leadership, has an absolute duty and obligation to acknowledge the mental health issues that oncologists, nurses and other oncology clinicians experience,' Hlubocky says. 'We must normalize and speak of mental health issues to minimize the stigma that presently exists.'

Does it strike anyone else as sadly ironic that one of the most dire health issues of our times is presided over by a profoundly unhealthy physician population? The current model of cancer care serves no one, leaving complex patient needs unmet and exacting a cruel toll on clinicians. We are all – patients and doctors alike – casualties in the war on cancer.

17

THE CURL

I'VE WRESTLED WITH THE question of whether I should continue working since my diagnosis. Managing my health can feel like a full-time job – exercising and meditating daily, sourcing and preparing healthy food, staying on top of medical appointments and exploring supportive therapies, participating in clinical trials for exercise and medicinal cannabis. With an unlimited budget and no need to work I could easily put all my time and energy into staying healthy, but that isn't my reality. And having a focus beyond cancer self-care seems important if I am to not be entirely defined by the disease.

I've managed to maintain what you might call light duties and am trying to master the three-hour workday. The magazine gig I had editing a quarterly lifestyle journal, *Slow*, started to feel like too much eighteen months in and my aversion to tight deadlines and the stress they entail has only hardened over time.

Kirst has stepped up to take on more of the provider role, but I still need to be contributing to the family finances. Then I'm made an offer that seems too good to refuse.

It's early 2016, I've recently finished chemo and my hair's just beginning to grow back. I'm nearly bald, with an alarming grey pallor, but as the toxicity starts to leach from my system I'm feeling better by the day. As fate would have it, I have to renew my driver's licence photo a few weeks after finishing chemo, so I'm stuck with this image that resembles an escaped criminal or death mask for the next ten years. I'm waiting for a cop to look at it, look at me, and declare the licence a fake.

A proposed reunion of my old workmates from *Tracks* days at Mason Stewart Publishing in Sydney is a welcome distraction from the world of oncology. I might once have been lukewarm about these sorts of reunions and celebrating the supposed bond I share with a group of people I worked with for a few years close to thirty years ago. But with the heightened awareness of my mortality comes a new appreciation for past friendships. I'm in.

Kirst is keen to join me so we jump on a couple of cheap fares, recruit the grandparents for a bit of kid-sitting, and we're off to Sydney for the weekend. The venue is a stylish bar close to the old *Tracks* office in Darlinghurst, which was once surrounded by brothels and junkies. The local corner pub, the Tradesman's Arms, attracted a colourful clientele of petty crims, bent cops and us magazine-publishing types. The Tradoes was the favoured watering hole of the notorious rogue detective Roger Rogerson, where he did his dodgy deals when Sydney's criminal underbelly was in its prime. Mason

Stewart published a stable of lifestyle magazines including *Australian Playboy*, *Australian Cricket*, *Slimming*, and *Waves*. We were a disparate bunch; surfers, cricket nerds, smart inner-city women, fashionistas and pornographers, who stood out among the Tradoes' regular, hard-bitten clientele.

A bunch of Maori scaffolders used to favour the Tradoes for a Friday arvo, after-work ale, and for some reason the biggest, meanest, roughest-looking bloke among them took a shine to me. He'd collar me as soon as I arrived and drag me into the men's room to smoke hash. 'We start fights at other pubs, but we come here to relax,' he'd reassure me. We'd occasionally arrive at work to find junkies shooting up in the car park or ripping off someone's car stereo. Sex workers hung out the windows and upstairs balconies of surrounding terraces or patrolled nearby Williams Street. All a world away from the quaint timber beach house overlooking Whale Beach with a resident red setter I had envisaged when I gleefully accepted the *Tracks* gig.

Like most of inner-city Sydney, Darlo has been through a serious gentrification in recent years and is barely recognisable from the grungy old neighbourhood that inspired Paul Kelly's eighties hit 'Darling It Hurts', a pained love song to a street sex worker. I spent a formative five years of my early adulthood here, from the age of twenty-one to twenty-six, and ghosts and memories linger round every corner. Lobbing into Sydney with a suitcase and surfboard to begin my new life, not knowing a soul. The office intrigues and romances. The *Tracks* office bong. The former ad manager who kept a dinner plate piled high with cocaine in his desk drawer to get him primed for the next sales pitch, like a smooth-talking Scarface insisting you book a double-page spread.

Our urbane English publisher seemed to despise surfers, even while profiting handsomely from their patronage. Big Phil would get around in cream linen suits, resembling a pale and pastier Bryan Ferry, and referred to *Tracks* readers as 'spotty-faced little fuckers'. Yet he deferred to the virile, red-blooded blokes running *Tracks* to appraise his latest choice of *Australian Playboy* cover models as a litmus test.

'Is this one high on the horn, boys?' he'd ask us comically, in his plum English accent, waving cover proofs of naked women around theatrically in the boardroom, the only time we slovenly surfers were allowed to set foot in his hallowed inner sanctum. Legend has it Phil once hosted some bigwigs from the US *Playboy* head office checking on their antipodean licensee. When it came time to give them a tour of the building, he told them the *Tracks* office was a storage cupboard rather than reveal the barefoot, pot-smoking, sun-tanned layabouts he employed on his empire's most profitable title.

It all feels like a lifetime ago. We're older, balder, a bit worn around the edges. I'm just a bit balder and more worn than most. The usual exchange of news, updates on career, families, kids, health, has a sharp edge to it now as I assess how much information to provide about my new circumstances, but my appearance gives it away. 'You look like you've been through some kind of trauma,' Cheryl, one of the old advertising graphic artists, observes insightfully.

Yet, the reunion is a joyous, uplifting occasion just the same. Karaoke provides the raucous social focus of the evening and we quickly revert to old roles – the party animal, the joker, the extrovert, the messy drunk, the flirt. Among the many folks I'm happy to be reacquainted with is a bloke I first hired as *Tracks'* travel writer. Neil Ridgway was a young uni graduate from Maclean, on the NSW North Coast, when I gave him a start ghost-writing the travel column for our entirely fictitious resident surf travel expert, Daryl Davenport. Neil did this with enough aplomb he eventually rose to the role of editor, long after I'd moved on, then successfully launched UK men's magazine *FHM* in Australia at the height of the lad magazine fad. With exquisite timing, just as print began to circle the drain, Neil pivoted to a marketing job at surf brand Rip Curl with enormous success, now claiming the grand title of marketing chairman for Rip Curl International.

His new esteemed position doesn't stop Neil and his old assistant editor Wayne Dart from thoroughly dominating the karaoke mic, with a string of enthusiastic duets of Oz pub rock anthems and old crooner classics. Neil and I've been friendly without ever being especially close, but he's never forgotten that first freelance gig. So it feels like he's returning the favour when, a few months after this glorious reunion, he calls me out of the blue to see if I'd be interested in writing a book on the history of Rip Curl to mark their upcoming fiftieth anniversary. It sounds like a sweet gig, with a realistic budget, some international travel, and enough time to do the job properly. And I'm touched by his faith – it'd be easy to write me off as a bad bet in my current condition. Even I'm unsure if my health is up to it.

I have a sneaking suspicion writing books – the uncertain financial returns, the gruelling deadlines, the long hours stooped over a computer keyboard – contributed to my health crisis. Is it crazy to consider taking on another? But I still need to earn a living. I settle on an age-old freelancer's strategy: quote high, so if you get the job, it's enough of a windfall to make it worthwhile and if you don't get it, you don't really mind. 'I'd need to earn enough that I could afford to do nothing but this book for a year, to do it justice,' I tell Neil seriously. I suggest a generous monthly retainer for twelve months and a travel budget, and he doesn't blink. Turns out budgets in successful iconic surf brands are healthier than they ever were at middling magazine publishers. Looks like I'm writing another book.

Yet, I'm still beset by doubts. If my time here is limited, shouldn't I be doing something more meaningful, that makes a greater contribution to humanity and leaves more of a legacy than producing marketing material for a surf brand? Will it take too much of a toll on my health? How will I handle the overseas travel at a time when I often find myself feeling profoundly brittle and vulnerable and just wanting to hide under my doona?

In the end, the income and opportunity seem too good to pass up. The money will allow me to do everything I need to do to look after my health – all the herbs and supplements and Pilates and yoga classes and naturopathic and integrative doctor's appointments and organic vegetables I require – while supporting my family and continuing to ply my trade. I also don't want to let cancer stop me from doing things. I like writing. I think I'm reasonably good at it. It's all I've ever done for paid employment. The prospect of a healthy income, with trips to France, Portugal, California, the Rip Curl head office in wave-rich Torquay, and winter excursions to Mount Buller to ski with the founders, Doug 'Claw' Warbrick and Brian Singer, on their annual winter retreats proves irresistible.

The other pay-off is I get to take Alex to the annual Rip Curl Pro at Bells Beach, the world's longest running surf contest, with VIP passes and accommodation at the no-frills brown brick Surf City Motel. Thus, our Easter is spent surfing Bells or neighbouring Winki Pop at dawn, feasting on the VIP catering in the Rip Curl stand while watching the action, sneaking out for a sly sesh at Winki when the contest's at Bells, and scouring the surrounding coast for waves. Alex meets many of his surfing heroes and shares an ice cream and a friendly chat with seven-time world champ Stephanie Gilmore after dinner one night. We're blessed with perfect Victorian autumn weather with consistent swell, offshore winds and mild temperatures, and after a week of it, Alex wants to relocate to Torquay permanently.

'Tell him to come back in August,' Neil suggests.

As I write in *The Rip Curl Story*:

> With Alex frothing for maximum surf time, I decide to test that old adage: "No one at Rip Curl ever got sacked for going surfing" . . . I rationalise that in some way the Rip Curl story needs to seep out of those ancient cliffs and reefs and illuminate to me the spirit of place that fuelled this whole outlandish adventure. No one at head office seems to mind a bit.

Come winter, I spend a couple of weeks at Mount Buller with the Rip Curl founders, enjoying generous hospitality in their neighbouring mountain-top apartments, and trying to keep up with Brian on the slopes. Despite being twenty years his junior, and it being eighteen months since Brian has had a knee replacement, I fail miserably, and he waits patiently for me at the bottom of each run. 'I hope I'm not slowing you down too much,' I offer apologetically.

Brian's a straight talker. 'It'd be different if it was a powder day. There are no friends on powder days,' he growls.

We ski in the mornings, lunch on the mountain, then talk story in the afternoons before adjourning for dinner at one of the village's better restaurants. If I can call this work, despite my mortal peril, I seem to have done something right in this life.

Shortly before I head to Europe to document the Curl's spectacular growth in the key markets of France and Portugal, a rising PSA with appalling timing necessitates a return to ADT.

One of my great comforts during this vexed time is Vivi's blossoming poetry career. She's been a star of her school's 'Wordsmiths' writing club for some time, but in year 10 she ups the ante considerably by taking out a national high school poetry prize. Then she discovers the world of slam poetry and a star (and a formidable feminist instinct) is born. I accompany her to a poetry slam at a local café and marvel at this intriguing hotbed of youth activism, teenagers railing against gender stereotypes, climate change, domestic violence and racism, the youthful audience clicking their fingers to acknowledge their favourite lines. One moment, my teenage daughter is a bundle of nerves sitting by my side in the audience, the next she is a force of nature up on stage.

Vivi takes out the Gold Coast heat of the Australian Poetry Slam with a scorching, posthumous take down of Edgar Allen Poe for calling the death of a beautiful woman 'the most poetical topic in the world'. A few weeks later, Viv heads to the Judith Wright Centre in Brisbane with her mum for the Queensland final. I'm at home with Alex wondering how she's going when Kirst sends me a short but euphoric text: 'SHE WON!!!'

We decide to make a weekend of it in Sydney for Vivi's performance at the Australian Poetry Slam Final at the Opera House, puffed with pride at our talented offspring's literary glory. Viv doesn't take out the national final, though obviously she should have.

We all catch the train to the airport on the Sunday evening after a joyous weekend. I'm flying straight on to France for the Rip Curl gig while the family are returning to the Gold Coast. They disembark at the domestic terminal, and I wave them off through the train window as it pulls away from the platform, feeling utterly bereft.

Normally this would be a dream assignment, but I'm beset by anxiety just negotiating check-in and hire car desks and foreign roads. The airline manages to lose my bags for two days so I'm without my meds and my surfboard and wetsuit, which heightens the stress. And I've chosen not to take the risk of travelling with my cannabis oil. A perfect mental health storm is brewing.

Eventually I make it to the south-west surf town of Hossegor and check in to the historic Hotel de Mercedes overlooking the scenic Lac d'Hossegor. The Quiksilver Pro has just finished in the pounding French beach breaks of La Graviere, and the hotel quickly empties of contest personnel until the few remaining guests are suddenly outnumbered by hotel staff.

My old mate Maurice Cole, who lived here for ten years after that cruel drug bust back in the seventies, has returned to his former stomping ground for his annual French shaping stint, and kindly takes me under his wing. Maurice picks me up in a clapped-out old Renault station wagon to go surfing in those same sublime beach breaks that led him to settle here four decades ago. Well into his sixties, he's still a commanding presence in the busy line-up, chatting amiably in French to old surfing buddies, casually picking off set waves, riding them with an easy grace. Later, he sets up a breakfast date with Rip Curl Europe's elusive and mercurial founder François Payot, whose ebullient storytelling over coffee and croissants in his magnificent converted farmhouse in the French countryside proves one of the highlights of my research.

Maurice seems to be managing his own cancer diagnosis successfully, still charging in the surf and shaping beautiful boards, and his inspiration and companionship mean the world to me. Even so, my own anxieties give me little peace. I come in from a pleasant enough surf one morning at La Graviere and for no apparent reason suffer what I assume is a panic attack. My heart pounds and my head swims, questioning what I'm doing so far from home, desperately missing my family, feeling lost and adrift. I walk back to my hire car trying to stifle tears, unsure what to do or where to be. I manage to keep up a brave face and get the job done, assiduously interviewing, note-taking, writing, observing. But back in my hotel room I stare at the ceiling and wonder what the hell I'm doing here.

An old friend from *Tracks* days (let's call him Caleb) has settled here picking up a rundown house cheaply in the forests behind Hossegor back in the nineties and turning it into an informal backpacker party house. Caleb invites me over for dinner and despite some reservations about how I'll cope in a large social setting, it's as if we're in our twenties again, young and foolish, with no responsibilities. Caleb's lifestyle has changed little in thirty years. All his guests are on holidays, every night's a party, but I sense it's a dangerous lifestyle for my old friend, who never needed too much encouragement.

Upon arrival, he drags me into the bathroom where an Italian surfer is racking up lines of cocaine on the marble benchtop. It's been decades since I last succumbed to the seductive white powder and I politely decline, but Caleb's always been persuasive. 'It's really pure,' he insists. 'It'll do you good just to forget about everything for a while.' He passes me a rolled-up twenty euro note and it's as if old muscle memory kicks in and I'm soon hoovering up two generous lines; behaviour not recommended in any of the integrative cancer protocols I'm aware of.

The party's warming up around the kitchen table, littered with a platoon of Kronenbourg stubbies, the little green hand grenades resembling old Victoria Bitter throwdowns, and they prove as easy to imbibe while losing count. A pair of demure young English women have just arrived straight from the airport and seem both shocked and charmed by the unexpected nature of their holiday accommodation. An old nylon string guitar is passed around the United Nations round table of surfer/slacker/stoners and I take my turn, banging out some of the Frothies' old beer-drinking anthems. The crew are soon joining in with the bawdy singalong lyrics and suddenly I'm thirty again, when the Frothies were banging out these appalling ditties to packed houses at the Gold Coast's seedier dives. Turns out, Caleb's prescription has some merit.

But the long shadow of cancer is never far away. A friend of Caleb's has recently been diagnosed with a brain tumour; she's in complete denial and doesn't want to talk about it, but Caleb insists I offer her some wise counsel. I feel like a bit of a phony proselytising on the virtues of a plant-based diet, meditation, exercise and a healthy lifestyle, having just inhaled a jumbo serving of Bolivia's finest and partaken of the party joints being regularly passed around the table. Ian Gawler would be unimpressed.

A few people have asked me for lifestyle advice since my diagnosis and it's a role I've been happy enough to play, sharing whatever I've learnt about cancer self-care, short of offering actual medical advice. But I've yet to encounter someone who's coping strategy appears to be pretending it isn't happening. My heart aches for this tortured soul, a single mum who simply can't contemplate the reality of her situation, but I feel like an imposter offering even the most rudimentary guidance.

The raucous night out feels like a naughty detour from my own self-care regime, but I manage to convince myself one night of misbehaviour is fairly harmless. And the endorphins of hysterical laughter have got to be good for you, right?

Yet I'm surprised how quickly I regress. I return to my lonely hotel room in the early hours of the morning, predictably enough entirely unable to sleep, listening to my heart race, the four walls closing in.

The next day, my old mate asks me if I'd be interested in a drive to Plum Village, a Buddhist monastery in the French countryside, home to Vietnamese Zen Buddhist monk and author Thich Nhat Hanh – an entirely unexpected development. Thich Nhat Hanh has been hugely influential in my own nascent Buddhist instincts and meditation practice and his books have helped guide my evolution since a beautiful Portuguese woman in Hawaii gave me a copy of *Peace Is Every Step* twenty-five years ago. His classic rumination on mortality, *No Death, No Fear,* and the Buddhist view of impermanence and reincarnation provided much comfort in the early, bewildering days after my diagnosis. Plum Village is as close to a Mecca as this old atheist is ever likely to embrace. Caleb wants to have a thorough cleanse from his decadent lifestyle, which has caught up with him in his fifties, and he figures the strict monastic traditions of a Plum Village retreat might do the trick.

In a parallel universe, I set aside my Rip Curl commitments and drive the three hours to Plum Village with my mate, embrace its simple, Buddhist lifestyle and might have remained there to this day, head shaven, saffron-robed, omming and chanting and meditating my days away until I attained enlightenment. A sliding doors moment I might yet come to regret. But my stubborn old work ethic won't allow it. I'm due in Portugal for the Rip Curl Pro in Peniche, to examine how this once sleepy fishing village has been reborn as one of Europe's most thriving surf cities. Enlightenment will have to wait.

On my first overseas assignment for *Tracks*, as a green 21-year-old, I drove a little Citroën 2CV, or Deux Chevaux (two horses, in reference to its tiny engine's capacity), from Paris to Lisbon and back via the European surf hubs of Ericeira in Portugal, Mundaka in Spain and the French surf centres of Biarritz, Hossegor and Lacanau over the course of a month. Carefree, footloose, my whole life in front of me, I bought cheap red wine by the litre, decanted from oak barrels into plastic water bottles, subsisted on baguettes and cheese and ham, slept in my boardbag on people's floors. Embarking on the dream life of a surf writer, that trip could not have been further removed from my current anxious existence. Yet here I am, over thirty years, a marriage, two kids and a cancer diagnosis later, still plying my ludicrous trade.

Portugal is kinder to me, perhaps because I'm closer to heading home, halfway through a two-week trip, over the hump. I've been to Peniche once before, in the late nineties, and adored it – the smorgasbord of fresh seafood straight off the fishing boats, the easygoing temperament of the Portuguese, the rugged coast and historic waterfront fort, the wonderfully varied surf and familiar stands of eucalyptus trees lining the highway north from Lisbon. The story of how surfing, and Rip Curl in particular, has taken root and flourished here is fascinating. A decade ago, with local fisheries in decline, Peniche's gregarious mayor António José Correia embraced surfing as a new source of economic prosperity. Rip Curl's presence, in the form of a world tour event and enormous retail store, has been embraced like a saviour. My great photographer pal Ted Grambeau is in town for the event and my anxiety seems to dissipate in the face of his unfailing bonhomie. Still, I'm relieved when the job is done and it's time to fly home.

The return to family feels like a life raft after the disorienting sense of being all at sea. What drew me to the gig – the opportunity to travel and practise my craft and catch up with old friends like a final global farewell lap – now feels like a burden. The ravages of my ADT leave me wanting to crawl into the nearest cave and never leave. Yet duty, and a meeting with one of the great quixotic surfing talents of the modern age, calls.

After a brief home pit stop to do laundry and hug the family, I'm off to California for an audience with Rip Curl's enigmatic, legendary team rider and three-time world champ Tom Curren. Since his unstoppable pro tour heyday in the eighties and early nineties, Curren's cut a mysterious figure in surfing, riding bizarre, skimboard-style craft, travelling to far-off coastlines, putting at least as much energy into his folky, bluegrass-tinged music as his surfing.

I fly into Los Angeles early on a cool autumn morning, pick up a rental car and brave the six-lane freeways south to Laguna Beach, where I am again booked into the Pacific Edge Hotel, three years after my last visit – though it may as well have been a lifetime ago. I reach Laguna by 8 am and despite my request for an early check-in I'm left to bide my time. Fortuitously, I pick up a local street press magazine, full of gig guides and band profiles, and a double-page ad announcing the opening of 'Orange County's first legal cannabis dispensary'. With time to kill, and without my precious oil, I figure, *why not?*

South Coast Safe Access takes some finding, tucked in among suburban homes, car yards and fast-food joints. The car park's busy with customers coming and going, a security guard stands impassively by the entrance, and ID is required at reception. But once granted entry, like an exclusive nightclub, a world of delights opens up. Jars of buds and small vials of oil and smoking paraphernalia are arranged in neat rows on shelves and in glass counters. Courteous and knowledgeable staff explain the virtues and characteristics of each product as discerning customers sniff and examine their colour and discuss provenance like wine buffs. I ask for something to assist with sleep and am directed to a small bottle of THC oil for US$35, which I'm told should last a week or two. Done. I've still got time on my hands before check-in, so I hit Laguna's farmers' market and stock up on fresh salad greens, carrots, blueberries, sprouts and freshly squeezed pomegranate juice. When I finally check in, my little hotel bar fridge looks rather different to the last time I was here, when it was stocked only with beer and salsa.

I busy myself conducting interviews with notable figures from Rip Curl's past while I wait for the man I flew all this way to speak to grace me with his presence. Tom Curren is notoriously tricky to pin down and so it proves for my visit. The Great One is in Israel on some unspecified mission despite our agreed rendezvous. Curren's so central to the Rip Curl story, particularly in the United States, I can only hope he resurfaces before it's time for me to return home. In the meantime I visit Rip Curl's new, purpose-built headquarters in the surf industry hub of Costa Mesa, dubbed Velcro Valley – the surf equivalent of the tech industry's Silicon Valley. The oil helps take the edge off at the end of a hard day's interviewing and transcribing and I find myself dancing about my hotel room with my UE Boom speaker blaring. The mercurial Mr Curren eventually returns from his mysterious mission to Israel, and I spend a couple of intriguing days in his company at his home in Santa Barbara with his Panamanian wife, Maki. Curren's as eclectic as ever, his answers ranging from vague to garbled to profound, sometimes in a single sentence.

The task of pulling all these disparate elements together is joyful, like roughing out a large mural, then filling in the detail in each section as I work across its vast expanse. I hadn't appreciated how much my self-identity was wrapped up in being a writer until I felt my vocation threatened by my illness or, more accurately, its treatment.

I've spoken to men who abruptly quit work when they were diagnosed, putting all their energy into managing their health. These are usually older men close to retirement who can afford to stop work. Even so, some eventually return to their trade when they find there's no real impediment to them working, and they seem to derive meaning and satisfaction from it. For others, work is almost entirely out of the question while managing pain, anxiety and the side effects of treatment. Everyone's different and work occupies a different place in each person's life. For me, continuing to work has been a healthy and supportive focus, as well as a financial necessity, but work will never again be all-consuming. The lunacy of ruining our health to make money has never been more apparent.

The Rip Curl Story is launched at Easter 2019, at a gala event at the Torquay Golf Club with no expense spared. There's an open bar, three-course dinner, Vegas-style showgirls inexplicably teetering about on stilts, a gallery of surf magazine covers featuring Rip Curl surfers through the decades, and a line-up of local surfers modelling a timeline of Rip Curl's classic wetsuits, from the stiff old things of the early seventies, the garish fluoro of the eighties, to the pervasive black and techy innovations of the 2000s.

Everyone's presented with a copy of the book. People seem to like it. Claw and Brian and Neil are happy. I've managed to keep myself alive and my family fed, housed and clothed for another year. But financial management has never been my strong suit, and I've barely saved a cent of my generous remuneration. A cancer diagnosis tends to undermine efforts at delayed gratification. It's a sobering day when the final monthly retainer lands in my bank account. Having put all my work energies into the book, I'm abruptly unemployed and without income. I go from living high on the hog to scraping the barrel in the blink of an eye.

18

FATHER'S DAY

THERE'S NO BREKKY IN bed, no socks or undies or hankies or morning cuddles for Father's Day at our place. I'm too busy falling apart.

I don't even want to get out of bed. I'm sobbing uncontrollably for no particular reason, hiding out in the bedroom so the kids don't see me like this. Kirst isn't sure what to do with my despair. I thought I was sailing along wonderfully . . . until I wasn't. But I know this feeling, the creeping stealth of ADT quietly overtaking me and pulling me under. I'm short with the kids, lose my shit at the slightest trigger, feel completely unable to regulate my emotional responses, become teary at the drop of a hat. I must be miserable to be around.

I'm not alone. I google my ADT to try to understand its side effects and find a website called 'Ask a Patient' where people leave accounts of their experiences with various medications.

TripAdvisor for meds. Side effects from ADT and the extent
to which they influence a man's wellbeing may vary, and the
entries describing some people's negative experiences of it are
chilling. It's a familiar roll call of misery, telling of mood swings,
brain fog, lethargy, suicidal ideation, men declaring they'd rather
not live than live under the depressive yoke of this medication.
One woman describes her once loving husband as a Dr Jekyll
and Mr Hyde. And then there are some side effects I've been
lucky enough to dodge – insomnia, sensitive skin, joint pain.
There are calls to take the drug off the market and warnings to
other men to avoid it at all costs. I can't tell if I'm appalled or
comforted to learn I have so much company in my struggles.

Many men on the same ADT I'm prescribed use it quite
happily for long periods with nothing like these severe side
effects, but I tend more to the nightmare side of the experience. Many times I've thought life is not worth living if I have
to continue taking it, which is the emphatic recommendation
of my oncologist. I'm baffled that oncologists can routinely
prescribe a drug that quadruples the risk of suicide; compro-
mises bone density, cardiovascular health, sexual function
and cognitive function; and increases the chance of diabetes,
without putting any supportive therapies or even monitoring
in place. I don't even feel like I've been adequately informed
of the ADT's cruel impacts.

In a 2015 study, 'Adverse effects of androgen-deprivation
therapy and their management', researchers reported:

> ADT is usually prescribed at a time when patients are
> told of the devastating nature of their disease and outlook.

The hormonal vicissitude from ADT may then compound the psychological distress of the patient already in a state of crisis. In a survey of men newly diagnosed with metastatic disease, about a third of patients were identified as highly distressed and this level increased over the first 12 months. The risk of suicide was also substantial, with the risk being as high as four-times the matched peer control. Further, ADT has been found to impair memory, attention and executive functions.

Not an ideal impairment as you navigate your way through an often complex and confounding medical system. The authors concluded:

> There are numerous adverse effects of ADT that require pro-active prevention and treatment. Ranging from cardiovascular disease, diabetes and osteoporosis, to depression, cognitive decline and sexual dysfunction, the range of adverse effects is wide. Baseline assessment, monitoring, prevention and consultation from a multidisciplinary team are important in minimising the harm from ADT.

I'm now convinced I was suffering undiagnosed PTSD for several years post-diagnosis, exacerbated by the added trauma of concurrent hormone therapy and chemotherapy within a couple of weeks of diagnosis. The effects manifested in mood swings, depression, sudden and disproportionate outbursts of anger and suicidal ideation that wreaked havoc with my family life.

Hormone therapy can creep up on you, slowly eroding your mental health, cognitive function, sense of self, and your ability to regulate your emotions. This can feel like a slow descent into madness, except you don't even realise it until the latest bout of madness has passed. I've lost my shit in airports, train stations, shopping centres, over family meals, where some mild stressor suddenly tips me over the edge and I'm shouting and blaming and accusing others of some imagined wrongdoing. My conduct in airports has become infamous in our family. I recall checking in for a domestic flight, determined to maintain my composure, when the lady at check-in mildly scolded me for being impatient, for dumping my bags too close to the people already checking in ahead of me, rather than waiting in the allotted place. 'Next time, can you just wait there?' she asked calmly, but with a trace of annoyance, indicating the metal poles and barrier of the check-in queue.

In my addled mind this was a gross injustice, requiring a rabid defence. I was the aggrieved party here, being unfairly singled out for censure when I'd been focused only on navigating the airport experience without incident. 'I was waiting!' I bellowed in outrage. 'I wasn't doing anything other than waiting.' To me this seemed an entirely reasonable defence, but I noted a look of alarm on the woman's face. 'Okay, look, I think we've just got off on the wrong foot. Let's start over,' she pleaded, with real fear in her eyes. I looked to my family for support, confirmation the other party here was behaving very strangely indeed. Instead, I saw our teenage daughter in tears, embarrassed by her father's deranged behaviour. At the time, I had no idea how to account for this dissonance, yet this is an entirely predictable response to hormone therapy. Prescribing this drug to men and sending them out into the world without better preparing them for its ravages seems borderline negligent.

Some nights I lie in bed and hear trucks roar by at the bottom of our street and think, *If I were to just walk down the hill and step in front of one, all this would be over in an instant.* Kirst would have my life insurance; she's young and gorgeous enough to meet someone else. The kids would be better off without my moody, brooding presence. What's to be gained by dragging this whole thing out? I never feel in serious danger of acting on these dark thoughts, but it's still an alarming place to find oneself at 3 am. Usually, in the light of a new day I can regroup and muster the energy to carry on, but not this day. Kirst can see it and knows we need help.

Kirst used to work at an upmarket health retreat in the Gold Coast hinterland and still has friends who work there. She makes a call to a pal who handles bookings and, as luck would have it, they have a special on for friends and family of staff to fill a few last-minute vacancies in their spring detox week starting today at 50 per cent off the usual price. Soon I'm packing a bag, pulling myself together to say goodbye to the kids, explaining that this is my Father's Day gift, a week off by myself to be pampered.

It's humbling to have to wave the white flag and concede I'm not coping. But there's a kind of relief too, to let go of effort, to surrender, acknowledge that this thing is bigger than me. Kirst drives me out along winding country roads and through lush, subtropical rainforest to the grand entry and imposing driveway to the retreat's spectacular hilltop position.

The steep climb leads to what appears to be a small, historic village, a cluster of re-purposed old timber buildings, a church for yoga, quaint timber cottages for the reception and dining areas, augmented by modern accommodation and a grand spa and fancy gym, all set amid towering eucalypts and groves of fruit trees. I'm hearing strains of 'Mrs Robinson', as Simon and Garfunkel encourage me to look around and appreciate the sympathetic smiles, to stroll around the gardens until I feel at home.

I'm no longer the heroic cancer survivor defying my medical prognosis. I'm someone who needs to be packed off to a fancy sanatorium to be fixed and put back together, who's not coping. The outside world feels so big and loud and complex and confronting and overstimulating, all I want to do is hide away. Yet stripped of all distractions, with the opportunity to really stop and be still and feel into my core state, I fear that I will just . . . lose it completely, unravel, fall apart and struggle to put myself back together again. I imagine myself bawling for days as all the pent-up pain and angst and fear of the past three years comes tumbling out. Kirst kisses me goodbye with a kind of weary relief that I am someone else's problem for a few days, and I can sense her thinking, 'God, I hope this works'.

After a short induction explaining the rules and routine, I'm shown to my quarters. I drop my bags and gaze about its opulence, slightly awestruck. It's . . . beautiful, the sort of well-appointed and comfortable safe space I feel like crawling into and never leaving. The high ceiling and timber beams and floorboards, the queen-sized bed and spacious granite bathroom, the second bathtub on the back deck that can be made private by sliding screens to enjoy a discreet outdoor soak. All this luxury feels like a buttress for my emotional fragility. Even at 50 per cent off this constitutes a grand splurge and I realise with a pang of guilt how desperate Kirst must be feeling to even suggest it. It's easy to forget how my emotional condition impacts those around me when I'm in such a dark place, a black hole that sucks the energy out of everything within my gravitational field.

I settle into the retreat's gentle routine happily enough, relieved to have someone else map out my days. Early morning qi gong on dew-dropped lawns gazing out over panoramic views of the Gold Coast, the rolling hills, surreal beachfront high-rise towers and the shimmering Pacific beyond. Rainforest walks with our ebullient resident guide, Johnny, who points out edible plants and other vegetation of note as we traverse the surrounding hills, skirting neighbouring farms and country roads. A healthy breakfast begins with a shot of apple cider vinegar to kickstart the metabolism but, sadly, no coffee. A variety of morning activities are offered depending on your tastes and energy levels. High intensity training, tribal dance sessions, meditation and yoga classes, information sessions on health and diet and relationships, a kind of free-form movement workshop that has me leaping and twirling and rolling about the room imagining I am a dolphin. And all this before lunchtime.

Afternoons are given over to what's called dreamtime, when you can book treatments in the opulent spa, see a qualified counsellor for emotional healing, or just do nothing. I opt for plenty of nothing, with a couple of massages punctuating my week. I keep waiting for my cork to pop – for the accumulated trauma to come spilling out but, strangely, it never happens. Instead, an entirely unexpected thing occurs. I feel . . . joyful. Not just happy, but a deep-seated, contented gratitude and wonder and appreciation for all this . . . loveliness.

So, this is what it's like to be wealthy, to have your every need catered for by attentive staff. Sure, the opulence and pampering and healthy food are nice, but I've been fortunate enough to enjoy those kinds of indulgences before, usually on media junkets to high-end surf resorts. This is different. It's not so much about the luxury. I'm exactly where I need to be, doing exactly what I need to be doing. I've felt a similar sense of relief amid the spartan environment of a Vipassana meditation retreat, without the five-star treatment, a feeling of being insulated from the world, without the stress and noise, and that more than anything seems to be what I need.

One rainy afternoon, I luxuriate in the outdoor bath in my suite and can't recall when I've felt so deeply at peace, fat raindrops splattering on the tin roof as I gaze out over orchards of mango, avocado and citrus trees and the forested hills beyond. I've deliberately left the laptop and phone behind but brought good old-fashioned pen and notepad and spend the afternoon scribbling, a stream of consciousness vent of the past three years pouring out of me.

My fellow guests are a mixed bunch – burnt-out business-people; middle-aged folks who appear to have stayed at the party too long, now belatedly attempting to cleanse body and soul; a young woman from North Queensland escaping a toxic relationship; an older couple on their annual retreat and reset from busy lives; a larger-than-life Middle Eastern restaurateur who has more outrageous life tales than anyone I've ever met; a thirty-something New York Jew whose entire extended family immigrated to New Zealand after the September 11 terrorist attacks and its subsequent Islamophobia that felt too familiar for comfort.

Gradually, through the week, over meals and rainforests walks and fireside chats, our stories come out with a rare honesty. Mine always elicits great sympathy, which is both comforting and disconcerting. People are lovely but I don't want to be the object of pity. I'm okay, I try to reassure people (and myself). I'm doing well and plan to keep it that way. But in the warm embrace of the camaraderie building up over the course of the week, I feel a kind of collective support or espirit de corps that has been missing for much of my cancer journey.

This is no slight on the amazing levels of support I've enjoyed from family and friends, but there's time and space here – freed of household chores and family and work respon-sibilities – for us to really see and hear each other. It strikes me as odd this is such a rare circumstance in modern life, that I am having heartfelt conversations with virtual strangers I rarely manage with friends and family.

I sign up for a counselling session, The Journey, based on the work of author Brandon Bays. The woman conducting the session, more than the spurious promo spiel, attracts me; a fifty-something, soft-spoken American who's led some of my favourite sessions of the week with a gentle but commanding authority. She leads me through a guided meditative journey (there's no other word for it) in which I descend a flight of stairs into some unknown darkness and confront my childhood self. In a dream-like state and through much sobbing and wailing, I comfort my inner child and a kind of healing takes place. Afterwards I can recall only vague details, but the sense of lightness, of having tended to old wounds, is deeply comforting.

I'm unsure how to categorise whatever trauma my childhood may have contained. My older brothers picked on me (I know, boo fucking hoo). I found it hard to have my voice heard. Our family moved around a great deal. By the time I was eight I'd changed schools five times. My father and older brother had a particularly vexed relationship. Our parents split when I was fourteen but, in reality, had been emotionally distant for years. Nothing that really rates high on the scale of human traumas, no events that would trouble The Hague. Yet, I sense I grew up with a feeling, like so many of us, of not being enough, of there being some vague, undefined thing wrong with me that needed fixing.

Are these challenges enough to give me cancer? It hardly seems plausible, yet I remain determined to heal on every possible level, to live a happy and healthy life for however long I get to hang around. The week's pampering and introspection seems to do the trick. I get to the end of the retreat feeling an unfamiliar lightness, unburdened, ready to live my life differently, on my terms, deeply sensitive to my old habit patterns.

On the final night there's a farewell gathering after dinner, in a lounge area with an open fire and strong après-ski vibes.

Someone (okay, perhaps show-offy, frustrated performer me) suggests a talent show, an open mic night of the soul, if you will, in which anyone can get up and do more or less anything they feel inspired to that doesn't involve the removal of trousers.

One of the waiters performs a stunning original poem that sets a warm intimate mood. I spot an old acoustic guitar languishing in a corner of the room and bust out an original ditty about personal change and growth, with the requisite three chords and within my limited vocal range, which seems appropriate in the circumstances.

The staff comment on what a remarkably bonded group we've been, that these final night gatherings sometimes fall flat or are poorly attended. No one has missed this one. Perhaps this is a function, someone suggests, of several of us being here under the family and friends discount, enjoying an experience that would normally be beyond our financial reach, inordinately grateful for the entrée to a world we'd otherwise never know. Someone else wants to start a Facebook group to stay in touch and check on one another's progress on our various paths. Everyone's keen. (It lasts a month, tops.) There's much hugging and exchanging of email addresses, exhortations to keep going on the idealistic paths we've forged.

On departure day, I'm as nervous as a teenager on a first date, waiting for my beloved to collect me. I have all this new . . . awareness to practise, insights to share, intimacy to rekindle. Kirst, on the other hand, has been working and studying and dealing with two teenagers at home and may not be as wide open to redefining our lives and relationship, to ascend to greater levels of connectedness and emotional honesty, as I.

I'm pacing the car park when I realise her car is already there but she's nowhere to be seen. I find her in the gift shop chatting with an old friend, in no particular hurry to be reunited, and I feel a familiar stab of hurt. Where's that acute awareness of old habit patterns when I need it?

The drive home is uncomfortably quiet. I know the drill. I've been away on enough surf trips and meditation retreats and various healing 'modalities', while Kirst has valiantly held the fort, managed the kids, her own work and study, myriad domestic duties, to know it doesn't go down well to come on too strong with my newfound wisdom and insight and aware-ness. I can play the long game. 'So, how was your week?' I proffer.

I know this is the right thing to do, but it's still a buzzkill. The litany of little household chores and challenges, parenting conundrums, financial and professional and academic stressors – each is a pin in my helium bubble of newly acquired idealism, and I find myself hurtling earthwards at a frightening clip. The kids at least are happy to see me and hug like they mean business, and the love I feel for them in that moment, the determination it instils in me to do better, to stay well, to just . . . evolve, is the most powerful tonic of all.

Later that night, Kirst and I have some time to ourselves in front of the TV and I wriggle in for a bit of that intimacy I'm so keen to rekindle. I can sense her coolness, a distance between us I feel powerless to bridge. In the moment I decide to go for complete emotional candour.

'I know our relationship feels broken, but I'm committed to doing all I can to fix it,' I blurt. Kirst has recently been taken with the work of Brené Brown and her wildly popular TED Talk on vulnerability, so I figure this'll work a treat.

She takes a while to decide how to respond and, as is her way, chooses her words carefully. 'I'm not sure I can see a future for us.'

Oh, look. There's the earth.

Thud.

19

MENDING

In the mountaineering book and film *Touching the Void*, two friends, Joe Simpson and Simon Yates, are the first to climb the west face of Siula Grande in the Peruvian Andes. But on their descent, Simpson falls and breaks his leg. In an attempt to lower his friend safely down the mountain by ropes, Yates inadvertently lowers him over the edge of a cliff. He's unable to see Simpson or pull him up. After an hour and a half of grimly hanging on to his friend's lifeline, he realises he can't hold his footing any longer and they will both fall to their deaths. Yates's only option is to cut the rope connecting them, to allow his partner to fall to almost certain death and save himself.

I imagine Kirst's predicament feels a little like this. Or perhaps this is how it feels for me and I'm projecting. My emotional distress, my wild mood swings and bouts of depression, her efforts to keep us both afloat and our family together, seem doomed to pull us all down. With the benefit of hindsight, I can see Kirst was struggling to maintain her footing, felt she had no choice but to cut the rope, to emotionally distance herself, before we were all pulled into the abyss. At the time I'm just angry and hurt and panicked.

Kirst has had to step up as the main breadwinner since the Rip Curl gig ended. She's simultaneously working at a health clinic in Burleigh, running a community acupuncture practice in Brisbane for people with a history of homelessness, substance abuse, mental illness, or some combination of the three, and completing an Honours research project based on this selfless work. It's a case of dealing with hardship by helping people worse off than yourself, and I'm full of admiration for her altruistic endeavours. 'It's a hell of a way to channel grief,' she observes.

But it does render her largely emotionally unavailable. While our relationship hangs in limbo, she begs for a four-month amnesty, to get to the end of the year and complete her studies, before we wade into the messy business of trying to sort out our future.

'All I can tell you is that I love you, I am here, but I just can't think about the future right now,' she explains, with a heavy sadness that offers little comfort. I have more time on my hands to fixate on our fractured relationship, and this purgatory feels like torture. How can she do this to me? Didn't we vow to stay together in sickness and in health? My health insurance and life insurance can't just ditch me because I've become a bad deal, a drain on their resources. They have to honour our contract because no other insurer would touch me now. How can Kirst just ditch me when the going gets rough? I also realise how much I've been leaning on her and the toll it has taken. I'm heartbroken to begin to understand that she's also acting out of her protective instincts as a mother, that she doesn't want our children to have to live with their father's dark moods.

We try counselling but the session is so hostile and full of blame and unprocessed grief I actually feel sorry for the counsellor. Far from mending our divide, the session just consolidates the chasm between us. What's becoming increasingly clear to me is that Kirst finds life easier when I'm not around, that she welcomes my absences, the break from my capricious moodiness and my volatility around the kids.

In my distress I turn to my old friend Vipassana and book into a ten-day retreat. If I have to build a new life on my own, I'm going to have to get a grip on this spiralling sense of panic and crisis, a feeling that I am going to be abandoned, that my health will deteriorate and I'll die a sad and lonely death. In the grip of my ADT, I feel powerless to stop this catastrophising and the only solution I can think of is ten days on the meditation cushion to let it all unravel, to allow myself to fall apart and then reassemble in some new form to prepare for a new life.

This will be my third Vipassana retreat and I'm expecting them to get easier each time. But I should know better. Goenka makes it clear in his discourse at the end of each day that we're not here to chase pleasant sensations or to avoid unpleasant ones, but to sit with whatever arises with equanimity.

This proves a greater challenge than I'm prepared for. I've arrived in a state of high agitation and as soon as I step into the meditation hall and lower my arse on a cushion, my mind and body give me no relief. I'm beset by excruciating physical aches and pains and my mind cycles through a range of doomsday scenarios. I'm going to be estranged from my kids. I'm going to be living in poverty in my van, on a disability pension, a homeless vagabond as my health declines. Kirst will re-partner. The kids will have a stepdad. There's also the cold, hard, statistical reality that married men with prostate cancer tend to live longer than men who are single, separated or divorced. The idea of focusing on my nostrils and calming the mind seems preposterous.

I don't know that I've ever experienced such sustained emotional pain. The moments of bliss I've been craving never arise. Every sitting is another descent into physical and psychological torture. Sittings of strong determination, in which we are instructed not to move, are entirely beyond me and I often end up hugging my knees to my chest, resting my head on my knees and quietly sobbing to myself. Each hour feels an eternity. The days crawl by. I'm close to doing a runner, pulling the pin and jumping in my van in the dark of night and getting the hell out of here. But I've no idea where I'd go anyway. My troubled mind leaps to worst-case scenarios and Kirst's four-month amnesty has landed like the death knell of our marriage. Something in me tells me I need to go the distance, to get to the other side of this agony and discover what life looks like after ten days of this self-imposed exile.

As the days pass, I begin to construct a picture of a bearable existence on my own. I'll live nomadically out of the van, migrating between this Vipassana retreat, spending time with the kids, and cruising the NSW North Coast hunting waves. I'll join WWOOF Australia (Willing Workers On Organic Farms) and work for my food and board at a series of alternative lifestyle communities down the east coast. In short, I think I'm going to become a hippy, fifty years after the Summer of Love – meditating, growing veggies, tilling the soil, the full *Morning of the Earth* trip, surfing and writing as I go.

It's not until the final session of the final day that I feel anything approaching peace and then I don't want to leave at all. This will be my new home. They are building a new meditation pagoda and calling for volunteer labour. I'll move in and help. I have no practical skills to speak of but I'm desperate. After the final morning's session, when other people pack up and flee the retreat as fast as they can, to talk, drink coffee, see loved ones, I linger, unsure where I want to be and who I want to be with.

There's another midmorning meditation session for the regular Vipassana community in the local area so I hang around and join in and finally, after ten days of struggle, I find some peace and stillness on the cushion. I've managed to convince myself this new life might just be tolerable, even enriching, a step forward in my personal evolution.

I begin to sense a parting of the clouds, a gradual return to more rational thought, the crisis passing. I'm going to be okay. Whatever happens, I'll survive. And there's another realisation. I know Kirst is a good, kind, loving and compassionate

229

person. If she has got to this point, then her whole experience of my cancer must be way more traumatic than I realise. I've been so self-focused, on my diet, my meditation, the roller-coaster of test results and scans and my own suffering, I've been oblivious to hers.

When I return home, the mood seems to have thawed a little in my absence. I'm thrilled to see the kids and Kirst is warmer towards me. When we have a chance to talk, I share some of my insights from the retreat. 'I'm sorry I didn't realise how all this has been impacting you,' I offer, sincerely.

I sense an immediate softening. 'That makes me the most hopeful I've felt for our future in months,' she says quietly. Our circumstances are so out of the ordinary, I don't think I can apply any normal relationship template to our situation. We love each other. We're committed parents. We're both good people. For now, that seems to be enough. But I'm going to take a bit of time away from home when I sense I need to, or as my ADT dictates. It's as if I have discovered I turn into a werewolf on a full moon and have to lock myself away to avoid doing any damage.

My mate Graham lives in a 100-year-old farmhouse in the Gold Coast hinterland surrounded by abundant avocado trees, rainforest and towering stands of hoop pine. He has a spare room and I start spending a bit of time out there when I'm struggling. It proves the perfect circuit-breaker, for me and the family. I set up office in the spare room and stay over a day or two each week and there's something deeply healing about these forested surrounds, the old farmhouse, Graham's empathetic company. I return to the family renewed and ecstatic to see them and slowly, over time, a quiet mending seems to take place. Kirst and I begin writing to each other while I'm away from home, exchanging emails giving voice to our private torments and offering comfort to one another in a way that beds down a new kind of relationship.

Nothing is predictable about my circumstances; there is no guarantee of how long various treatments will remain effective, the mercurial fluctuations in PSA, how severely the ADT will wreak havoc on my life. The only way to achieve any kind of peace is to strive to live in a kind of perpetual present, not speculating on the future or dwelling in the past. And yet I'm asking Kirst for a cast-iron guarantee she will never leave me, that she will endure any amount of suffering and anguish to adhere to our marriage vows. In our entirely unnatural circumstances, I come to understand how unrealistic this is. There's an old trope that an intimate partner can't just walk away from a relationship with someone living with cancer, but in reality, many relationships falter under its cruel, multi-layered strains. Over time, I recognise that Kirst's presence – that she is here, and she loves me – will have to be enough. If I become a danger to my own children, if my dark and volatile moods threaten the well-being of my family, how can I demand that she commits to this?

Raising a teenage boy while lacking testosterone yourself presents another unique challenge to family harmony. As our boy experiences his first testosterone surges, as his underdeveloped prefrontal cortex promotes impulsive behaviour and sabotages emotional regulation, we make a volatile mix. One awful evening, trying to wrest Alex's mobile phone from him at bedtime, we almost come to blows. I seem to lack the emotional ballast to regulate my own reactions, and Kirst is often left feeling like she has two teenagers on her hands. I get better at simply removing myself from stressful situations, rather than risk another blow-up, but this burdens Kirst with an unfair parenting load.

Intermittent hormone therapy is my saviour; the periodic break from the eviscerating effects of my ADT affords us all some relief, a return to a kind of normality, when I can fulfil my parenting duties with a semblance of equanimity. I'm trying my hardest, but Kirst is sometimes frustrated with the slow progress, the seemingly inevitable lapses into irrational behaviour.

'I'm doing the work,' I plead in my defence.

'I just want the work to work,' Kirst counters.

It's a precarious dance, but gradually over time we seem able to achieve a kind of equilibrium. I still fuck up periodically, lose my temper, snap at the kids for no good reason, or lose my shit entirely, usually in the grip of another dose of ADT. But Kirst has become more understanding and forgiving of these lapses. And I'd like to think I've become more mindful. I don't need our relationship defined or locked into a non-negotiable contract when forces swirl and shift around us. She is here. And she loves me.

Our good mate Steve calls by for a cuppa. He's been a source of comfort throughout my health journey; a counsellor by training, and as emotionally intelligent and empathetic a character as you could ever meet. 'How are you two going?' he asks in a way that is rooted only in concern, without judgement.

I look to Kirst for her response.

'It's like we've mined to the bedrock of relationship and become best friends,' she says.

I can ask for no more than that.

In *Touching the Void*, Joe Simpson survives the fall into an ice chasm and crawls back into base camp three days later with a broken leg, suffering dehydration and frostbite, but miraculously alive. He harbours no resentment towards Yates, knows he would have done the same thing if the situation was reversed.

I, too, feel like I've crawled back to base camp, battered and bruised but still breathing, my partner and I bonded by the shared ordeal, a sense that no one else can understand what we've been through.

20

THE NON-DISCLOSURE AGREEMENT

EVENTUALLY IT SEEMS SOME karmic balance is restored to our family life. An extended break from my ADT consolidates the healing process, and our personal fortunes take a welcome upswing when Kirst lands a PhD scholarship to continue her public health research. I'm invited to a writer's conference in Macau, that surreal gambler's paradise a short hop from Hong Kong, that proves an unexpected joy, mixing with a multicultural cast of writers from across the Asia-Pacific. The conference leads to an offer of a creative writing PhD scholarship of my own, and I land a publishing contract to write this book.

Then, on New Year's Eve 2019, I receive a message from a woman in California named Andrea representing legendary surf charter skipper Martin Daly. Widely regarded as the world's foremost surf explorer, Martin is a former swashbuckling salvage diver working the islands of South-East Asia

who became the accidental pioneer of the global surf exploration and surf charter business. Andrea and I have been going
back and forth for a few months over the possibility of me
writing a biography of his extraordinary life and career.

'Martin is on the honey pot, and I want to know if you're
free to jump aboard Jan 3 or 4. It's all about timing so let me
know if you can do it,' she writes.

Andrea makes it clear she has been canvassing other writers
for the gig, which strikes me as . . . odd. I've never auditioned
for a book project before but if I must, a couple of weeks
aboard one of the world's premier surfer charter boats in a
largely unexplored part of Melanesia sounds like a reasonable
way to do it. Martin wants to see if we're 'compatible', which
I imagine might involve throwing myself over the ledge of
some particularly nasty remote reef waves to prove my bona-
fides for the gig. In my current condition, I may well be found
wanting.

This is extremely short notice, complicated by the fact that
I have family visiting from interstate until 5 January, but it's an
intriguing offer, nonetheless. What is the honey pot? A spectacular wave discovery? A new luxury pleasure craft? A polite
euphemism for the salty old skipper hitting the sauce too hard
over the festive season and my services being required for some
kind of drastic intervention?

Martin stumbled upon the wave riches of the Mentawai
Islands off the west coast of Sumatra, Indonesia, while salvag-
ing a sunken bulldozer for a logging company back in the
early nineties. Since then, he's converted his original old tug,
the *Indies Trader*, to a basic but highly functional surf charter

boat. He's undertaken the Quiksilver Crossing mission for the booming surf brand, circumnavigating the globe three times over seven years on an epic mission of surf discovery. And he's expanded his surf charter fleet to the progressively more opulent *Indies Traders* *2, 3* and *4*, like ocean-going Thunderbirds. The last of these comes with its own helicopter landing pad on the roof, catering to an elite clientele of surf-industry moguls and hedge-fund managers.

But the old sea dog seems wearied by the commercial shit fight his grand discovery in the Mentawai Islands has descended into, and the machinations of the surf industry he's had to navigate, as hazardous as any reef, during his seven years at the helm of the Quiksilver Crossing. Those chapters have emphatically slammed shut, with the overcrowding of the Mentawais – fifty-five charter boats and a dozen land camps in the island chain he once plied alone with a few mates – and the sale of the big surf brands to larger corporate predators.

And so, he's retreated ever deeper into the wild, like Colonel Kurtz in *Apocalypse Now*, not maddened and deluded like Marlon Brando's tortured character, but gripped by an insatiable case of surf lust and the quest for the next great wave discovery. He's famously fashioned a magnificent surf, dive and kite surfing retreat on a remote atoll in the Marshall Islands that's become a kind of aquatic Davos (that gathering of global elites) as the rich and powerful jet in from all corners of the world for a taste of this improbable tropical idyll. And he's re-focused his surf charter business on Melanesia in the hope history will repeat, and he might discover another largely untrammelled wave-rich region to bring guests to.

The offer strikes a nerve too, because over twenty years ago, well before marriage and kids, I'd passed up one of Martin's spontaneous invitations and lived to regret it. I bumped into Martin in a bar at Jakarta airport on my way home from the Mentawais in 1998, while researching an article for US *Surfer* magazine on the booming surf charter industry there and the increasingly hostile rivalries between its main players. I was nursing a beer and ruminating on the complex journalistic challenges of this assignment when Martin walked in and told me he was picking up a fresh crew of passengers for a bold journey of surf exploration along the coasts of Java and Sumatra in the original *Indies Trader*. There was a spare berth if I wanted to jump aboard and a fax machine to file my story. (Imagine! A fax machine!)

Reporting on this bitter power struggle between surf charter operators while enjoying the hospitality of one of its main protagonists seemed like an alarming compromise of my journalistic objectivity. Besides, after two weeks at sea, I was looking forward to the comforts of home and the warm embrace of a girlfriend awaiting my return. I had half an hour, Martin told me bluntly. I sipped my beer and weighed my options, and when he returned I politely passed; romance and journalistic integrity winning out over surf adventure. When I next spoke to Martin six months later, he said it had been the trip of a lifetime, uncovering numerous new discoveries without another soul around. That decision has haunted me ever since. Twenty-plus years later, now married with two teenage kids and managing a cancer diagnosis, maybe this is my shot at redemption.

Kirst and my extended family give their blessings, god love them. Kirst has one request – can I take Alex along so she can focus on work and her PhD studies. A father–son surf trip appeals as a path to mending our volatile relationship. I ask Martin and he replies with an emphatic *No problem*. Flights are a confounding obstacle course of convoluted routes and long layovers, island hopping from one remote airstrip to the next, and astronomically inflated fares due to the late booking, but it looks possible. Things begin falling into place and that familiar rumble of excitement at the prospect of an impending surf trip takes hold.

Then I pull out Alex's passport on Thursday afternoon before our intended Sunday departure and discover, to my horror, it has expired. It's 4.45 pm. In a panic, I sweep him up from where he's lounging in front of the TV, hightail it to the post office to gather the necessary paperwork and get head shots taken, doubtful this latest hurdle can be cleared. The woman behind the counter is sceptical but takes the photos and hands over the application form anyway. As I head towards the bench to begin filling out the form, I spot a familiar figure addressing a post-pack. 'Ted!' I almost bellow with excitement. My great pal and celebrated surf photographer Ted Grambeau turns and beams his trademark cheery grin.

Ted is close to the most unflappable, well-travelled and obliging man in the world, and he knows a bit about express passport applications. He quickly takes charge of the situation, signing the back of Alex's passport photos and the application form as guarantor to confirm his identity. His advice is clear and upbeat. Lob at the passport office in Brisbane at opening time the next day, plead your case, have Alex look imploringly at the bureaucrats with wide-eyed pleading and trembling bottom lip and throw yourself at the mercy of officialdom.

We follow Ted's instructions to the letter. Just for good measure I do something I rarely do and play the cancer card, with a heart-wrenching statement on the official form outlining my compelling need for the express service on compassionate grounds. Living with an advanced cancer diagnosis, this might be my last opportunity for an overseas surf trip with my son, I write, while not believing a word of it. A medical certificate confirming my diagnosis does the trick. The woman processing my application looks across at Alex, a cute, blond-haired boy sitting patiently while his dad pleads his case. It would take a heart of stone to remain unmoved. 'Come back at 2.30 and I'll see what I can do,' she tells me, very nearly shedding a tear.

Alex and I head to a nearby inner-city skate park so he can ride out the pent-up emotional energy. I pull out my laptop, activate my iPhone hotspot, and continue my trawl through the bewildering labyrinth of internet airline booking platforms. The stifling Brisbane summer heat is only relieved by the shade of a sprawling Moreton Bay Fig as the city traffic whizzes by. At 12.30 pm my search is interrupted by an email from the passport office informing me that Alex's new passport is ready. Holy shit! A new passport within three hours seems miraculous and perhaps a sign we are destined to go.

It's a triumphant drive back to the Gold Coast but finding flights that align and are affordable remains a confounding maze. Later that afternoon, after hours of searching, I think

I've finally cracked the code. I email a prospective itinerary through to Martin to see if it'll work with his schedule, delaying his preferred departure by a couple of days. He thinks he can do better. 'Leave it with me,' he says.

I head out for dinner with the extended family to try to make up for my impending absence but before I've taken a bite, an email lobs in from Martin. Having scoured the internet, he's convinced my proposed itinerary is the best available option. 'Book 'em Danno,' he instructs. Heart pounding, I excuse myself from dinner, dash home, pull out laptop and credit card and start tapping in details. I have the first and second legs locked in for Alex and me, clocking up over $3000 on the Visa card, then embark on the final flight booking from one obscure island outpost to the next when my heart sinks. The flight is full. I've blown three grand, my son and I will be stranded god knows where and the mighty *Indies Trader 3* will set sail without us! This can't be happening. It seems too cruel.

So begins a frantic new search. Mercifully, I find a flight that looks like it will work, but the booking form refuses to accept my Visa card. I try Kirst's. No dice. In a panic, I ring Martin and he suggests these obscure local airlines might recognise his Indonesian credit card and benevolently dictates his details over a patchy WhatsApp connection as I type them in with trembling hands. Bingo! We're on!

Yet one more hurdle looms. My pharmacist can't get my meds delivered in time but scours an online database and finds a chemist in Beenleigh with stock, conveniently located en route to Brisbane airport. They close at 4 pm on our day of departure. After seeing off my dad, my brother and his family at Gold Coast airport, Alex and I race an hour north in my HiAce van to Brisbane International, the accursed M1 a veritable car park with holiday traffic, Google Maps predicting we'll make it to the chemist ten minutes before closing. Through some swift detours and fairly elastic observance of speed limits, we make it with only minutes to spare.

It's just as well. Before we leave the chemist in Beenleigh, I re-check my itinerary and discover to my horror that I've misread our departure time by an hour. This is by now almost comical. The Keystone Cops marathon continues with a final dash for the finish line: installing the van at the distant, open-air, long-term car park (its height won't allow it to fit in the covered parking closer to the airport) and anxiously waiting for the free shuttle bus to deliver us to the international terminal. We make check-in as our flight's about to close.

Three flights, two extended airport hotel layovers, Alex's first encounter with a teeming city in a developing country, and a fresh fish lunch at a harbour-front restaurant later, and Alex and I arrive at a tiny South Pacific airstrip, the *Indies Trader 3* anchored offshore, froth levels at fever pitch. The young fella's been a star traveller, rolling with every unforeseen eventuality, never complaining, even while overawed and unnerved by the sometimes confronting realities of travel in the developing world.

The exquisite irony now is we have arrived to discover the weather has turned bad, and Martin is awaiting the arrival of a part for his generator, so we are dry-docked for another day.

Sometimes I feel as if I'm living some sort of surreal double life – one week undergoing blood tests and awaiting results, consulting with earnest medicos, wrestling with vexed questions over treatment options, the next flying by the seat of my pants on an international surf junket with our young son at the mere whiff of new wave discoveries. An integrative doctor I consult is very big on the emotional dimensions of a cancer diagnosis and his prescription at my last appointment was simple: 'Get busy living or get busy dying.' This whole exercise is my emphatic vote in favour of the former.

One of Martin's crew checks us into a hotel right across the road from the airport, a sprawling old timber structure where you can see slivers of light between the floorboards, and we worry about mozzies and malaria in these equatorial parts. The power tends to go out at random moments, like in the middle of dinner, and no one appears to be in any hurry to do anything about it, so we sit in darkness for several minutes before our waiter produces candles for our table. The hotel appears to have few other guests as we wander its long, dimly lit hallways. I'm half-expecting Jack Nicholson to hack his way through our door with an axe, but we survive the night unscathed.

The next day we hire bikes and ride the couple of k's into town and check out the waterfront markets, where fresh fish, fruit and vegetables and the ubiquitous betel nut are displayed on rough wooden tables under makeshift plastic shelters. Alex buys an overpriced shoulder bag in Rastafarian colours, but seems a little unnerved by the attention his blond hair and pale skin attracts and is keen to return to the hotel. Soon enough one of Martin's crew collects us to board the *Trader 3* and we get to clap eyes on our new floating home.

I've set foot on the *Trader 3* once before, nearly twenty years ago, not long after Martin acquired it in partnership with one of his wealthier clients. I'd been invited aboard a leg of the Quiksilver Crossing on the original *Trader 1* back in the early 2000s, with Quik's A-team – Kelly Slater, Tom Carroll, Ross Clarke-Jones and a few others. Late one night, after another day of perfect tropical surf, I was asleep in my bunk with my head next to a porthole when I was awoken by the sound of a boat pulling up alongside us. I opened my eyes to the sight of the sleek, gleaming blue hull of the *Trader 3* an arm's length away. I stumbled out of my bunk rubbing sleep from my eyes as if I was dreaming, stepped out onto the deck and there was Martin beaming.

'Come and check out my new boat,' he announced proudly, extending a hand and pulling me aboard. Back then the *Trader 3* was the height of surf charter opulence, something way beyond the simple, utilitarian old salvage boat we were on. I surveyed its plush interior, the long dining table with padded seats, a large map of the world mounted on the wall, and a timber bar down one side of the saloon with industrial size fridges for drinks. The master bedrooms came complete with ensuites. I figured it was the kind of luxury I'd never get to experience as a paying guest, and gazed around me, awed that surf travel had become so extravagant.

Now, my son and I are boarding the *Trader 3* to embark on ten days as the only guests aboard the ultimate surfing pleasure craft. It's hard to believe. The honey pot, as it turns out, is a long, Indonesian-style left, a rarity in these waters, previously unsurfed as far as Martin knows and among the best waves he's discovered, in a life full of great wave discoveries. He shows us video of it at 5 to 6 foot and it reels for hundreds of metres through barrel sections and long walls perfect for open-faced carves. We're beside ourselves. The swell has dropped out so we're unsure where Martin is taking us but by late afternoon, we anchor adjacent to what looks like a small, fun left, chest to head high on the sets without another surfer for hundreds of miles. None of the anxiety of other boats turning up and crashing your session. This, it turns out, is the honey pot and Martin has decided to share it with us. Having seen many of his discoveries overrun by crowds I understand the significant bestowal of trust. I'm sworn to secrecy about precise locations and forbidden to publish any unapproved images, though I literally have no idea where we are.

Alex and I trade waves; Martin mans the tin boat and picks us up at the end of each ride and tows us the couple of hundred metres back to the take-off spot. We're at the western end of a large bay and long crescent beach lined with the ubiquitous coconut trees, and we may as well be the only people in the world. As the sun sets and the sky catches fire, Martin calls last waves, and we head back to the mother ship. The Indonesian chef Casmen has prepared beef rendang for dinner followed by his signature dessert – deep-fried Oreo cookies with ice cream. My dietary guidelines are out the window and Alex is in heaven. Ten days of this, huh?

The next morning, we go exploring. In a soon to be familiar pattern, Martin orders us into the tin boat with a brusque, 'Grab your sunnies, hat, sunscreen'. There's nowhere to hide from the relentless equatorial sun on the tin boat. Martin appears to have some sort of sixth sense for where to find waves and we're soon idling next to a wobbly right-hand reef break off a small and seemingly uninhabited island. We've no way of knowing if it's ever been surfed or how safe it might be. But Martin's mission here is to log as many waves as he can find in the region, get a photo of someone surfing them (even if that's an ageing surf journalist and his teenage son) and move on to find the next one. He's building the case to run surf charters here and assembling images to woo his customers.

'The first to catch a wave gets naming rights,' Martin announces, as Alex and I prepare to jump off the tin boat. Father and son paddle towards the shifty line-up, initially competitive then strangely deferring to each other politely.

'You go.'

'No, you go.'

But youth wins out over age, and Alex scratches into the first wedging peak and rides a quick, zippering right, the reef flashing by underneath. A magical moment off an unnamed cluster of islands I couldn't reveal the location of even if I wasn't sworn to secrecy.

Alex paddles back out beaming. 'What are you going to call it?' I ask. We toss around ideas. Martin has dubbed my son the crash-test dummy of this little exploratory mission and Alex suggests Dummies. Or Towers for the large communications tower inexplicably protruding from the nearest picture-postcard tropical island. He settles on Oreos, in honour of last night's dessert.

'It's going to be a big afternoon in the tin boat,' Martin announces after lunch on day two of our voyage. It sounds exciting. We're going wave hunting. But Martin adds a cautionary note. 'You're going to be sick of the tin boat by the end of the day.' They're prophetic words.

There's an interesting duality to life on the *Indies Trader 3* during an exploratory mission like this. On the mother ship, it's all luxury, fine dining, spacious bedrooms with ensuites and high-thread-count cotton sheets and plump pillows, a well-stocked bar with chilled beers and afternoon bar snacks. You come in from the surf and are greeted by the ever-smiling Indonesian crew – Eco, Romanus, Tarfiq and Casmen – with neatly folded beach towels embroidered with the Indies Trader brand, and tall glasses of chilled water. There's a hot hand shower on the rear deck to rinse off, complete with shampoo and conditioner, and little packs of toiletries supplied in each cabin.

But an afternoon in the tin boat with Captain Daly on the hunt for waves is another thing altogether. After lunch, we load the tin boat with surfboards, an esky full of bottled water and beer, and three eight-gallon tanks of petrol (which should have raised some red flags). The mother ship stays well out to sea and continues its journey eastwards as we speed towards a large island, with a planned rendezvous later in the afternoon at the eastern end of this verdant land mass. Dark brooding storm clouds hug dense green jungle and jutting hilltops as the coast pulls into sharper focus on our approach. 'You want to see whitewater before you see beach,' Martin bellows above the roar of the outboard.

He's scoped out a likely point break here on the charts, so we are going in for a closer look, then surveying the northern coastline of this entire island for possible set-ups. It's like no other surf mission I've ever been on – a painstaking search for glittering needles in a haystack of close-outs, infuriating 'almost-waves' and random beach breaks. As we get closer to the coast, he shares other gems of knowledge from the wave hunters' handbook. 'If you see whitewater exploding straight up it means it's too shallow,' he says. 'When you see a barrel staring at you like a stationary wave, that's the real deal.'

As we approach the point, distinct lines come into view, a tantalising prospect, and it's easy to see how this has become a lifelong obsession for Daly. There are no paying passengers on this leg, making it a wildly expensive undertaking. There is a commercial imperative, of course, quite apart from work-shopping his memoir. With the Mentawais overrun and an expensive charter boat to maintain, Martin's looking for a point of difference, as he puts it, and is engaged in a deliberate pivot to the Pacific. But there are easier ways to earn a quid. More than anything, it's clear Martin loves this shit.

Martin's point looks promising, with a couple of distinct sections divided by a rocky outcrop. 'Little Mali', my son dubs it, bringing to mind the rocks that divide Snapper Rocks from Rainbow Bay at home. The swell's small, 'just background stuff', Martin says, but enough to produce a few clean peelers that hold promise of what might be in larger swells. This was his target for this exploratory mission and it's encouraging without being mind-blowing. We press on, but things soon take an upward trajectory.

Around the corner lies another cobblestone right point – fun, user-friendly, shoulder to head high and ideal for the clientele Martin envisages transporting out here, the well-to-do, successful businesspeople of a certain age who want to relive some of the wave-riding elixir of their youth without risking life and limb. Alex and I paddle out and catch a couple each before Martin waves us in, setting the pattern for the day.

There's about 30 kilometres of coast to survey before dark so there's no time to waste. We find ourselves paddling out at one break after another for a series of short sessions along an extraordinary concentration of promising surf, even in the absence of serious swell. Two more right point breaks, each better than the last; a short, shallow, slabby right that has me and my boy spooked; another short, peaky, hollow left, which we reject as too risky; and yet another right that wedges against a sheer rock face, producing quick little barrels. By midafternoon I estimate we've surfed six previously unsurfed waves, as far as Martin knows, seen another six or so, and my boy's named three surf breaks. How many fourteen-year-olds can say the same?

But Captain Daly's wave-hunting appetite is not yet satisfied, and we press on. It's already been just about the most productive day of surf exploration of his life, apart from his Mentawai glory days. But the second half of the afternoon is not so fruitful as we pound up the coast past endless miles of random beach breaks and occasional villages. As the afternoon grows long, and storm clouds gather, my boy and I stare back longingly at the mother ship way out to sea with its mod cons, but Martin is on a mission. Five hours bouncing over chop in the tin boat jars the body and everything aches. Our mood darkens with the weather as the euphoria of our surf discoveries wears off and I can see my boy crumpling. But Martin's in his element, ordering me to fetch another Bintang from the cooler, surveying the coast through binoculars, snapping photos. 'This is how you find waves, boys,' he barks. 'It's as important to know where there isn't surf as where there is.'

Finally, as the sun gets low, we reach the end of the island and pause in a picturesque cove, bathed in the golden twilight, a tiny left hugging a rocky point under the shade of dense, overhanging foliage. You could just about surf the little peelers here without risking sunburn. Sipping a cool beer in the afternoon glow, all seems right in the world, despite the fruitless last half of our search and aching bodies, anticipating warm showers and a hot dinner. But Martin has other ideas. 'Just one more spot to check,' he announces brightly, and Alex and I exchange dark glances.

We bounce across the mixed-up cross chop of a broad channel to the next island in the fading light as a gathering breeze whips up the ocean's surface. Martin's four or five beers in, the sun's low in the sky, and my boy's slumped in a dejected stoop in the front of the tinny. Floating logs litter the water from local logging operations, and I start to feel uneasy. There's nothing to see at the north-western tip of the island, just more formless beach breaks and boiling ocean currents, and we finally head back to the mother ship.

It's been an extreme day, exhibiting the yin and yang of surf exploration with Captain Daly, but he's oblivious to our suffering. We get to the *Trader 3* and the crew look stressed, ushering us aboard in the pitching sea and fading light. We descend straight to our cabins, shower, change, and my boy's in bed asleep before dinner's even served. Martin descends from the bridge brimming over with bonhomie, joie de vivre and the glow of a man who has made carpe diem a way of life.

'Where are all the surf explorers?' Martin asks me rhetorically over dinner, as if he's an endangered species, the last white rhino. 'I don't see them out here.' This kind of endeavour takes a lot of resources, I suggest, and can't be done overland out here where the coast is mostly dense rainforest, with only the occasional village and even fewer roads. 'A yacht's only fifty grand,' he counters. 'That's not a lot of money these days. That's six months in the mines.' A fair point.

'Do you think I'm obsessed?' he asks me, point blank.

'Yeah, absolutely,' I reply.

At age sixty-two, when most are plotting retirement, Daly's obsessive energy seems boundless. No nook or cranny goes unexplored. Charts are pored over. He makes no written record of any wave discoveries lest they fall into the wrong hands, and wants no photos published of his most treasured recent find, having learnt first-hand how one betrayal can spell the ruination of a region. It's a torturous dilemma for a man who makes his living taking people surfing in remote regions but fears the incursions his mere presence will almost inevitably inspire.

My son and I return to Australia after ten days of empty waves, long ocean voyages and gourmet catering, to make way for paying passengers and the start of the school year. But Martin has decided I'm the man to write his story and I'm soon summoned back onboard for a subsequent leg, along with my photographer friend, Ted Grambeau, and a couple of local surfers, for a journey deep into one of surfing's last frontiers. We're advised to be coy about precise locations, but in a region that's been rocked by civil unrest and foreign interests exploiting natural resources, surf tourism is seen as a small glimmer of hope for a better future.

Between trips, I send an email to my literary agent with the immortal words, 'I like the way 2020 is shaping up'. Clearly the hellscape that follows is entirely my fault. Our second journey begins as the coronavirus is sweeping the planet, borders are closing and each country's responses to the looming pandemic changes daily, sometimes hourly. 'We're in the best place to be in the world right now. On a boat,' says Martin, when we're safely back on board the *Trader 3*.

Local customs, immigration, police and quarantine staff appear to disagree and descend upon us en masse at our next port, complete with face masks and, alarmingly, rubber gloves. They're on high alert and a boatload of foreign surfers represents an unwelcome threat. The stern immigration official's mood is impossible to read behind the face mask. When he discovers that officials failed to stamp Martin's passport at his last port, he announces flippantly that Martin is in the country illegally and will have to go to jail.

'I hope you are joking,' Martin quips.

'I'm not joking,' he deadpans.

Tension lingers in the air. Our local guide, Shaun, does some judicious name-dropping and explains our mission here is to promote tourism, to have visitors return after the horrors of the civil conflict of the nineties. I'm gently strumming the

Trader 3's onboard guitar hoping it might soften the mood. Martin finds a copy of the local visa he applied for online among his old emails and the immigration official's desire for incarceration seems quelled. Our star local surfer, Titima, discovers he went to school with one of the police. I study the immigration official and sense a softening in his eyes and a smile beneath the mask. The tension eases and soon it's smiles all round and a warm welcome. The officials depart in their longboat wishing us well, with a couple of bottles of Johnny Walker for their troubles.

After stocking up at the local markets, we head out the next morning, hungrily eyeing the twin lefts and rights that zipper down the flanks of the large passage to open ocean. There's no real swell and it looks only a couple of feet, but their form is unmistakeable – that hypnotic geometry of evenly peeling lines and almond-shaped barrels beloved of surfers everywhere.

The coastline is all sheer cliffs that bring to mind the Bukit Peninsula in Bali, but abrupt drop-offs to astounding depths mean the surf options are limited. After a couple of days' travel and several fruitless missions on the tin boat we eventually reach more fertile shores. The coastline has changed to an endless series of bays and reef passes and tiny offshore atolls that suddenly present a dizzying array of options even in minimal swell.

We find half a dozen promising set-ups in a day and surf three of them – a fun but fullish left that reminds me of Namotu Island in Fiji; a short hollow right; and another bowling left that breaks way offshore in a reef pass, where we are joined by a local father and his two teenage children who ride the lumpy lefts on battered old boards with a smooth familiarity. Titima is dazzlingly at home in these reef breaks, immediately reading the line-ups, finding prime position, lancing lips, racing zippering walls and finding tight tubes. I feel like a clumsy interloper in his company.

Quality surf breaks, when you finally find them, seem to come in clusters. Think the Seven-Mile Miracle of the North Shore of Oahu, the long lefts of the Bukit Peninsula, the tropical reef playground of the Mentawais, the long right points of Byron Bay and the Gold Coast. Something about the geology and bathymetry of one classic surf break seems to logically extend to its neighbouring region.

Later, Martin, Shaun and Titima head off in the tin boat to explore a likely river mouth sandbar where a couple of locals and a white guy are surfing small, crumbly lefts, despite the ever-present risk of crocodiles lurking in rivers. The white guy has a diving knife strapped to his calf in case of attack, a surfing accessory that might lead you to question how badly you really need to go surfing. The five-minute mission drags into hours as Martin inevitably decides to check out a string of nearby islands and an intriguing bombora out to sea; Ted and I congratulate ourselves on having the good sense to decline the invitation and stay on the mother ship. Shaun and Titima eventually return with familiar haunted looks.

The next day the swell is up, and the mission is to assess as many potential set-ups as possible along the south-eastern end of the coast, its myriad reefs and islands. We find picture-perfect twin lefts and rights peeling down the sides of neighbouring islands, but they're punctuated by outcrops of dry reef that make it look a bad bet. Further along, we brave a serious offshore reef, rearing up in menacing peaks like a mini–Sunset Beach in Hawaii, at a solid 8 feet. I paddle out tentatively, scare the shit out of myself and retreat to the boat with my tail between my legs. There are more islands to explore within eyesight but an invisible maritime border, closed due to COVID-19, separates us from their secrets, so we retrace our path and find more waves on the return journey – a fun wrapping left with a challenging backdoor end section, a playful right running down the flank of a gorgeous little island, a horseshoe-reef with a fast, shallow and hollow left and right peak.

We're greeted warmly wherever we go ashore, and engage in long chats with the locals about how the arrival of surfing and surf tourism might impact their lives and how an established surf management plan successfully rolled out in Papua New Guinea could work in neighbouring islands to ensure local communities benefit and crowds are limited. Martin is determined not to see a repeat of the Mentawai gold rush out here. Traditional land rights extend to offshore reefs and islands 3 miles seaward, so villagers here are legally the custodians of their own wave resources.

We meet colourful expats who've forged unlikely lives out here – yachties and aid workers and rogue refugees from the modern world who prefer the challenges of island life to the work-earn-spend hamster wheel of Western society, despite some alarming hazards. While we're here, a Thai geologist is shot dead for suspected illegal gold prospecting. We meet another charter boat skipper who had his tenders stolen, and was threatened with having his arms hacked off if he tried to retrieve them, for anchoring and surfing without seeking permission from local landowners. A jocular expat tells us all is well in this neck of the woods as long as 'you don't get a hole in ya', his Aussie slang for getting shot. Recent local elections went well, another yachtie tell us, because there were only two deaths. Another yachtie was robbed at gunpoint and his abandoned catamaran sits anchored in a harbour for sale, acquiring a thick green layer of marine growth while its asking price plummets. Sudden crowds are unlikely to be an issue here.

And yet there is a magical allure, an intoxicating edge to this surf exploration business in one of the surfing world's last true frontiers, where risks and rewards are high. When I'm safely home, I try to work out where we surfed on Google Earth, but I'm left entirely confused, and perhaps it's best that way. Martin's the only one who knows precisely where these waves are located, committed to memory rather than maps or GPS coordinates. And he's not telling. Perhaps it's enough to know they, and who knows how many others, are still out there awaiting the intrepid surf traveller. I do know where there's a catamaran going cheap if anyone's keen.

The post–surf trip glow does not last long, however, as the reality of COVID-19 hits, with lockdowns, home-schooling and hard border closures. And an unsettling blood test and scan result reminds me I'm not the carefree wave hunter I've been posing as for the past month.

21

THE TURP

I return from my second mission aboard the *Indies Trader 3* in late February just before the world shuts down. But while humanity battles the looming pandemic, I have more immediate concerns. I can barely piss. My PSA, which had been slowly rising at a rate which didn't cause my oncologist too much alarm, suddenly spikes. A subsequent scan shows 'subtle progression' and a new metastasis in my pubic bone. One helluva way to lose that delicious, post–surf trip glow.

Out there, on the high seas, pioneering new surf breaks, landing super-sized mackerel, treating myself to a cold beer at the end of another wave-filled day to salute yet another psychedelic South Pacific sunset, it had been easy to forget all this – the blood tests, the scans, the fluctuating PSA, the slow trickle when I attempt to relieve myself. Not for the first time, I come back to earth with a thud.

My oncologist refers me to a urologist, a former neighbour as it happens, to attend to my 'urinary retention' issue. An ultrasound shows that even after I attempt to relieve myself, I'm retaining about 800 millilitres of liquid, a dangerously large volume of piss to be swilling around in one's bladder. The logical explanation is that subtle progression of the cancer has caused my prostate to enlarge further, restricting the urethra.

Proponents of intelligent design, those anti-science creationists who posit there must have been a grand, brilliant architect to life on earth, might want to explain the shoddy architecture of the male urinary system to me. Specifically the way the prostate surrounds the urethra, so that the high incidence of prostate cancer or even the more benign and common prostatic hyperplasia (enlargement of the prostate) condemns older men to a life of broken sleep, frequent trips to the toilet and embarrassing accidents. Surely a benevolent creator could have come up with a more intelligent design than this.

My urologist neighbour is alarmed by the scan results, tells me we have no choice but surgery – a charming procedure known as a TURP (trans-urethral resection of the prostate), or 're-bore' in common parlance. Without it, there's a very real chance I could block up altogether, he warns, which can quickly become a life-threatening medical emergency. If it had happened during the aforementioned exotic surf trips, I might well have died, unless the good skipper or one of my shipmates happened to be packing a catheter and were prepared to shove it up the eye of my cock to release the trapped liquid before my bladder burst. I'm booked in for surgery in a week's time.

The progression of my cancer also means the hormone therapy I'm on is no longer effective, and I'll have to return to my dreaded ADT, a drug that had rendered me almost suicidally depressed, or face more chemo. A dispiriting choice. In the midst of a pandemic, when being immunocompromised might prove deadly, my oncologist and I agree to give the ADT another go, to see (a) if it is still effective and (b) whether I will tolerate it any better this time round. A year of travel and adventure, writing books and living a full life rapidly evaporates.

I had hoped to mark the upcoming fifth anniversary of my diagnosis with another surf trip to somewhere exotic, perhaps Martin's fabled Marshall Islands resort, in defiance of my dire prognosis, thumbing my nose at the medical orthodoxy. Instead, I face a new round of medicalisation that threatens to drastically impact my quality of life. The TURP surgery is not without risks, even in men without prostate cancer – risks that are heightened when you add cancer into the equation. My greatest fear is incontinence, and the unsettling need to wear pads for the rest of my days. For men without prostate cancer the risk is around 1 per cent, but it is higher for men with prostate cancer, my urologist says.

'Can you quantify that?' I ask.

'No,' he replies bluntly.

I voice my concerns, the threat of incontinence, nappies, the blow to quality of life. 'This procedure is in the name of quality of life,' he assures me. 'My TURP patients are my most grateful patients.' It is also a procedure both my father and father-in-law have been recommended, even without prostate cancer, in their eighties and seventies respectively, a fact that does nothing to shore up my faltering sense of self. Am I now medically an old man, beyond repair, being patched up and kept on the road with increasingly drastic interventions?

Going back on my ADT feels like returning to an abusive relationship. I'd left my abuser but hadn't been able to survive on my own and so will have to slink back to its promises of protection, even as it wreaks havoc on my physical and mental health. Like so many, my hopes for 2020 are quickly turned on their head. I was told at the outset of this journey that I could expect five years of reasonable health and, right on cue, it seems like my time is up and I face a new phase of more invasive and debilitating treatments. Instead of surfing new waves on distant shores, will I be wearing nappies, descending into depression in the grip of ADT, or facing more chemo?

The deterioration in my health is also deeply humbling. All my optimism about defying my prognosis, my faith in complementary or integrative therapies, my confidence I could somehow juice and meditate and exercise my way to lasting health evaporates with alarming speed. Who am I to think I will be the miraculous exception? The idea I can disprove decades of medical science and find a path through this minefield that has eluded millions of other men and countless medical researchers suddenly seems like a grand folly. The need for surgery and the return to ADT is a cruel double whammy I'm not at all sure I'll survive, at least with my sense of self, dignity and quality of life intact.

I've been reading *The Biology of Belief* by American biologist Bruce Lipton, and its central message, that our thoughts affect our physiology, resonates deeply. I've also been seeing an integrative doctor who emphasises the emotional dimensions of a cancer diagnosis – that cancer cells are angry and the key to taming them is more joy and love in your life. I've embraced this concept and the surf trips had arrived like confirmation I was on the right path, instilling in me a deep sense of vitality and well-being. Now, all that idealism seems hopelessly naïve.

After my initial freak-out, after the tears and despair and hopelessness have played out, I am pleasantly surprised by my next response. Without a conscious decision or concerted effort, a quiet calmness and gratitude arises. I put it down to the accumulated benefit of five years of meditation practice. As trite as it sounds, I start reflecting on all the things I am grateful for. A functioning, First World health system. Our low pandemic numbers in Australia generally and Queensland in particular. A well-resourced hospital just down the road, and private health insurance. My family. Surfing. An almost miraculous flow of interesting and rewarding work opportunities even as the global economy goes into freefall.

In many ways, the pandemic seems like the global crisis I've been training for, as a freelance writer living with a life-threatening illness. Financial insecurity – check. Confrontations with mortality – check. Working from home – check. While the rest of the world adjusts to its radically altered circumstances, it's business as usual for me. *Welcome to my world*, I feel like announcing to a panicked global populace.

I front up for my ADT injection with a new resolve to make peace with my abuser, to cut a deal of sorts. If it can keep the cancer at bay, I'll endeavour to tolerate the mood swings, the bouts of depression and crippling lethargy with a new mindfulness. My PSA has continued to rise after the initial spike, from twenty-three to fifty, well into the danger zone for progression. In the two weeks after my return to ADT, it plummets to fourteen, a tremendous result and one that makes my oncologist 'very happy'. Since switching oncologists, I've enjoyed a warm rapport with my new guy and his openness to discussing my lifestyle efforts. Now for the TURP.

On my recent surf trips, our skipper had explained how much he hated going into port, dealing with officialdom, enduring the multiple hurdles of bureaucracy he had to clear each time – customs, immigration, harbourmasters, refuelling and, in the age of COVID-19, quarantine officers, even in remote Melanesian outposts. It's out on the high seas searching for surf he felt most alive. Ports were 'like glue', he explained, where you could become stuck for extended periods entangled by unforeseen complications and bureaucratic systems that often seemed confounding and contradictory. I know how he feels. I view hospitals and the medical system similarly. I want only to get through the surgery with a functioning urinary system and be able to get back out on the ocean of life without the need for catheters, colostomy bags or incontinence pads.

I arrive at the hospital with a little overnight bag, a few healthy snacks to supplement the grim hospital food, and a bottle of cannabis oil for comfort. I go through the rigmarole of check-in in the plush lobby of the large private hospital our health insurance affords us. I kiss Kirst goodbye and disappear through sliding double doors into the sterile, fluoro-lit world of pre-op. Here I strip off and change into the pale blue surgical gown, hairnet and slippers, climb aboard the wheely bed, or gurney, and am shunted into the operating theatre. I briefly meet my anaesthetist, who wants to know why I have such a fat medical file for one so young. (*Oh, stop it!*) It turns out she is the same anaesthetist who had put me under when I had a vasectomy twelve years earlier.

The last thing I recall is being shuffled from the gurney to the surgical bed, blinking under the dazzling theatre lights. The next thing I know I'm in my hospital room with a catheter up the eye of my penis and a post-anaesthetic haze not quite masking a distinct tenderness in my nether regions. The feeling of vulnerability in such a state is profound. Any movement sets off waves of pain. I take surreptitious sips of my homemade cannabis oil when no one is looking, eventually drifting off into a pleasant state of mild sedation.

This feels like a new stage in my cancer journey from which I'm not sure there will ever be a complete return. My sense of self is instantly altered. I am no longer the brave cancer survivor defying my dire prognosis and living my best life. I am now at the mercy of a medical system I remain deeply suspicious of – the profit motives, the potential for monumental fuck-ups, the all-too-cosy relationship with Big Pharma, the uncomfortable sense that my fate is no longer in my own hands – even while grateful for the skill of my urologist and dedication of the nursing staff.

Only a few months earlier I'd been the intrepid wave hunter scouring foreign shores, surfing new-found waves and mingling with remote villagers. Now, as I shuffle to the bathroom carrying my swollen bag of piss, grimacing with the pain of the catheter, regarding my pitiful figure in the mirror, I find it hard to shake off the spectre of a bleak future of increasingly aggressive treatments, slowly eroding my quality of life. I don't even want to look down at what has become of my phallus, at the protruding tubes and dried blood and the source of those sharp stabbing pains. The idea this misshapen organ could have ever been a source of pleasure seems almost inconceivable.

I'm only meant to be in hospital for two days. In on a Thursday morning, surgery that afternoon, twenty-four hours' rest and recovery and observation, whip the catheter out, establish that you can pee freely and you're on your way. And therein lies the catch. A nurse awakens me at midnight on Friday night to remove the catheter, a rude awakening if ever there was one. I query the timing. 'The idea is that you go back to sleep, wake up in the morning and take a pee as usual without overthinking it. You don't want to overthink it,' the nurse explains breezily, ensuring I will definitely overthink it.

What happens if I find I can't piss post-surgery? I wake around 6 am and arise free of my catheter, rejoicing in the sense of liberation but still nursing a delicate tenderness downstairs. I shuffle to the toilet, take aim and wait, trying desperately not to overthink it, an effort that grows increasingly difficult as the required free-flowing stream of urine fails to materialise. I breathe deeply, try to relax and soften my swollen bladder. Nothing.

'Try going for a little walk or take a shower. That sometimes helps,' a nurse advises. I shuffle up and down the empty corridors of the hospital, a veritable ghost town on this Saturday morning, and take up my position again at the toilet bowl to no avail. I take a shower. Nothing. 'It's early days,' soothes the nurse. 'We'll just give it some time.'

What now? More surgery? Do I wind up with a catheter and a bag permanently? Worst-case scenarios flood my consciousness. I struggle to keep panic at bay. As the morning wears on the nursing staff become more attentive and serious. 'Don't let it get to the point where you're in discomfort,' the nurse warns, seriously now. 'We may have to reinsert the catheter and keep you in for another couple of days. Sometimes it just takes a little time to settle down.'

I'm growing desperate. I just want to go home, eat proper food, be with my family, and I want nothing more to do with that catheter. Until, quite suddenly, I do. An ultrasound shows I'm holding nearly a litre of fluid in my bladder. At the same time, the mild discomfort I've been experiencing quite quickly escalates and all I want is for some compassionate soul to shove that damn catheter back in and drain my bladder before I explode. The nurse is remarkably swift and efficient. I could never imagine I would feel so relieved or grateful to have a thin metal pipe stuck up the eye of my cock. As my bloated bladder drains, waves of relief flood my body.

I'm now faced with a choice of two pretty unappealing options — I can take my catheter and bag, go home for a few days, come back on Tuesday to have it removed and try again. Or I can stay in hospital for another couple of days and have another try on Sunday night or Monday morning. Given how vulnerable I feel with the catheter back in place and how carefully I have to move to avoid a searing pain shooting up my old fellow I opt to stay, desperate as I am to go home. If there are any further complications, I want medical help close by. And I want that catheter out and this whole sorry chapter over as soon as possible.

One thing I learn from my protracted hospital stay is how appalling most free-to-air TV is, as I forlornly flick through channels looking for diversion. My cannabis oil has run out by the third day so I'm without the comfort of the cosy green cardigan. My sleep is broken with the regular pinging of the nurse's call button as other patients press their buzzers for attention. Kirst proves my salvation, bringing in more healthy snacks and encouraging me downstairs and outside into the sunlight for a picnic and a game of Scrabble – a welcome dose of normality.

But as the days wear on my mood darkens. A sense of having been irretrievably mutilated takes hold. Over the past five years, my cancerous prostate has been pricked with a needle a dozen times to extract samples for a biopsy. I've been pumped full of toxic chemotherapy drugs that made my hair fall out, rendered me listless and miserable, and turned my skin a pale grey. I've been prescribed hormone therapy, AKA chemical castration, leaving me sexually impotent and almost suicidally depressed, nearly costing me my marriage, my family and my career as well as my mental health. All this in the name of keeping me alive. And doctors wonder why cancer patients go off in search of far-fetched alternative treatments.

In a dark moment, I curl up on the hospital bed and sob to Kirst, 'What else do they want to do to me?' Four days in hospital might not sound like a long time but it changes me. I have less confidence that I can disprove the medical orthodoxy. Mortality has circled closer, the very idea seems less abstract. I've lost some of my bravado to stare down my disease. Life feels at once more tenuous and more precious.

The days, and the darkness, pass. Late Sunday night, a nurse comes to remove the catheter. I sleep restlessly, anxious about my next trip to the toilet, wake at 3 am with a strong urge to pee and make my way gingerly to the toilet, trying not to over-think it but haunted by the what-ifs of failure. Before I know it, a strong, steady stream of urine is arcing magnificently into the bowl, of a volume and duration I haven't known in years. I feel as triumphant as a toddler who's earnt his toilet-training stripes. I send my wife a text with the joyous news, eat one more bland hospital breakfast, and pack and dress for depar-ture. I've cleared customs, immigration and quarantine, I'm throwing off the bowlines, leaving port and heading back out on the high seas.

The outside world looks unfathomably bright and sparkly on this autumn morn. Was the world always this shiny? Admittedly, the COVID-19 interruptions to air and road traffic seem to have made our atmosphere clearer but, even so, I'm dazzled by the brilliant luminescence of it all and euphoric to get home, catheter-free, and be with my family. It will be another three to four weeks before I can surf or undertake any strenuous exercise, but for now I'm free and every moment, every day, week and month from here on in will be a blessing.

And yet I am altered – I've been shunted a few steps further along this dastardly board game towards one inevitable conclusion. My old self, my old life, now seems hopelessly distant and a new reality has arisen in its place. It's as if I am swimming between islands and have lost sight of my starting point before my destination has come into view. I am now all at sea and have no choice but to keep swimming towards some unknown goal or risk sinking altogether.

22

NOBODY TOLD ME THERE'D BE DAYS LIKE THESE

ONE OF MY ABIDING philosophies through this whole ordeal has been: Don't get on the rollercoaster. That is, don't get too despondent about bad results and don't get too excited about good results. PSA bounces around over time, and you can't allow your entire emotional state to be governed by a number on a blood test. Equanimity, smooth sailing, homeostasis, is the goal.

My darkest hours are often followed by a new dawn, and I've learnt through harsh experience to try to ride out those troughs until the next peak comes along. Not to go up and down too drastically, to try to appreciate the small joys along the way. One of those small joys has become my drives into the rolling green hills of northern New South Wales to score my buds. A friend who lives in a multiple occupancy community down a secluded dirt road has been growing her own and supplying a few close friends, and she's become my go-to drug buddy. The New South Wales–Queensland border closure means I now need to print out a border pass, take a long and circuitous route and brave a police checkpoint each way – my newly purchased stash on board the homeward journey, giving a thrilling covert edge to these missions.

But that edge gets a bit too sharply honed for comfort on one fine winter's day in 2020. My favoured mountainous route is closed to all traffic at the state border, where a cattle grid prevents even wandering cows breaching border security. I do a wide swing via Murwillumbah to reach my destination, turn off at the familiar dirt road and wind my way along the rough track to my friend's property. Her driveway's too steep for my van so I park at the top and walk down. Susie's an old hippy chick from way back, a mellow flower child, but she opens the door in a state of high and uncharacteristic anxiety. 'You're just going to have to grab and go,' she blurts, eyes wide, handing me a brown paper bag. 'My neighbour's just been raided by the cops. I think he's got a meth lab down there.' This is not the news you want to hear while doing a drug deal. She'd opened her front door that morning to half a dozen uniformed police, who quickly realised this demure hippy earth mother was not the hardcore ice manufacturer they were looking for and charged on down the winding driveway to the neighbour. Susie reckons she was relieved, there'd been a lot of strange characters coming and going at all hours of the day or night. Life in these lush green hills is not always as idyllic as it appears. She was going to call me and tell me not to come but figured she'd be better off not having the ounce in her possession if they returned to her place. In Australian football parlance I fear she might just have sent me a hospital handball, one that loops through the air and lands in your hands just before the opposition's biggest and meanest defender mows you down.

I take my stash and leave feeling a little rattled, heart pounding as I labour up the steep mountain driveway, and not just from the physical exertion. Safely back in my van, I drive down the mountain through winding roads and emerge into the canefield flats under a perfect blue dome studded with cottonwool clouds, my bucolic environs in stark contrast to the tense scene I've just departed and my own nervous energy. I'm just starting to relax when my phone rings. It's my oncologist calling for our regular telehealth appointment in the time of COVID. He's usually running late, and I figured I'd get home in time. But today he's punctual so I pull over, cane fields swaying in a gentle breeze as far as the eye can see. I can almost hear the soft wafting strains of the Go-Betweens.

My PSA has dropped again, he announces, from 0.34 to 0.15, the lowest it's been since my diagnosis five years ago. Since going back on ADT, and enduring the TURP, it's plummeted from 50 to 0.15 over the space of three months. A normal PSA is anything below three, so this is exceedingly good news. As nasty as the side effects of the ADT I'm on are, the stuff definitely works. I ask my oncologist if this might be a good time to consider the targeted radiation my integrative doctor has recommended while we have the cancer on the ropes. I've read radiation is generally more effective while on ADT and the cancer cells are already weakened.

'I think if we scanned, we wouldn't find anything to radiate,' he says calmly. It takes me a moment to process this statement.

'What do you mean?' I ask.

'I think you're in remission,' he replies.

I contemplate this news. A group of cyclists whizz past. The goal I have been assiduously working towards for five years has finally arrived. Yet I hadn't pictured the moment quite like this. I'm not sure what I'd imagined. Balloons? Streamers? Party poppers? Marching girls? Instead, I sit in my van with my cracked old iPhone 6 on speaker as my oncologist tells me to keep doing whatever I'm doing, that these results are near miraculous and given the response I've had I should be able to take a break from the ADT should I need to. If I feel like I'm struggling I can just skip the next injection if I'd like. *Fucking oath, I'd like!*

There is no way of knowing definitively if I am indeed in remission without re-scanning. But I only had a scan a few months ago and I try not to have them unless I really have to, because they aren't great for you, with their radioactive dye and one in 200,000 chance of death. For now, I'm happy to accept my oncologist's judgement. I'm not getting too carried away either, acutely aware the medication could become ineffective at any time, that prostate cancer cells mutate and become hormone resistant so that any form of hormone therapy would prove useless, and palliative chemo would be my next option. But a win's a win and I'll gladly take it, like a footy coach who's snatched a late goal from a dubious free kick, taking it one week at a time while plotting a season's long campaign. Except this season stretches into years with no ultimate premiership in sight, just the avoidance of being booted from the competition all together. For now, I'm happy to be running around the paddock for another month, getting a few kicks, laying the odd tackle, maybe a few score assists. I'm not at all sure this metaphor is working – what it really feels like is that I've scaled a mountain only to find countless peaks yet to conquer stretching off into the distance, an oncological Himalayas. But for now, the view is magnificent, my lungs are full of sweet mountain air, every cell humming with the exhilaration of a lofty and sometimes unlikely goal abruptly realised.

Oddly, I feel little urge for wanton celebration. There is relief, a quiet relaxation of the survival instinct, some room to breathe. But this is not a cure. The medical orthodoxy assumes the cancer will return at some stage, that cancer cells still circulate in my system and will coalesce into new tumours at some undefined point in the future, when hormone therapy fails to keep them at bay. While I don't feel bound by this pessimistic assessment, I also feel a celebration would be tempting fate. I'll never boldly declare I have 'beaten' cancer, as some seem so quick to proclaim. I frame it as making peace with my cancer and don't want to inspire any spiteful vengeance, any humbling slapdowns for my cockiness. I'll be hosting no 'How to kick cancer's arse' webinars or writing breathless exposés of the evil conspiracies behind mainstream oncology.

Instead, I find myself in limbo, a netherworld of neither ailing cancer victim nor triumphant cancer survivor. I hadn't anticipated this condition I'd craved for so long would come with its own set of challenges. I don't know what to attribute my remission to, and neither does my oncologist. 'This is a one in a million result,' he gushes. 'I wouldn't believe it if I hadn't seen it with my own eyes.' This is exciting but not entirely useful in assessing what my ongoing maintenance program should be. Logic would suggest I keep doing what I've been doing.

Did the cannabis regime help push me into remission? I'm unqualified to make a judgement, beyond my own first-hand experience. Even integrative oncologists sympathetic to the role of medicinal cannabis in cancer treatment concede the jury is still out, or that studies on the subject are generally small and inconclusive, perhaps because funding for such studies is hard to come by. But even without a medicinal, anti-cancer benefit there's much to recommend the use of cannabis oil in managing symptoms and side effects.

A 2020 systemic review of animal studies into the use of cannabinoids in the treatment of prostate cancer, published in the *International Journal of Molecular Sciences*, concluded: 'Cannabinoids were shown to reduce the size of prostate tumors in mice and as such, it can be concluded that they possess anti-cancer properties.' Animal studies can't simply be extrapolated to humans but given the encouraging results, and the toxic nature of existing treatments, one might think further study would be a high priority. Yet mainstream prostate cancer research still focuses on various combinations of the existing, highly debilitating treatments.

A 2012 study published in the *Indian Journal of Urology*, 'The role of cannabinoids in prostate cancer: Basic science perspective and potential clinical applications', was encouraging of the use of medicinal cannabis to manage pain, given the scourge of opioid addiction, and the promising signs of an anti-cancer benefit as well:

> Cannabinoids should be considered as agents for the management of prostate cancer, pending support from *in vivo* experiments . . . Among the patients suffering with chronic pain and receiving opioids, one in five abuse prescription-controlled substances, and it is not difficult to see that opioid dependence and abuse is becoming a public health problem. Different methods of managing pain should be addressed to avoid these scenarios.

> The presence of pain in men with advanced prostate cancer is an immediate indication for aggressive management with analgesics, while adequate treatments that address directly the cause of the pain are pursued. Cannabinoids possess attributes that have impact in both cancer pain and prostate cancer pathophysiology. These compounds harbor analgesic properties that aid bone cancer pain, reduce opioid consumption, side effects, and dependence, as well as exhibiting anti-androgenic effects on experimental prostate cancer cells.

I can only hope a brave and well-funded cancer researcher somewhere, unafraid of being labelled as some sort of maverick hippy tripper, takes up the gauntlet. The study authors noted the worldwide prevalence of prostate cancer, the difficulties in managing bone pain in metastatic disease and absence of curative treatments for advanced prostate cancer as well as the

dire quality of life challenges: 'For these reasons, it is fundamental to invest time and intellectual resources into finding
new and novel targets for the treatment of prostate cancer.'

'Hallelujah,' I feel like hollering when I read these words.

As a postscript, my hippy friend eventually goes to court and
cops a $700 fine for the couple of plants she had growing on her
back verandah. I'm not sure what happens to her ice-cooking
neighbour, but I hope his penalty is somewhat harsher. As
far as I know, there's no therapeutic application for ice. But
the upshot is my regular supply of bush buds is gone. The
ounce I've just procured will last me another couple of months
but I'm going to need a new source. Given my results I'm keen
to maintain my current regime.

The hurdles, time lag and expense of accessing legal medicinal cannabis seems prohibitive and I doubt I'd qualify anyway.
I have no pain and mainstream medicine is yet to recognise
any therapeutic properties of cannabis in cancer care other
than treating the side effects of chemo or for pain relief.

The Nimbin Hemp Embassy in northern New South Wales
has been on my radar for a while as a likely source of medicinal
cannabis, an underground operation that manages to operate
in plain sight. But then the total closure of the New South
Wales–Queensland border puts paid to that idea. Cancer in
the time of COVID throws another curveball.

23

THE HEMP EMBASSY

I RUN OUT OF oil three days before they widen the border zone between Queensland and New South Wales to include the hippy, hemp-centric town of Nimbin.

No problem. A couple of days off the oil will probably do me good. I've been using it intermittently since my diagnosis. I figure regular breaks will stave off dependency on the thick, pungent green oil and its sedative effects, but that horse may have already bolted.

I sleep terribly without my precious . . . I mean, my oil. Up every couple of hours to piss. Wide awake between 3 and 4 am, unable to sleep. I meditate for an hour and maybe snatch another hour dozing post-meditation, but it isn't enough. I'm fast acquiring an unsustainable sleep deficit to rival the country's rapidly growing, COVID-induced financial deficit.

I use cannabis oil predominantly for sleep. I always let my

oncologists know I'm using it, and none have ever had any objection. 'About half my men with prostate cancer use cannabis oil,' my oncologist tells me with a chuckle, as if amused by this eccentricity in his patients.

So, off to Nimbin it is as soon as border restrictions allow. There's precious little herb around the Gold Coast; I envisage a convoy of jonesing Gold Coasters speeding to Nimbin as soon as the border zone expands. The alternative lifestyle crowd first famously descended on this otherwise sleepy dairy and banana farming community back in the early seventies for the Aquarius Festival, Australia's own belated blossoming of the Summer of Love, flower power, or whatever tag you wish to give the counterculture's grab bag of psychoactive, eco-friendly, anti-authority and anti-materialist living. Nimbin has been well-known as an alternative lifestyle centre ever since, the little country town that turned on, tuned in and dropped out. The town's been through some dark chapters since it was first re-imagined as a Utopian alternative to the mainstream capitalist model – with hard drugs, homelessness and poverty all sullying those youthful hippy dreams. Yet Nimbin is still there, with its rainbow colour palette (long before the marriage equality debate), and street dealers eager to offload overpriced ounces to conspicuous tourists.

Today, most businesses in the bustling main strip celebrate this heritage – happy herbal highs, hemp cafes and clothing, the wonder herb infused in everything from smoothies to custard tarts and herbal tonics. The iconic embassy is the town's beating heart, its cultural epicentre, running the annual Mardi Grass festival since 1993, advocating for decriminalisation, providing information and education around the much-maligned and misunderstood herb they seem to believe can save the planet. A sly speakeasy dispensary downstairs caters for those with chronic illness, promising relief for everything from epilepsy to cancer.

I haven't been to Nimbin for twenty years and found something at once alluring and melancholy about the town back then, the dreamy alternative lifestyle lustre tainted by a stoner malaise that seemed to leave many inhabitants adrift and directionless.

A mate of mine we'll call Kevin, with a modest recreational appetite for the herb, proposes a daytrip in his smart, late model Mini Minor and the offer of a driver and companion is too good to refuse. Off we go, border passes dutifully printed out, on a glorious spring day, traversing the delightful country roads and verdant hills of the rainbow region, the wind in our hair and a song in our hearts – even if that song is 'Everybody Must Get Stoned'. We meander along the banks of the Tweed River heading south, through the old logging and farming towns of Murwillumbah and Uki, through cane fields and rainforest and farms before reaching the turn-off to Nimbin.

Kevin is something of a style king, with the latest and greatest of everything, always immaculately groomed, a far cry from my dishevelled personal aesthetic. My cheap servo sunnies have recently broken and he loans me another much nicer pair. Kevin's a keen, perhaps even compulsive, online shopper. He'd seen Matt Damon in a movie and liked the look of his shades and so searched and found a pair online. He'd done the same thing when Tom Cruise's sunnies had caught his eye in another flick. We're not so much Thelma and Louise as Tom and Matt. I imagine we resemble a well-heeled, middle-aged gay couple as we roll into town in his gleaming Mini with the Queensland numberplates, resplendent in our designer sunnies, he in his black Nike action wear. I'm disappointed when no one attempts to sell us weed on our first cruise of the strip and conclude the town's streetwise dealers must suspect we're undercover cops.

A band of middle-aged blokes is setting up under a rotunda in the town's central park and soon they're banging out a crude rendition of the Doors' 'Light My Fire' as a homeless man performs an interpretive dance around the nearby streetscaping. An art exhibition is underway in a large hall in the middle of town. Families and couples and colourfully dressed locals happily wander the main street, grazing in cafes, chatting in happy clusters, no masks or social distancing to be seen. This is likely a hotbed of the anti-vaxxer/5G/plandemic crowd, but the vibe is friendly with no hint of the dark energy I'd once associated with the place.

'Would you rather I was legally drunk?' asks a chalkboard sign out the front of the embassy, a provocation to the old pub and bottle shop next door. Inside you can shop for bongs, hemp clothing, an array of literature extolling the many virtues of cannabis, t-shirts emblazoned with cannabis leaves in the Rastafarian colour schemes. Weed worship appears to possess all the traits, the cultural accoutrements, rituals and devotion of a religion. Kevin leaves me to visit the dispensary downstairs while he heads to the cafe next door for a coffee and to negotiate the purchase of some bush buds.

I approach the counter and say I'm here for medicinal cannabis oil and a friendly silver-haired lady directs me to a door at the back of the shop. I step through into a hallway decorated with large posters proclaiming the wonder properties of cannabis to treat an array of health conditions – epilepsy, anxiety, cancer, insomnia, chronic pain, the list goes on. A flight of rickety timber stairs descends to a small open-sided room with three desks and chairs set up for consultations and a reception area.

They do a brisk trade as customers of all stripes come and go, anxious middle-aged mums with brooding teenage daughters, twenty-something tradies, shuffling seniors . . . and a veteran surf writer staving off cancer.

I ring a brass bell and am quickly attended to. The old hippy women who staff the enterprise are a delight. A cheery lady who we'll call Debbie serves me with prompt efficiency and we sit at a small table exchanging details, the specifics of my condition and the various products she recommends, their dosage and price. Something about her manner is immediately reassuring, though I have no idea what, if any, qualification she might possess for this role, other than years of experience. Behind her, a busy office whirrs away on various tasks – they offer a mail-order service, advocacy, legal advice, all apparently tolerated by the authorities.

Debbie recommends a 5 millilitre vial of THC oil (the psychoactive stuff) she calls Phoenix Gold for $220 to take at night to assist with sleep, which seems a bit steep for the thimble-sized bottle, along with a topical hemp cream (to be massaged into the perineum twice daily) and a raw CBD paste (non-psychoactive) to be taken orally in the morning. She assures me I'll only need three drops of the oil and that the tiny vial should last a month, but given my prolonged daily use, and high threshold of tolerance, I'm sceptical. They only accept cash. I have $300 on me and her prescription comes to $335.

'I'll have to leave something out,' I suggest, proffering my wad of notes.

'Take the lot,' she offers kindly. 'We don't do this to make a profit.'

I leave with my little brown paper bag of goodies and find Kevin in the cafe, perched on a bar stool happily chatting to the dreadlocked young bloke behind the counter, sipping a latte and negotiating the purchase of an ounce of buds. Kevin eagerly endorses the hemp custard tart. It's all so convivial and civilised, Amsterdam on the Northern Rivers, a glimpse of a world where pot is legal and freely available and its efficacy for all manner of ailments can be openly researched and acknowledged.

We drive back to the Gold Coast in high spirits, tinged only with the slight anxiety of negotiating the border crossing with our contraband. Coolangatta is not Nimbin, after all. The local coppers once smashed in the doors of young surfers in early morning raids to bust them for tiny amounts of weed. When we display our passes and are waved through by bored border police, we bump fists, feeling more like Thelma and Louise than ever, returning to Kevin's hinterland home to better explore our purchases.

I sample my oil for the first time that night, the prescribed three drops, wondering if they'll do anything. I sleep soundly for six hours, an impressive stretch for me, meditate, doze some more, and eventually awaken feeling slightly groggy. But it's the best night's sleep I've had in days. Phoenix Gold, indeed.

So begins a pleasant monthly ritual. I look forward to the scenic drive through the northern NSW countryside, the stop in Uki for its famous pies. The pleasure of these jaunts isn't just about the oil. There's a liberation, a naughty sense of absconding, like wagging school, truancy for grown-ups, tossing aside midweek work commitments for a country drive just because I feel like it. There's plenty that sucks about having cancer and if you can't use it as a leave pass to just take off when you feel like it, or watch a midday movie, to flout our archaic drug laws, smoke a spliff or microdose shrooms, what's the point?

I remember feeling deeply challenged when I first received a pensioner concession card, after I went on a part–disability support pension as hormone therapy rendered me incapable of working about four years into my diagnosis. I reckon a cancer diagnosis should come with a 'do whatever the fuck you want' card, carte blanche to follow your every whim and fancy without guilt or recrimination.

These monthly excursions proceed swimmingly until one cool autumn day in May 2021 when I take the familiar turn-off to Nimbin and am soon confronted with a police random breath-testing unit. A large sign declares they're testing for drink *and* drug driving, lest there be any doubt. Unbeknown to me, the weekend of Mardi Grass, Nimbin's annual celebration of all things weed-related, starts tomorrow culminating in a colourful parade through town with a giant ceremonial papier-mache joint, under the watchful eye but generally passive presence of the local constabulary.

I've been fully aware of the chances I've been taking for years now – the reality of using medicinal cannabis (even self-prescribed) means you either give up driving altogether or risk prosecution, loss of licence and heavy fines. Cannabis stays in your system for days, or even weeks, yet there's no acceptable legal limit as there is for alcohol, even though multiple studies have found cannabis use does not impair driving after eight to ten hours, maximum. Taking a few drops before I go to bed impacts my driving the next day no more than having a couple of glasses of wine with dinner, yet attempting to manage my health criminalises me in the eyes of the law.

Pressure is mounting to overhaul Australia's irrational drug-driving laws to better reflect the science and the high use of medicinal cannabis in the community, to make the focus on road safety not prosecuting the chronically ill. But that's little help for me now as I approach the RBT and the cars in front of me are waved over to the side of the road by police. My heart pounds. I've been told Fisherman's Friends, those potent throat lozenges allegedly beloved of fishermen, help mask the presence of cannabis in breath tests. I carry a pack with me for just such occasion and quickly pop one in my mouth.

I've thought if I got pulled over and tested, I'd boldly take on the system, go to court and contest the charge as a fearless advocate for cannabis law reform. But as I approach the RBT all that bravado seems to evaporate and I'm shitting myself. The two cars in front of me are pulled over and then, as if my grey HiAce van camouflages me as an innocent tradie going about his legitimate business, I'm waved through. I give a little silent thanks to a higher power I don't believe in and drive on, adrenalin surging from the close shave.

But I still need to make it out of Nimbin, this time with my little stash of prohibited substances. I procure my product as usual from the dispensary downstairs, then retire to the Hemp Café for a fortifying soy latte and some local intel before attempting the drive home. Every road in and out of town is similarly patrolled, the barista, a gregarious forty-something Frenchman, tells me. He also recommends Fisherman's Friends to escape detection. I note they're for sale on the counter of the general store across the road and imagine Fisherman's Friends HQ pondering why they have such a lucrative account in this little country town, far from the nearest fishing fleet.

Hopefully the RBT is still on the side of the road to catch drivers on the way into town, not out, and I decide to run the gauntlet. I'd have to remain in Nimbin for days or weeks and not partake of any more cannabis products to legally drive home, which would be a tall order on Mardi Grass weekend when I'd likely become passively stoned by the ambient cloud hovering over the town like a London fog.

Happily, I make it out unscathed and continue on my way. But this zealous policing of the chronically ill seems like an absurdity, criminalising cancer patients trying to manage their condition as best they can, when mainstream medicine fails to address their needs. The push for sensible law reform is gathering steam.

A 2021 study led by Danielle McCartney, clinical research associate at Sydney University's Lambert Initiative for

Cannabinoid Therapeutics, and published in the *Neuroscience & Biobehavioral Reviews* journal, found cannabis users had a window of impairment of between three and ten hours. 'Our study shows that cannabis is unlikely to impair driving for more than five hours when inhaled, or for more than eight hours when taken orally,' she tells the *Sydney Morning Herald* in April 2021. 'It's becoming increasingly clear that our drug-driving laws are not only out of date but hugely unreasonable now that we have tens of thousands of Australians using legal, prescribed medical cannabis. Our drug-driving laws should be about enhancing road safety and minimising injury, not about criminalising drivers who have only the mere presence of a drug in their system.' Her views are echoed by Iain McGregor, academic director of the Lambert Initiative, who says prosecution based only on the presence of THC in blood or saliva is 'manifestly unjust'.

Having cancer is hard enough. Getting yourself to medical appointments is kind of important. Being criminalised because you want a decent night's sleep and to try to manage the toxic side effects of treatment doesn't help. If depressing that little eye-dropper a few times into my gob before bed makes me a criminal, then call me Pablo Escobar.

24

SURFEBRUARY

A WORK COLLEAGUE, EX-PRO surfer Richie Lovett, pops up on my Instagram feed in early 2021 spruiking something called SurFebruary. I'm intrigued. Partly because, well, surf. Dur. But also because Richie is a cancer survivor and still rips with the kind of sharp elegance he plied on the pro tour for a decade. A malignant tumour in his hip bone ended his pro career and necessitated a hip replacement, at thirty-one. He's gone on to a successful career in the surf industry, in sales and marketing, contest commentary and, more recently, surfboard design.

If Richie is pushing SurFebruary, I'm listening. The idea is to surf every day for the month of February, seek sponsors, and raise money for Chris O'Brien Lifehouse, an integrative cancer hospital in Sydney that provides supportive thera-pies like acupuncture and meditation alongside conventional oncology, with the admirable and apparently novel aim of treating the whole patient, not just the tumour. The kind of holistic cancer care I'd like to see become standard.

Lifehouse was the bold vision of Professor Chris O'Brien who, as director of the Sydney Cancer Centre, imagined a more patient-centred, integrative approach to treating cancer. When he was diagnosed with an aggressive brain tumour in 2006, he continued to pursue his vision for Lifehouse, where cancer patients could find complementary and mainstream oncology treatments under one roof. He lived just long enough to see his vision realised, with the opening of the Chris O'Brien Lifehouse in April 2009, only two months before he died.

I visited Lifehouse soon after my diagnosis, to get a second opinion on my treatment options from one of the country's leading authorities on prostate cancer. To walk into their natural-light-filled foyer and gaze about at its stunning architecture while a pianist tinkled away on a grand piano, to walk past rooms for acupuncture, massage and yoga in a cancer hospital was revelatory. If I can support their work by going surfing every day for a month, why the hell wouldn't I?

It's late January, with only a few days left to begin my fundraising, but I'm in. I have selfish as well as altruistic motives for signing up. In the last couple of years, my surfing has become less frequent, my sessions shorter, my already modest abilities apparently in decline – dulled reflexes, fatigue, poor balance. A sad downward spiral.

I've always suffered from a kind of performance anxiety about my wave-riding abilities. Surfing alongside pro surfers for much of my working life has been both a blessing and a curse.

I admire their supernatural ease and how effortlessly their surf-boards seem to transport them wherever they wish to travel on a wave. Why doesn't my body or board work like that? Increasingly, I paddle out and I feel like a drunk on an ice rink struggling to stay upright. Yet even my compromised surfing has become a potent and essential part of my self-care, more about time in the ocean, connection to nature, getting lost in a sense of something greater than the self, rather than any ego-driven performance agenda. Which is just as well.

For Christmas 2020 I'd bought myself a new board on sale, the most modern, high performance shortboard I'd ridden in years, in an act of blind optimism to somehow arrest the slide, an ambitious roll of the dice to reclaim my surfing. The gleaming white 6 foot 6 inch Mayhem Sub-driver, designed by Californian shaper to the stars Matt Biolos, is a beefed-up version of the kind of refined equipment favoured by elite pro surfers, not middle-aged cancer patients. Yet something about its sleek curves called me.

The Mayhem passed the underarm test – when I tuck it under my arm, it just feels right. This – more than dimen-sions to 1-16th of an inch (surfboard measurements are still stubbornly empirical), volume, rocker, tail and fin configura-tions – ultimately guides the discerning surfboard buyer. I'd recently favoured thicker, wider boards to compensate for my own expanding dimensions and declining abilities. I could barely get my arm around their girth, like my grommet self, struggling to carry my first old yellowing barge forty years ago.

The Mayhem feels sexy, flighty, alive, like an unbroken horse compared to those tugs. I'm smitten. Yet my first few sessions on it are deeply humbling. Its skittery nature has me struggling to get to my feet, falling, missing waves altogether. Mayhem, indeed. Then there are moments when I manage to successfully stand erect on the thing – a clean, sharp, carving turn, that lively, sensitive, responsive feeling under my feet, the board and me as one. Those few glimpses hold enough promise to convince me I might not only be able to arrest the decline and maintain my surfing abilities, but even turn back the clock, improve as I get older, defy my dire prognosis and slow the cruel march of time.

And, so, SurFebruary it is. I fill out the requisite online form, upload a profile pic, compose a stirring biographical blurb about my deeply personal motivations and begin my social media blitz to shame my friends and family into donating. More than these noble instincts, surfing every day for a month as a rock-solid commitment and an act of virtue holds a deep appeal. Who can begrudge me, a cancer patient raising money for cancer care, my surf time? Work, household chores, family commitments, will all have to fit around this altruistic mission. The ultimate, guilt-free surfing leave pass.

I begin my campaign a few days early to build some momentum, get into a groove by getting up at the crack of dawn for the early session. I'd lost this habit over the years as I'd begun to observe what's politely termed the 'gentleman's early' once those pesky kids and the gainfully employed are at school or work. The relentless crowds on the Gold Coast mean I rarely surf its famed point breaks – Burleigh, Currumbin Alley, Kirra, Greenmount, Snapper – and content myself with its fickle beach breaks with fewer people.

Hitting the points at first light is a revelation. I rise in near darkness, around 4.30 am, and am in the water before the sun is up. This used to be my favourite time of day, that magical, shadowy half-light as the new day's waves reveal themselves through the sea mist. Why had I forsaken it for so long? Babies, sleep deprivation, school runs and then the fatigue brought on by chemo and hormone therapy led me to prioritise sleep over wave riding. I'd chosen the comfort of the doona over the sublime confines of the tube.

Just three or four dawn patrols in succession awakens something in me, a pilot light of surf stoke flickering back to life. I start getting a feel for the greater sensitivity of the Mayhem. The view of the rising sun while bobbing in the ocean is a magical, enlivening elixir.

The early birds I share the line-up with seem to be a chirpier, friendlier bunch than your average, snarling, GC point break crowd. I get maybe half an hour in and half-a-dozen sweet rides before the hordes descend, leaping off the Alley rock like penguins hunting for a feed. It's my cue to drift down the line to pick up a few more waves on the less crowded end section, before giving in to the weight of numbers, happily satiated before most people are out of bed. I remember this feeling, like being part of a secret society, supping on the pure prana of the new day before it's sullied and diluted by human noise and nonsense.

There's just one hitch to my dastardly cunning SurFebruary scheme. Our daughter Vivi is moving to Melbourne to begin an arts degree at Melbourne University, and we have scheduled a trip south to help her settle in. It's hard to believe our little girl's leaving home. She's had a decorated academic career to date – a scholarship to one of the Gold Coast's top private schools, poetry prizes, the school captaincy, an OP3 in year 12 that would have gained her entry to any university in the country. We've tried extolling the virtues of the University of Queensland, just up the road in Brisbane, the lure of coming home for weekends for home-cooked meals and to do laundry. But Viv's always loved Melbourne, even as a little girl, and her heart is set. It's bittersweet as a parent to see your offspring step so confidently and independently into the world. We console ourselves that these are signs of a job well done, but the Vivi-shaped hole in our lives will be difficult to fill.

SurFebruary also happens to coincide with a reunion of some old surfing buddies down at Phillip Island, on Victoria's south-east coast, where my surfing life truly began. My best mate in high school, Pat, and his family had a modest timber beach house on the Island, which an entire community of friends helped build over a couple of years, like an Amish barn raising, except with beer and the odd sly spliff. As the junior members of the construction team, in our early teens, we helped dig out post holes and punched nails into the timber deck. We were rewarded with an informal timeshare arrangement that afforded us free coastal accommodation on our sporadic teenage missions to the surf. Pat's parents are now in aged care, the family has decided to sell the largely unused beach house and Pat's called for one last hurrah.

The idea of revisiting the scene of so many of my adolescent highlights with some of my oldest mates, riding the waves we enjoyed as floundering but eager learners, is irresistible.

This is where we got drunk, had many of our early fumbling sexual adventures, first felt true independence and freedom, half-a-dozen of us cramming into bunk beds, living on pasta and baked beans and beer. When our non-surfing, Pommy schoolmate Nigel joined us down the Island for the first time, he wanted to know what to bring. 'Just the essentials,' we told him. He arrived with a box of provisions that included mint sauce and paper table napkins and we mocked him mercilessly.

So, I'll be sweet for my daily surf during the Island component of my Victorian visit. But Melbourne is another matter. Fortunately for me, a former corporate lawyer (and one-time nightclub cage dancer) by the name of Andrew Ross has spent the past five years fundraising, planning and ultimately building Australia's first surfing wave park open to the public, UrbnSurf, located conveniently right next to Tullamarine airport. I've been taunted by social media images of pro surfers, surf media freeloaders and various surfing celebs and influencers enjoying the perfect, man-made waves of UrbnSurf for months. When a pal on Twitter posts photos of his latest session, I can't help a slightly cynical response that my invite appears to have been lost in the mail.

Within hours, UrbnSurf's head of marketing, Rupert Partridge, messages me on Twitter apologetically. It appears my UrbnSurf invite has genuinely been lost in the mail, or at least my inbox, perhaps ending up in my junk folder. He wants to make amends and invites me to book in free of charge whenever suits me. This seems like fate. I'm giddy with excitement. I dare not even breathe a word of it to our surf-obsessed teenage son or he'll lose his shit and beg to stow away in my board bag. I need only to clock up a wave or two each day, I assure Rupert, but he buffs me out with two one-hour sessions for four straight days regardless; COVID-19's version of an Indo boat trip in Tullamarine.

My old school chum Pat scoops me up in his ute from outside Tullamarine airport on a balmy Friday afternoon, I throw my board and bags in the back, and we're headed down the Island as if it's 1983 all over again. That delicious ease between old mates settles in. There's no substitute for shared history. Pat was always a hit with the ladies, with his long blond locks, in the heyday of that straw-haired surfer look. But he was also resolutely monogamous in a series of long-term relationships, while we imagined the fun we'd have if we enjoyed his pulling power.

Now there's precious little of that teen heart-throb hair left, just a close shave of peach fuzz to blend in with the expanding bald spot. He wears it well, I'm sure still sending hearts aflutter among women of a certain demographic. I find myself staring at him with a kind of plutonic love, the sweet bond of an old friendship that has somehow endured not just time but physical distance, multiple relocations, divergent paths, health crises. He's an urban planner, a partner in a busy consultancy firm, but has pulled a tree change with his young family to Central Victoria, commuting to the city only when necessary. We stop in the thoroughly unremarkable country town of Tooradin, as tradition demands, for fish and chips.

Our third musketeer Mark is holed up in Jakarta with his young family (Pat and Mark were both late starters) teaching at an international school. He's doing it all remotely now from the safety of their apartment due to COVID-19, and is planning a return to Australia. He's sorely missed. We thought of ourselves as Matt, Jack and Leroy from the seventies Hollywood surf movie *Big Wednesday*, written and directed by the great John Milius as a heartfelt homage to his own surfing youth. *Big Wednesday* got panned by critics and most serious surfers at the time, but we loved the raucous depiction of sixties Californian surfing and it has achieved a certain cult status more recently.

Mark was Matt – the best surfer of the three, with his nimble, wiry physique – but he didn't share any of his avatar's self-destructive alcoholism. Pat was Jack, the responsible one, predestined to do the right, morally sound thing in any given circumstance. And I was Leroy the Masochist, the wild one, prone to food fights and binge-drinking.

I can still quote much of the script from *Big Wednesday*:

'I think I'll throw my food at ya.'

'I'm Leroy the Masochist, I'm here all the time and I'll do anything.'

'Jack went in, gung-ho all the way, man.'

'I never, and I don't know who would do such a thing, but I never pissed in your steam iron.'

And the timeless surf forecast from the salty old surfboard builder Bear: 'That's just the lemon next to the pie.'

In Mark's absence, we're joined by a couple of other old mates, Mup and Danno, who formed their own dynamic duo at high school and dubbed themselves the Water Rats, for the spartan deprivations of their coastal missions. Their modus operandi was to arrive with almost no money or provisions and somehow survive by their wits, which usually meant petty shoplifting, bludging off us or scoring free day-old bread from the bakery, where Danno worked on summer holidays.

We meet up at the old beach house late in the afternoon, four middle-aged men revisiting the set of their most treasured teen adventures, like a real-life *Friends* reunion but forty years on, with less botox and more visible signs of ageing. We shuffle about the stage awkwardly, recalling favourite episodes, quoting bits of dialogue, memories ambushing us around every corner. But I've got limited time for sentimentality. My first order of business is to rack up a surf to fulfil my SurFebruary commitments before dark. The surf's small, cold and uninspiring but the beach is so rich in memories I don't mind a bit.

To our teenage imaginations this little bay housed a multitude of possibilities. The little right running into the easterly corner which we used to boast broke in any swell, any wind and any tide, and a short, sucky left that occasionally peels towards it over a flat shelf of reef. The nondescript close-out beach breaks in the middle of the bay that we somehow convinced ourselves produced a surfable left. At the western end of the bay is a dribbly little right, dubbed Peppermints for no apparent reason, best suited to longboards. And out off the rocky ledge that protrudes from the base of the western headland is an optical illusion we called Mums, though I can recall no explanation for its name either. Mums would begin to break promisingly in a gaping right barrel but almost immediately flattened out into deep water. Generations of surfers were sucked in to paddling way out to try to surf it, like sailors lured to the rocks by a siren's song, and always came back disappointed, the enticing peak rarely offering anything more than an abrupt drop and a fat shoulder.

Yet this unremarkable beach and its surrounds formed our early surfing universe. The fearsome barrels of Express Point, a short walk eastwards, was our own North Shore, a serious big wave challenge way out of our league. And the beach breaks of Woolamai offered genuine quality when we could scrounge a lift there. We were flailing kooks who surfed maybe a dozen weekends and a few weeks of school holidays each year, whatever progress we'd make was quickly lost when we returned to the purgatory of landlocked suburbia. We'd wear our holiday tans and sun-bleached locks with pride, dry-docked in the endless flat expanse of Melbourne's outer eastern suburbs, standing out like foreigners amid the suburban subcultures of punks, sharpies, skins and footyheads. The flags on top of the Forest Hill shopping centre car park would torment us as we trudged to school when the wind puffed gently from the north, indicating the coast was offshore and the waves would be on.

I'm the only one surfing today, and our little posse of middle-aged blokes joins me for the walk down to the beach, cheering me on as I manage to trim unsteadily across a couple of tiny peelers in the fading light. Mission accomplished.

I thought we'd get to be a bit older before health issues began to dominate our conversations, but we've all had our brushes with mortality. Girls and footy and surfing have been replaced by medical procedures and ageing parents as chief topics of conversation. Mup's been through treatment for throat cancer and received a clean bill of health. Danno's had a brain aneurysm and miraculously survived. Pat seems to have got this far reasonably unscathed but is dealing with a mum with dementia and an ailing father. You have to squint to recognise the carefree teens we once were.

The house itself is like an old friend, a powerful presence in our youth, like an ageing, weathered sea salt who quite literally accommodated our surfing dreams, an endlessly patient elder enduring our youthful excesses without judgement. A physical manifestation of, and a temple to, our friendships, something we'd helped construct with our own hands. We'd camped out in the bare timber shell when it first got to lock-up stage, terrorised by the great bogong moth plague of 1980, as huge swarms took flight through the house every time you shifted a loose plank of timber. I remember hearing that bogong moths were edible and an important food source for Indigenous people, the focus of festivals and feasting when the large brown swarms migrated south from Queensland in their millions each spring, but I was never tempted to sample their reportedly nutty, sweet flavour, even when provisions were low.

We gather round a backyard fire in the cool Victorian evening with a few beers. Someone produces a spliff, god bless them. In the glow of the fire, I look around at these balding, battle-scarred friends and feel the kind of deep affection only a connection over decades can give rise to.

Around this time I catch Scottish author Andrew O'Hagan interviewed on ABC Radio National about his novel *Mayflies* and the close male friendships from teenage-hood to middle age it celebrates. 'When it comes to storytelling, romantic love gets all the big headlines and all the Oscars, but the love of friends is actually, if you're lucky, the other very stable thing in your life,' O'Hagan says. *Mayflies* focuses on the friendship of the charismatic ringleader Tully and the book's more, well, bookish narrator, Jimmy. O'Hagan is asked who his Tully was growing up.

'His name was Keith Martin. Keith was a fantastic record collector, he had the highest cheekbones in Scotland, he had the best record collection in Europe, and he was the most politically engaged 16-year-old that anybody had ever met, and Keith was my best friend at that age. And it was like getting permission to be who you really wanted to be, having a friend like that.'

My Tully was Pat. He had the best record collection in Blackburn, the longest blond hair at Nunawading High School, a complete set of the *Herald* cartoonist WEG's classic VFL Grand Final posters dating back decades, along with vast archives of *Tiger* and *Roy of the Rovers*, English soccer comic books. He single-handedly made it cool to wear shorts to school in the stifling heat of the Victorian summer, rather than sheepishly complying with the nonsensical fashion for long pants. His parents were staunch Labor supporters and the most socially progressive people I'd ever met. They took me to my first anti-nuclear protest when I was fifteen, a fact that outraged my parents, and my first inner-city theatre restaurant on the same day. His older sister Rachel, a drama student, would somehow corral our motley crew of teenagers into her amateur theatre productions annually, with intensive rehearsals over school holidays in this very abode.

'I think best friends are the guardians of your potential,' O'Hagan says in that interview, and it's one of those statements that chimes like the crisp, clear peel of a bell. Pat called out our bullshit, wouldn't just laugh along with sexist or racist jokes, treated women with respect and expected the same of us. Our running gag was that Pat was always late because he just had to hand out a few how-to-vote cards.

The very fact his parents had this beach house and maintained an open-door policy to their extended family and friends kept me on the surfing path, even when we had to go to such lengths to get there – hitchhiking, begging rides from parents and older siblings, or the all-day public transport marathon: train to Frankston, bus to Stony Point, ferry to Cowes, then hitching to the ocean coast.

Our adolescent folklore was written here. The time Danno lit a fart in our family tent and set it on fire. The fight we got in at a beach party, when Pat's older brother and his mates came to our rescue, lengths of pipe and four-by-two at the ready. The intimate teen grapples that went on in the upstairs loft bedroom. The nocturnal raids on the nearby Young Christian Workers Camp, which sounded a bit too Hitler Youth for our liking. A few of the boys dressed up in ski masks and garish clothing and ran through the joint whooping like banshees, then just as quickly vanished into the night.

We rode Sea Level surfboards shaped by underground Victorian shaper Rod Stock, round-nosed twin fins we called dunny lids that closely resembled the modern and fashionable fish design – flat, thick and wide with two broad-based fins. Under the next-door neighbour's house, we had access to a quiver of classic longboards – the Keyo, the Klemm Bell, the Pyke. We were unwitting, suburban hipsters before our time, minus the facial hair, man buns or posturing.

We played in a fairly awful high school band, The Head Toks, our slang for the kind of short, sharp blows or 'crow pecks' that would be delivered to unsuspecting students in the crowded corridors of Nunawading High School. Our set included crude covers of the Sports, Elvis Costello and the Beatles as well as our own dubious attempts at songwriting – my trite anti-war anthem, 'Soldier'; Pat's denouncement of commercial TV and radio, 'Media Attraction'. The Head Toks never played a paid gig but did the rounds of our mates' birthday parties, and Pat's mum Christine volunteered us to play at the local community centre for a monthly social gathering of kids with Down syndrome. They were some of the best gigs we ever played, like Beatlemania had come to Blackburn, the youngsters pogoing as if on pingers and mobbing us when we finished.

Now, I'm the only one who still surfs, Mup's the only one who still plays in a band, and Pat's the only one who hasn't had a life-threatening health crisis. I enjoy a deep comfort just being in their company, like my own circumstances aren't so dire or out of the ordinary – we all have our crosses to bear, our scars and, as Jim Morrison put it, 'no one here gets out alive'. I allow myself a couple of glasses of red for the occasion and between that and the spliff and the guitar passed around the fire like a conch, I'm sixteen again, belting out old Paul

Kelly songs or dredging those dubious originals deep out of the vault.

The weekend is over too soon. We've all got real lives to get back to – work and families and all the responsibilities of busy modern dads. Our goodbyes are oddly unsentimental, like we don't have the language for our feelings. As memorable as the weekend has been, realistically we just don't know how often we might be able to pull off this kind of thing – given physical distance and life pressures – but there's a renewed commitment to maintain these cherished friendships.

Ever the pragmatist, Pat recruits us to help load his trailer with all manner of junk he needs to get rid of before the sale, scraps of timber, broken furniture, old pedestal fans, the detritus of our adolescence here. But I'm carting something way more precious back to Melbourne with me.

25

URBAN TUBE HUNTERS

AN OLD INSTAGRAM ACCOUNT called Urban Tube Hunters (now defunct) once documented city-bound surfers' efforts to simulate the tube-riding experience in everyday urban settings, under overhanging trees, or in stormwater drains or pedestrian tunnels. I can relate. Growing up a surf-obsessed teen an hour's drive from the nearest rideable wave required similar acts of imagination.

I'd ride my skateboard around our hilly neighbourhood, imagining I was surfing, roaring down steep footpaths, then turning up the equally steep driveways that lined them, carving a turn back down before I ran out of speed and trying to string a few such manoeuvres together as a kind of surf simulator to hone my skills between coastal runs. Ottawa Avenue provided one of my favourite faux waves, a steep drop followed by two perfectly contoured driveways in quick succession, supporting the illusion I was mastering my backhand 'reo', or re-entry, in which the surfer turns hard off the lip of the breaking wave and drops back down. After rain, I'd ride my bike under drooping tree branches heavy with water droplets and run my hand through the leaves as I passed under them, producing a shower of spray that vaguely re-created the ocean experience. When my mates and I got cars and licences we'd careen onto the shoulder of dirt roads where there was an inviting embankment and perform the automotive approximation of a reo (not recommended in a clapped-out Toyota Corolla panel van).

Like so many aspects of modern life, such flights of invention and imagination are no longer required of the young, landlocked surfer, in Melbourne at least, and a growing number of locations around the world. UrbnSurf has allowed urban tube hunters to bag the real thing, authentic ocean-like barrels right next to an international airport in Melbourne's otherwise flat, featureless north. Would hunting barrels in captivity satisfactorily simulate the real thing? Would it feel like cheating, a soft, easy option like shooting the proverbial fish in a barrel? I'm about to find out.

I'm as excited as my sixteen-year-old self on one of those early coastal adventures forty-odd years ago. I still can't quite believe I'm heading inland to go surfing. I turn off just before the airport, past chicken shops and pizza joints, 7-Elevens and milk bars, car rentals and airport hotels, the unending brick and tile of northern Melbourne's vast suburbia. The Essendon AFL's team's training ground, the Hangar, looms up on the left, where bored suburban dads park their cars and stand at a cyclone fence to watch players train. It's hard to imagine an environment that feels less surf-like.

Soon I spot a concentration of black shipping containers piled one on top of another behind a high metal fence. Despite appearances, this isn't some international freight business. A left turn into the gravel car park brings me to the entrance of a surreal oasis on the outskirts of the airport. Cars with boards inside or on the roof are coming and going – tradies in hi-vis squeezing in a sesh between jobs, businesspeople ducking out in their lunchbreak, surf school groups, carloads of mates looking for a fix now that Mentawai boat trips are out of the question. The car park is packed on a weekday lunch time when I first lob at UrbnSurf for my debut in the pool.

I'm getting strong theme park vibes as I approach the front counter to check in – Wet'n'Wild for grown-ups. The front desk is busy with surfers checking in and the crew are friendly, prompt and efficient. I fill out an electronic waiver form on a touch screen, receive my wristband that records all my account details, flash it under a little scanner at the entrance and the turnstile magically opens for me. Before I've had a chance to orient myself, there it is.

I've seen the clips, read online accounts, spoken to a couple of mates who've partaken, yet nothing prepares me for the mesmerising spectacle. I watch dumbly in awe, eyes agog, as perfect lefts and rights peel away.

Surf journalism is a strange vocation, maybe excusable in one's youth, but surely a sign of stunted emotional development and perhaps a lack of career ambition in middle age. The pay's lousy, there's no job security, you write almost exclusively about whizzing along walls of water on slivers of foam and fibreglass and the people who are particularly good at it, documenting what they have to say about a whole range of things they have no particular qualifications for. As the ghost writer of surfing biographies, your job is to make surf stars sound more articulate than they are. For these indignities, the surf journalist is compensated chiefly in lifestyle, the occasional junket to exotic surf destinations and the dubious thrill of rubbing shoulders with famous surfers and attempting to ingratiate yourself to them. It all sounds a bit pathetic when I put it like that.

But right here, right now, in front of my bug-eyed incredulity, is the pay-off. I'm going to surf the pool, my every landlocked grommet fantasy come to life, all that doodling of waves during interminable maths classes made manifest. I've booked in last minute so take what spots are available. My pool debut is an advanced session on the left, a baptism of fire for a 56-year-old natural footer of intermediate ability, who rarely goes left, let alone one with stage four cancer, compromised bone density and an almost complete lack of testosterone. I'm a bundle of nerves. A hasty trip to the loo is required and by the time I get into my wetsuit and daub some zinc on my face it's time for the pre-surf briefing.

The UrbnSurf wave pool resembles a large baseball diamond with a pier down the middle, known as Roary, short for the Roaring Forties, because it generates the swells breaking either side of it. Perfect lefts and rights are pumped out every six seconds, in twelve-wave sets, with only a couple of minutes' break between. This frequency of waves and the ability to cater for large numbers of surfers is the key to UrbnSurf's success. Kelly Slater's Surf Ranch, by contrast, produces one wave every three minutes. With around fifteen surfers per session, on the right and the left, and a similar number of beginners having how-to-surf lessons in the small white-water waves, that's potentially sixty surfers per hour, each getting around a dozen waves for seventy-odd bucks.

Our group gathers on the lawn by the lifeguard tower as one of the instructors explains the rules. We paddle out single file next to the pier and wait our turn. We're told to stay well clear of the pier – when it starts generating swell you can get sucked towards it and people have lost fins on its protective wire mesh. When it's your turn and you miss a wave or fall, you go back to the end of the line, in which case you should turn and catch the whitewater in as quickly as possible to get out of the impact zone, so you don't get in the way of the next surfer. This is crucial advice because when the waves start up they are extremely close together, like a short period wind swell. If a couple of surfers blow the take-off in succession, things can quickly get messy. All this does little to ease my nerves.

And then, we're off. It's easy to imagine purists mocking the whole process, surfers handing over credit cards and flashing wristbands under scanners to get access to the surf, paddling out single file in neat rows to wait their turn on the artificial wave machine, the uniformed instructor issuing directions, the whirring of the machine, the high concrete wall you take off next to. It's all a long way from the sense of escape and freedom that drew most of us to surfing. And yet . . . there's something so magnetically hypnotic about the whole thing, I'm as excited as a kid at Christmas when I clapped eyes on my first foamie under the tree.

I'm also inordinately nervous. The concrete bottom and the 2-metre concrete wall that lines the pool are a bit menacing for someone who can't afford a serious injury. The apex of the pier and the wall create a tight little triangular take-off area where you feel hemmed in on all sides. When my turn comes, I'm freaking out. The surfer in front of me takes a wave, I paddle into position, the water starts receding as a swell builds in the narrow corner of the pool between the pier and the concrete wall and I turn and paddle like my life depends on it. I'm intent only on not blowing the take-off and disgracing myself.

Mercifully, I make the drop and take a conservative, low-risk approach to the wall that presents itself with a couple of gentle cutties and kick out, heart pounding. Backhand tube riding has never been my strong point. I find a variety of ways to blow the barrel section and never truly come to grips with it, though manage to miraculously avoid a close encounter with that concrete floor.

For the next three days, I gorge thoroughly like a pig with its snout in the feed trough before the rumblings of yet another Melbourne lockdown has me bolting for the airport a day early.

Is there a moral or ethical issue in riding man-made waves in the age of climate change? UrbnSurf claims that as long as you live at least a fifteen-minute drive closer to the pool than the ocean, your carbon footprint is smaller surfing the pool than driving to the coast. Solar panels supplement the energy supply, and the plan is to power it by 100 per cent renewable energy eventually. Is surfing losing something essential but intangible with the rise of wave pools? If wave pools aren't your kink, no one's holding a gun to your head to ride the things, and the ocean always awaits – vast, blue and free, with all its fickleness and beauty, hazards and mystique. If surfers are addicts and the ocean is our drug, then wave pools provide a convenient methadone program.

I've managed some quality time with Viv, enjoyed dinner with her on Brunswick Street at a hip taco joint, taken her grocery shopping to stock up her spartan uni student pantry, and wandered those same bohemian inner city environs with her that I first delighted in when I was her age. I've always thought of Viv as a Melbourne girl who just happened to be born on the Gold Coast and she appears entirely, effortlessly at home. We've been to visit my mum, cherishing the pleasure they so clearly derive from each other's company. But the hurried departure still stings, particularly as border closures throw the timing of future visits into question.

Safely back on the Goldy, I'm able to happily meet my SurFebruary obligations in the good old ocean and, while it's nice to be home, I have to confess to missing the ease and convenience of the pool. On the coast I drive around trying to figure out the most desirable location, battle it out with the unremitting crowds, and rips and currents and tides and fluky winds and the prospect of paddling for hours for only a couple of waves. I end up raising over $4000 for the Chris O'Brien Lifehouse, making me the eighth highest fundraiser in the country. I'm practically a professional surfer now. There's probably a new water cooler or massage table at Lifehouse with my name on it.

A year on, I catch an episode of *Catalyst* on the ABC about the Chris O'Brien Lifehouse, following the paths of several cancer patients receiving coordinated, integrative care. When one patient's chemo has to be halted because of high blood pressure, they bring in an oncology masseuse whose healing hands soon normalise the blood pressure so chemo can resume.

This is the future of cancer care I want to see, yet watching it in process makes me strangely emotional, even angry. Why doesn't all cancer care look this way? Why are cancer patients treated with such cold detachment elsewhere and offered nothing in the way of supportive therapies? The contrast with my own experience is stark and enraging. I've been left to fend for myself on so many fronts, it borders on negligence. Only my relative privilege and connections have allowed me to navigate the maze of the medical system, where so many others must flounder in despair.

We can and must do better.

26

THERAPEUTIC PSYCHEDELICS

I'VE BEEN ON AND off my ADT so many times I feel like a puppet on a string, unable to regulate my own behaviour, fearful of the impacts on my family, ashamed of my moodiness and outbursts of anger. My oncologist suggests antidepressants to counter the misery inflicted upon me by hormone therapy. Being prescribed one drug that makes me depressed and another to treat this medically induced depression doesn't make sense to me.

I don't see any stigma in using antidepressants or in suffering from poor mental health. But I'm fearful of what my GP calls their potentially numbing effects – treating depression by making us feel less across the board. Less crippling depression, yes, but will it be at the expense of joy, awe, wonder, and inspiration too? When so much has already been stripped away from me, must I sacrifice all feelings? Will I be able to write? Laugh? Love? Be a fully functioning, feeling human with a healthy emotional range? Not for the first time on this journey, I sense there must be a better way.

I'm driving back from a surf just over the border in northern New South Wales, when I hear an interview with US author Michael Pollan about his new book, *How to Change Your Mind*, on the study of psychedelics for therapeutic purposes. New research suggests enormous potential in the treatment of everything from depression, post-traumatic stress and anxiety to addiction, anorexia and obsessive-compulsive disorder. One study with terminal cancer patients showed guided psilocybin trips eliminated or dramatically reduced a fear of death in 80 per cent of cases. Psilocybin, the psycho-active compound in magic mushrooms, is also being used to treat returned war veterans with PTSD. Pollan calls the prohibition of psychedelics in the sixties one of the greatest impediments to medical research in human history. He also makes a compelling argument that psychedelics, like youth itself (according to the old adage), are wasted on the young, that they can be dangerous to the developing brain and are most useful to counter the rigid thinking and lifestyle ruts many of us experience in middle age. In his book, an international bestseller, he uses himself as a guinea pig for a variety of psychedelic experiences.

I've had limited experience with psychedelic drugs. A handful of nights on ecstasy (which is categorised as a psychedelic for therapeutic purposes) back in the decadent eighties, in my early twenties, when I found myself in Sydney amid the new party-drug rave scene. I first popped one with a group of friends in a noisy, sweaty nightclub in Oxford Street with New Order's 'Bizarre Love Triangle' blaring and topless men dancing with each other, sniffing small vials of amyl nitrate, or rush. *Toto, I've a feeling we're not in Blackburn anymore.* We had a ball, dancing like whirling dervishes into the wee hours. God knows what was in them – there were appalling comedowns, but that hasn't stopped a roaring trade in the pills.

One mild acid trip while roaming the New South Wales south coast with friends over twenty years ago, what I now recognise as a microdose, proved fun – no spectacular hallucinations, just an increased vividness and vibrancy to my experience of the world. We trekked through a eucalypt forest to find the largest spotted gum tree in the region and stood around the base marvelling at its girth, gazing awe-struck at its towering height.

I've never taken mushrooms, never experienced a full-blown, mind-altering trip. An older, more psychedelically experienced friend once asked me, 'Do you like your mind the way it is?'

'Yes,' I'd answered, without hesitation.

'Then don't take acid,' she'd advised.

Now, I'm not so sure I like my mind, at least in the grip of ADT. Pollan's suggestion that I can change my mind, that I might address trauma, anxiety and depression, not by feeling less but by feeling more, by experiencing the true interconnectedness of the universe, holds instant appeal. I feel like some of the trauma of my diagnosis is still trapped in my body, coming out in moments of stress to sabotage my efforts to live happily and be at peace with my condition. As Paul Kalanithi writes in *When Breath Becomes Air*, 'Even when cancer is in retreat it casts long shadows.'

Psychedelic experiences seem to dissolve the individual ego, making the struggles of our personal circumstances less significant as we're faced with the miracle and wonder of existence. I'm up for a bit of that. Maybe I've led a sheltered life, but I've no idea where and how to go about procuring psychedelic drugs.

I put some discreet feelers out through a couple of friends who are that way inclined. The psychedelic community is still very much a shadowy, underground scene, despite the recent mainstreaming of microdosing. The practice is apparently all the rage among young Silicon Valley professionals as a mental health tonic and performance enhancer in the hyper-competitive world of tech.

Rolling Stone first reported on the rise of microdosing in 2015, quoting an anonymous San Francisco IT professional they called Ken. 'Microdosing has helped me come up with some new designs to explore and new ways of thinking,' Ken says. 'You would be surprised at how many people are actually doing it. It's crazy awesome.' Even the otherwise sober business journal *Forbes* has reported on the phenomenon, claiming Apple maestro Steve Jobs was a disciple and mocked his rival Bill Gates for abstaining.

Melbourne's St Vincent's Hospital is running clinical trials using psilocybin to treat the existential dread of terminal cancer patients, with astonishing results. Lead therapist and chief principal investigator of the trial, Dr Margaret Ross, says:

We've never seen anything like this in terms of the most
dramatic and rapid reduction of symptoms alleviating
patient suffering . . . We see a lot of fear and despair in our
terminally ill patients, so to be able to offer a novel trial
treatment that has already shown such promise is excellent.
It's really a privilege to be able to conduct this
research. This is one of the most exciting developments
in psychiatric research in decades.

I get a cryptic voicemail message from a friend. He has
some 'goodies' for me. This turns out to be a small brown
bottle with an eye-dropper lid containing precisely one
hundred drops of lysergic acid diethylamide, or LSD, high
quality and quite pure, he assures me. Two to three drops
constitutes a microdose, ten drops a full trip. The bottle costs
$100, or $1 a drop, which seems like exceedingly good value
for money. We do the deal and I regard this small vial and
the clear liquid curiously, marvelling at its potent ability to
alter human consciousness. The vial's label is decorated with
a brightly coloured beetle, perhaps because I'll soon visualise these creatures crawling over my skin. Such designs are
intended to identify the origins of the acid for the discerning user, and some aficionados even collect the labels as
mini artworks.

I wait for a day I have the house to myself, no appointments,
no commitments, and take two drops. And wait. Nothing
happens. I take a third drop and wait some more. Perhaps I've
been scammed. I'm cautious about diving in harder, given my
brownie experience. But as the day wears on, slowly, almost

imperceptibly, I find myself fixating on small but inordinately fascinating elements of my surroundings – the wind through the towering Alexandra Palm fronds in our front yard, the play of light on the surface of our swimming pool and its reflection on the lounge-room wall, the view of a wind-ruffled ocean from our front porch. Then I notice I'm noticing these things. The effect reminds me of an old TV commercial for Crunchie chocolate bars that promised to 'change the colour of your day'. As the afternoon plays out there's little question the colour of my day has indeed changed. Subtle but undeniable. I'm in an exceedingly good mood, finding delight in almost everything around me – a cup of tea, the drifting and slowly morphing clouds, the affections of our toy poodle Lucky, whose incessant yapping usually annoys me, the simple pleasures of choosing to eat, read, rest, strum a guitar, stretch, or do a little writing as the mood takes me. If I wasn't high, I'd probably be stewing over some looming deadline or unpaid bill or the ever-present spectre of my next lot of test results.

There seems to be no downside to this state. I'm not *out of it* out of it. I can carry on a conversation, greet my children when they return from school without any anxiety (unlike with the brownies), perform most of the functions required of me as an adult – answer the phone, cook dinner, help with homework – with no loss of faculties. I wouldn't drive a car or attempt to land a plane, but fortunately I'm not required to. There's an urge to top up, to not let the magic wear off, but it's not like the manic, teeth-gnashing urgency of, say, cocaine, when you just need more every half an hour or so or you feel like life will descend into unremitting misery. If anything, there's a pleasant afterglow to the experience, a lingering memory of gratitude and awareness and vibrancy. I'm sold.

I enjoy my little eye-dropper of LSD over the subsequent weeks and months without it ever becoming a compulsion, microdosing once or twice a week. I spend some time out at my mate Kevin's property, and the former banana and avocado farm with its century-old, timber homestead proves the ideal setting. The verdant rainforest hums in unison with the cicadas and birdsong that provide the soundtrack to my day and my own gently harmonising cellular structure.

There's a little desk set up in the spare room and I manage to get plenty of writing done. A bush turkey is busy outside my window scratching the forest debris into an enormous nest. Avocados occasionally fall from an overhanging tree and bang noisily on the tin roof. I step out onto the verandah, and I'm struck by the energy of the dense foliage, a thousand shades of green staring back at me, almost like a sentient presence whose frequency I'm now tuned in to. As if answering a siren's call, I wander the surrounding forest, senses heightened, hyper-vigilant to the sounds of wildlife scurrying about unseen. At the end of the day, when the effects have worn off, I return home to my family like any other working dad to chat about our days over the evening meal. This all feels like the most exquisite, secret life hack, but I'm not just in this for shits and giggles.

The research focus when it comes to cancer appears to be on psilocybin. The acid has been fun, a soothing balm against the anxiety of my diagnosis, and if I could find a suitable guide

I'd be open to a full trip, but as a relative novice I'm hesitant. It's wild to think I could just depress that little dropper a few more times and be sent on a psychedelic journey of hallucinations for hours, but I resist the temptation, worried I might completely freak myself out, run naked through the streets and scandalise the neighbourhood.

Once psilocybin is on my radar, however, I seem to come across references to its wondrous properties everywhere, as if the fungi are wooing me. One of the key themes of Pollan's book is that there was much credible and promising psychedelic research going on in the fifties and sixties. While many credit counterculture figure Timothy Leary with popularising the use of psychedelics, among researchers he's seen as the guy who blew it. Once psychedelics escaped the laboratory and became a recreational plaything for Leary and his mainly youthful followers, the authorities quickly shut down the entire field of study during Richard Nixon's ineffectual War on Drugs.

But interest in psilocybin has started sprouting everywhere, like the magic mushroom itself in a field of cow pats after heavy rain. And, as fate would have it, a mate in northern New South Wales has a literal field of cow pats busily sprouting mushrooms of various species, including the magic variety, after recent rains. He gifts me a small package of the special ones, and carefully weighs and shows me the recommended microdose. Stu is planning a surfing road trip down the coast and asks whether I'd like to house-sit while he's away. I've been planning a bit of a writing retreat – this quaint old farmhouse with chooks, a veggie garden and outdoor dunny surrounded by fields of cows and a ready supply of psilocybin, not too far from the coast for the odd surf mission, seems like an offer too good to refuse.

Stu is a wiry sixty-ish surfer with a mop of sun-bleached hair who's living the *Morning of the Earth* dream – the back-to-nature, off-grid existence celebrated in that seminal seventies surf movie. With his solar panels, rainwater tanks, remote location and live-off-the-land ethos, I'm heading straight to Stu's place at the first sign of the zombie apocalypse. He suggests a tour of the paddocks to look for mushrooms, points out the different varieties and which to avoid. He turns off the electric fence that keeps the cows away from his veggie garden and we clamber over. The herd regard us impassively between mouthfuls of grass as we traverse the steep hillside, scanning for gold tops. Stu knows his stuff. I'm in good hands. Eating the wrong mushroom can be fatal so it's not something to be taken lightly. The psychedelic kind acquire a light blue-ish bruise when squeezed so that's a telltale sign, but I wouldn't recommended foraging for them without an experienced guide.

I experiment with the mushrooms at home when I again have the place to myself and at the recommended micro-dose, they're perhaps more subtle than the acid, and it's easy to assume there's no effect at all. But I resist the temptation to partake too liberally. I've heard a few horror stories of psychonauts who never returned to earth, once-great surfers who lost their minds on mushroom smoothies in Bali, or others who just remained forever out there. I have to remind myself too that my interest here is therapeutic and academic, that I'm a PhD student engaged in serious research.

Over a couple of weeks, I experiment, very gradually increasing the dose until I feel a more pronounced effect, but some way short of inanimate objects turning into dragons or swarms of bats attacking my eyeballs. Set and setting is everything, Pollan counsels in his book. To set an intention, and be in a safe, supportive setting is key. My intention is straightforward, to stave off the toxic effects of hormone therapy, particularly the wild mood swings and crippling depression, to release the trauma of my initial diagnosis and to try to overcome my fear of death. I continue the cautious nibbling of my little dried stash every few days and enjoy the gentle warping of my reality, a kind of stillness, the dropping away of extraneous thoughts and a powerful sense of being in the moment, deeply appreciating the small and ever-changing details of my surroundings.

Once I take up residence in the old farmhouse – on my own for days on end, just the cows and chooks and shrooms for company – I get a little bolder and spend a couple of quite blissful days exploring the outer reaches of what might reasonably be considered a microdose. I'm not sure how conducive this is to my other aim in being here, writing this damn book, but as I wander the surrounding paddocks hunting for more shrooms, I figure this is at least, quite literally, valuable field research. Days drift by with no sense of time, my activities governed only by the position of the sun, pangs of hunger, bursts of writing, simple tiredness, empty moments contemplating the fleet of vintage surfboards stashed in the rafters of the old farmhouse.

But I do write, in short, spirited, concentrated bursts. I'm feeling it, man, the ideas and words fizzing and popping and spilling out in a way that is most pleasing. When inspiration or interest wains, I go for another walk, visit the chooks, collect the handful of fresh eggs they lay each day, maybe gather an avocado or two off the ground, do another lap of the paddock searching for shrooms, without success, which is perhaps just as well.

I come to enjoy this loose feeling, my mind slipping its moorings and drifting unrestrained on the sea of my imagination – a sensation that lingers for some days after, before slowly fading. A glimpse of . . . I'm not entirely sure what. I'm reminded of a story told by a yogically inclined mate of mine about an Indian guru being given a hit of acid. The guru appeared to be entirely unaffected by it and when asked what he thought of the experience he replied, 'It is like trying to open a lotus flower with a crowbar.'

I sense this might be a state I can slowly, gradually cultivate through mediation, that psychedelics are a shortcut that give us a glimpse of what might be attained through the mental discipline and training that leads to transcendence. Most traditional cultures have used some form of mind-altering substances, usually with strict discernment and ritual and a qualified guide or shaman overseeing proceedings. We've all heard tales of ayahuasca ceremonies among Amazonian rainforest tribes, the use of peyote by Native Americans in Mexico, and the Western tourists drawn to these experiences in the quest for enlightenment, psychic healing, or transcendental thrill-seeking.

In the case of terminally ill cancer patients, the early evidence for psychedelic therapy seems so promising and the need for relief from emotional suffering so great, why wouldn't we offer people the opportunity to transcend their fear of death in their final months?

'You hit the limits of what medicine and psychiatry can provide,' says Dr Margaret Ross, of her work with terminal cancer patients. Speaking on the 'Mind Manifest' podcast in January 2020, Dr Ross says her deep drive to work in this area was tempered by an awareness of the risks she was taking. 'If I stick my neck out, publicly that's coming out in a way that I do support psychedelic research. People had warned me that you'll be forever known as the kooky psychologist who no one will employ. It will kill your career.'

Instead, she's been overwhelmed by the positive media interest and public support. 'Sitting with dying patients you're just stripped back to your raw humanity. That was a big driving force in overcoming that knot that said, Is this a good idea?' she says.

I'm not yet considered terminal, which is generally defined as less than a year or, in some cases, two years to live, when your cancer is unresponsive to any treatment. If I was, I'd be sticking my hand up for a jumbo mushroom smoothie or omelet. But the Shroom Underground proves a difficult community to infiltrate. I can source the fungi but I'm looking for an experienced and credible guide to oversee a full trip. The St Vincent's trial has been entirely overwhelmed with expressions of interest, but I decide to apply anyway, explaining my personal and academic interest in the therapy. I'm told my desire to write about the experience could corrupt the results and I'm knocked back. So, I turn again to my friends at the Hemp Embassy.

On my next visit, I ask the woman who serves me if she knows where I might find a psilocybin guide and she points me over the road to a herbal health store, but the woman I speak to there has no suggestions. As I leave, another woman approaches me on the street.

'I overheard your conversation,' she says, and gives me an email address for someone called Sam on a special encrypted email service, to protect his identity. When I get home, I jump online and have to open an account to be able to email him. I explain my interest in having a guided psilocybin trip to help deal with the anxiety of an advanced cancer diagnosis, as well as my academic interest, but never hear back. I discover an online forum, the Shroomery, which offers the psychedelic community the chance to ask questions and have them answered by other members, but my inquiry there also goes unheeded. I'm unsure where to turn next.

27

MIND MEDICINE

BEAUTIFUL BYRON BAY COMES to my rescue – an upcoming symposium is to be held there on psychedelic medicine and the campaign to have it legalised. The program, put together by a not-for-profit organisation called Mind Medicine Australia, includes an introduction to psychedelic-assisted therapy or what they call mind medicine, an exploration of the laws surrounding psychedelic therapies and instruction on how to train to become a psychedelic-assisted therapist. A group healing sound bath, in which the audience is lulled into a meditative state by a gentle symphony of chimes and gongs, rounds out the day.

The board of Mind Medicine Australia is made up of some heavy hitters in academia, politics and business. Founding philanthropic husband-and-wife team Peter Hunt, an investment banker, and Tania de Jong, a social entrepreneur, are both Officers of the Order of Australia. Fellow board members include Andrew Robb, former minister for trade, investment and tourism in the Abbott and Turnbull governments, and Admiral Chris Barrie, chief of the Defence Force from 1998 to 2002. These are not your typical Byron Bay counterculture hippy trippers.

The mounting COVID-19 case numbers in Sydney – the so-called Bondi cluster 800 kilometres away to the south – has meant a reduction in group sizes allowed to gather indoors in New South Wales, so the symposium has been split into two sessions to halve the audience. I'm in the morning session. The restrictions also mean the program has been compressed from six hours to three. We're assured we'll receive all the content as planned, but question time and panel discussions will be reduced and the planned sound bath at the end is off; presumably it is too difficult to social distance in a sound bath.

The symposium is a strikingly sober, even earnest affair, with what I imagine is a very conscious and deliberate focus on the scientific evidence for the therapeutic use of psychedelics, chiefly psilocybin and MDMA. There's no discussion of their recreational use, no use of their colloquial names – no mention of shrooms or tripping or ecstasy. And their goals are pragmatically modest – to have these drugs reclassified by the Therapeutic Goods Administration from schedule 9 (prohibited) to schedule 8 (controlled), at a federal level, to allow them to be prescribed for therapeutic use only by a suitably qualified health professional. Their mission is complicated by differing state laws – currently you can't even run clinical trials of psychedelics in Queensland.

After a thorough discussion of the compelling evidence base for their therapeutic use, a very clear explanation of the current legal landscape and the efforts to lobby government for reclassification is laid out. We could be sitting in any academic conference on the intersection of health, ethics and legal issues around medical research, except for a smattering of rainbow tie-dye and dreadlocks in the audience. When the floor is opened up to questions things get really interesting. An elderly man in the audience, voice quivering with emotion, explains he has lived with complex PTSD for most of his life, the result of an abusive childhood, that he has held a gun to his head to end his suffering and was only snapped out of it by the family dog jumping in a window. He says he can't wear a face mask because it triggers childhood memories of his mother trying to suffocate him with a pillow. He's now being treated with psilocybin and MDMA with an almost complete relief of symptoms.

'They work and these bastards are denying people life-saving treatment. People are dying because these drugs are being withheld and I'm angry,' he rages. There are murmurs of empathy.

Apart from self-education, I've come to do some sly networking, to try to find myself a qualified and experienced psilocybin guide. I've planned to simply explain my circumstances in question time and invite any such therapist to approach me after the session, understanding the need for discretion. But the reduced question time means I never get a chance.

Instead, I mingle outside the theatre as the morning crowd shuffles out and the afternoon one shuffles in, hoping to make some contacts. I find myself chatting to a delightful, raven-haired, forty-something lady we'll call Lisa, who's sympathetic to my story. Lisa says she can recommend a local therapist, a qualified psychologist who discreetly conducts psychedelic therapy sessions for a select clientele. She gives me her email address and says she'll arrange an email introduction to Jose. I must sign up to the same encrypted email service I already joined after my last Nimbin run, so I email Jose as soon as Lisa's email comes through. The next day, I'm excited to see a new message in my sneaky, super spy email account. But my excitement is short-lived. Jose's assistant says he is booked out for the next three months and not currently taking new clients, but they can put me on a waitlist in case he has any cancellations. I'm gutted. My return to ADT means there's a certain urgency to this quest, to find a way to manage the drug's side effects before they grow too dire. I politely express my disappointment and eagerness to be put on the list.

Fortunately for me, that same growing COVID cluster in Sydney means one of Jose's clients cannot travel up from Sydney lockdown and a vacancy opens up in a week's time – a group session with three clients in which he oversees an MDMA trip. It's not the psilocybin experience I've been after, but I'll take it. Jose recommends MDMA for new clients because he considers it gentler and more predictable than psilocybin, a way to build trust between the client and therapist before diving into the more intense shroom experience.

Jose sends me reams of reading material about the protocols and guidelines for the session. No coffee or other stimulants beforehand. Fast for five hours. Bring comfortable, loose-fitting clothing, a blanket, some trinkets, photos or keep-sakes that evoke happy memories to create a kind of shrine. The location is a quaint cottage on acreage in the foothills of Wollumbin (Mount Warning) in the Northern Rivers region; we are given written directions and asked not to use GPS. The directions are perfect: 'Take the first right after the solar farm. Look for the Tibetan prayer flags at the top of my driveway.' I'm tempted to point out, in northern New South Wales this doesn't really narrow down the location a whole lot.

I'm re-reading these instructions on the morning of my appointment, obediently foregoing my morning coffee. Kirst regards all this with a kind of wry amusement.

'This no coffee thing seems a bit extreme,' I comment.

She chuckles.

'The rest of it seems completely normal, but the no coffee thing raises some red flags,' I quip.

Kirst is doing her own PhD in public health, our parallel academic careers a fate neither of us would have predicted, and she expresses a certain envy for my research process.

'Funnest PhD ever,' I quietly gloat.

MDMA or 3,4-methylenedioxymethamphetamine, was first synthesised by German chemists in 1912 while developing other drugs to stop bleeding. When its psychoactive properties were recognised, chemical company Merck patented it in 1914, but it would be decades before its therapeutic applications were explored. The CIA experimented with MDMA during the Cold War in the 1950s as a form of mind control, and psychiatrists began taking an interest in its therapeutic use in the 1970s, before it became popular as a party drug in the 1980s, leading to its prohibition as part of the US War on Drugs. Despite this, research continued into its usefulness in treating a range of mental disorders, and in relationship counselling.

The drive south over the border is usually a surf trip for me, one I've always associated with a delicious sense of freedom; the high-rises and crowds of the Gold Coast giving way to cane fields and rolling green hills. But on this grey, wet, winter morning I'm on a different kind of trip. Wollumbin (Mount Warning), the Cloud-Catcher, that towering, extinct volcanic peak that dominates the landscape, is doing its job, shrouded in tufts of grey mist. I've got a CD of gypsy jazz playing on the HiAce's rudimentary stereo and the directions printed out next to me on the centre console. I find the turn-off, spot the solar farm and prayer flags, anticipation mounting. Thirty years ago, I would have chucked one of these pills down my gob on a wild night out with barely a moment's thought. Now, the feeling I'm about to cross a threshold and step into a heretofore unknown world reminds me most closely of the walk home from school in Year 11 with my then girlfriend, my teenage brain fizzing with the nervous anticipation I was about to lose my virginity. I'm hoping this experience lasts a little longer than that inglorious debut.

There are quaint cottages dotted throughout the gently undulating, heavily wooded hills, like the Shire in *Lord of the Rings*, handwritten signs imploring drivers to slow down, a few residents gently strolling on the side of the narrow, winding road, chook pens and veggie gardens, water tanks and solar panels. I pull into Jose's gravel driveway and park in front of a small, white adobe cottage. Jose is there to meet me on the front porch. He's a fifty-ish, bespeckled fellow with a tangle of curly blond hair, dressed casually in faded denim jeans, a worn grey t-shirt and sandals. He has a slight American twang and reminds me of Fred, one of the main characters in the satirical TV series *Portlandia*, about the alternative lifestyle couple who favour fair trade, organic, free-range, politically correct everything. There's a similar upward inflection to his speech that makes every statement sound like a gentle inquiry.

I'm led inside where my fellow MDMA adventurers are already lying down on mattresses around a central fireplace, headphones on, eyeshades in place, an ethereal soundtrack of world music vaguely wafting through the cottage. There's a youngish woman with long, red hair opposite me and a middle-aged bloke with a buzz cut lying on a day bed at right angles to her. My bed forms the other side of a U-shaped arrangement around the fireplace. Jose and I chat for a while to build a rapport, set my intentions for the session, go over the process and clear up any questions I may have. I've read all the literature I've been sent so have few questions.

'The medicine makes us porous to what needs to be acknowledged in order to be healed,' Jose's introductory email read. 'As the fight or flight centre of our nervous system/brain the Amygdala goes offline we can then feel safe to open to experiences that we usually dissociate from. Without the amygdala so activated we open to what needs our engagement . . . Your primary orientation is to simply be open to what may arise, acknowledging whatever comes up. The medicine/therapeutic process has its own direction and momentum, and we trust this direction.'

We've been told to just focus on our breath and physical sensations and emotions as they surface, without getting stuck in our heads analysing or interpreting these, just allow them to move through our bodies and consciousness. Vipassana has prepared me well for this.

Jose carefully weighs out my dose, hands me a small ceramic cup containing the MDMA powder in a capsule and a glass of water and invites me to ingest. Here we go. I take a sip with the capsule and swallow. No turning back now. The medicine takes up to forty-five minutes to come on, so I arrange my few little keepsakes by the side of my bed like a small shrine – photos of the family, a childhood photo of me, another of my two older brothers as kids, a photo book of our family trip around Australia, a surf shot of me pulling into a backhand barrel at Duranbah – my happy place. Then I too don the eyeshades and headphones, lie down, make myself comfortable and pull a blanket over me.

Am I feeling anything yet? I wonder, like an impatient child on a long road trip wanting to know if we've arrived – an odd, recurring question with no definitive answer. I'm feeling lots of things – all the feels, as the kids say. I'm thinking about the day the urologist told me I had cancer and that it had already spread to the bone. My intention is to take myself back to that trauma and release whatever remnants may have lodged in my body and psyche. I focus on my breath. The music rises and falls, inspiring waves of emotion, but nothing particularly transcendent. Is it even working? The others have been offered a small top-up and I'm about to request one myself when the question of whether it is working is answered by a steadily building sense of . . . it's hard to come up with any other word for it . . . bliss. I feel wonderful but I can't explain why, just a delicious hum of energy building and spreading through my body, a deep sense of release like I'm gently sinking into the mattress.

As the music rises and falls so too do the sensations, ebbing and flowing, building and receding, like a sensory magic carpet or bobsled ride – soaring, floating, a profound sense of opening and expanding through my chest, or heart centre, in the language of the chakras. People from my past, old friends, ex-girlfriends, family, drift through my consciousness. At one point I feel like I'm nursing our newborn baby daughter on my chest as I did the night she was born. Vivi's now nineteen. A wailing male vocal rises in intensity as the medicine seems to peak and I'm wrapped in an exquisite sense of euphoria, simply humming.

I manage to summon the memory of the urologist delivering my diagnosis – my wife and me seated in front of him, Kirst squeezing my hand in panic, the bone scan on the wall-mounted lightbox, the dispassionate explanation of the horse having bolted, the rising sense of crisis. Interestingly, I feel no grief or trauma but, unexpectedly, only compassion for the poor chump having to deliver the news. What must that be like, day after day?

Love, compassion, appreciation, are the overwhelming emotions, a powerful sense of what a wonderful life I've been gifted, the beautiful humans who've inhabited it, wonder at my own resilience, for still being here, alive and healthy and, for now, ecstatically happy.

Then, I feel like I'm surfing, reliving highlights from my wave-riding life, marvelling at the magic of whizzing across the ocean's surface and the miracle that a kid from the Melbourne 'burbs managed to fashion a surfing life through the ludicrous vocation of writing about it. I never want it to end but in the moment the experience is timeless. I have no sense of how long I lay here purring like a cat having its tummy stroked.

By the time these waves of bliss begin to gradually subside, and I stretch my arms and legs to see if they still work, peek out from under the eyemask, it is late afternoon. The grey day has given way to the golden light of dusk, the sun low in the sky. About five hours have passed since I arrived. My fellow travellers have also stirred and are sitting up while Jose prepares herbal tea and presents us with a fresh fruit platter. I haven't eaten a thing all day and don't feel especially hungry, yet each slice of watermelon or rockmelon or apple provides a juicy flavour explosion.

We finish with a sharing circle, describing our experiences. The woman across from me has been groaning like she might have been orgasming, or in pain, it's hard to tell through the headphones. She appears radiant and joyful, despite detailing a journey to the nightmare of her abusive childhood. She's a regular client who's been working with Jose for a year, with MDMA and psilocybin, and says the results far exceed any benefits she's gained from years of counselling. The other bloke, Matt, is fifty, with the hint of an Irish accent; he marvels at how different the MDMA experience is in this therapeutic setting compared to the party and nightclub environment he's usually partaken in. He's processing an adolescent assault and a string of failed relationships that followed. Matt announces that he's forgiven his abuser, realises he's sabotaged every relationship he's ever been in with infidelities, and wants to recommit to his current partner. Within the space of half an hour we're chatting as intimately as old friends and I feel remarkably clear and energised, with no signs of a hangover or having experienced any kind of altered state, other than a warm and pleasant afterglow.

We spend another hour or so chatting, sipping tea, swapping stories and biographical titbits. When my turn to share comes, I have no great trauma experience to report, just an unending tale of perfect bliss. I'm not sure if this means I have no buried trauma to unearth, that I have already processed it through my meditation practice and counselling, or whether it is so buried it will take a few sessions to emerge. We've been told the medicine will offer up what we need in that moment. 'Perhaps the medicine decided, this bloke has had it pretty rough and he just needs the bliss experience this time round,' I suggest. Every session is different, Jose explains, and I shouldn't expect it to be the same next time. Trauma and other unprocessed experiences arise when the time is right.

But there's something else – a pride in how far I've come since the terror-filled days following my diagnosis, a powerful sense that nothing is wrong with me, that I'm whole and healthy, that cancer has loosened its grip, or at least its power over me. I'm not suggesting MDMA is a cure for cancer, but rather that it has helped cancer's long, dark shadow recede a little, and left a feeling that I might at least be able to live out whatever time I have left with less fear and dread.

My experience is consistent with the research on PTSD patients. A 2021 experimental, double-blind, randomised trial, 'MDMA-assisted therapy for severe PTSD', demonstrated that three doses of MDMA together with regular counselling over an 18-week period provided lasting relief from PTSD and depressive symptoms for five weeks:

> . . . MDMA-assisted therapy induces rapid onset of treatment efficacy, even in those with severe PTSD, and in those with associated comorbidities including dissociative PTSD, depression, history of alcohol and substance use disorders, and childhood trauma. Not only is MDMA-assisted therapy efficacious in individuals with severe PTSD, but it may also provide improved patient safety. Compared with current first-line pharmacological and behavioural therapies, MDMA-assisted therapy has the potential to dramatically transform treatment for PTSD and should be expeditiously evaluated for clinical use.

A double-blind, randomised clinical trial in 2016 involving fifty-one cancer patients with life-threatening diagnoses and a history of depression found a lasting reduction in depression and anxiety in around 80 per cent of patients from a single dose of psilocybin. The study, 'Psilocybin produces substantial and sustained decreases in depression and anxiety in patients with life-threatening cancer', concluded:

> When administered under psychologically supportive, double-blind conditions, a single dose of psilocybin

produced substantial and enduring decreases in depressed
mood and anxiety along with increases in quality of
life and decreases in death anxiety in patients with a
life-threatening cancer diagnosis. Ratings by patients
themselves, clinicians, and community observers suggested
these effects endured at least 6 months. The overall rate of
clinical response at 6 months on clinician-rated depression
and anxiety was 78% and 83%, respectively.

Importantly, these studies reported very few adverse
responses, and characterised the few that did occur as mild
or moderate: an elevated heart rate or body temperature that
quickly normalised. Impressively, the benefits to mental health
reported were confirmed by family and friends of the trial
subjects, who noted improved mood, communication and
general relations following the therapy for months afterwards.

A meta-analysis of twenty-seven studies with over 4000
subjects across seven countries suggests up to 40 per cent of
cancer patients suffer from anxiety or depression. Existing
treatments have proven largely ineffective in alleviating these
kinds of mood disorders, as well as conditions like complex
PTSD. The current crisis in mental health is only likely to be
exacerbated in the wake of the COVID-19 pandemic. A huge
unmet need exists among millions of people across the world
living lives of mental torment and misery, or taking the ultimately tragic step of ending their lives, who could be safely
and effectively treated with a simple reclassification of these
drugs. To deny them such treatment, or make criminals of
them for seeking relief, seems criminal in itself.

In the days and weeks after my session I definitely feel a new lightness of spirit. I endure another two months on my ADT without any descent into depression and feel the most hopeful for the future since my diagnosis. When I meditate, I can drop back into a milder version of that state of flow or bliss or release, a subtle hum of energy. It's easy to see how people might want to do this just for kicks, or that those with an addictive personality might become attached to the experience. But as a mental health tonic I suspect it is inevitable that psychedelic therapy becomes mainstream. At a time when we face multi-layered stressors and existential threats, it makes no sense to deprive ourselves of the sort of mystical experiences that humanity has accessed for millennia as a spiritual balm. I only hope I live to see that time.

28

PATTING THE SHARK

A T THE START OF this journey, I imagined I'd face some agonising choices between quality of life and longevity, to endure
more aggressive and toxic treatments to extend life or opt
for quality over quantity, to die with dignity. And I always
figured I'd come down on the side of quality of life, here for a
good time, not a long time.

When I put this to my new oncologist, he replies brightly,
'How about we go for both?' I like the cut of his jib.

Seven years on, and counting, I'm now convinced quality
of life promotes longevity. Enjoying your day-to-day reality,
having some purpose and meaning, love and joy in your life,
a strong will to live, it seems to me, can only benefit your
overall health.

Discussing quality of life for men with prostate cancer
while chemically castrating them is a little like recommending

a good dentist while punching someone repeatedly in the face. Until we have less toxic and debilitating treatment options than hormone therapy, men will continue to suffer – living longer but with profoundly compromised lives, which doesn't sound like anyone's idea of good medicine.

I'd hoped by the end of this book I'd be gleefully reporting my array of successful hormone therapy hacks to deliver a rich and meaningful life, despite the challenges to mental and physical health. This experience has humbled me and moderated my ambitions. Lots of things help – nutrition, good quality sleep, exercise, meditation, immersion in nature, social connection, creativity. Love.

But hormone therapy, for me at least, feels like getting in the ring with Mike Tyson. You might get through a couple of rounds and start to fancy your chances, but you're going to end up on the canvas sooner or later. Life with advanced prostate cancer is hard, no question. I might never arrive at a place of complete acceptance of the way hormone therapy has impacted me. This quest is an often harrowing work in progress and some days are better than others, despair forever hovering on the horizon like storm clouds. Short of complete enlightenment, managing my diagnosis will always entail a degree of suffering. How I respond to that suffering is up to me.

Early on, inspired by my old mate Mick Fanning, I was determined to punch the shark, to put up my dukes and fend off my attacker. Over time, I realised this was a flawed and unsustainable strategy. I can't spend the rest of my life at war with my own body, battling an invisible foe within. Three or four years in, I decided patting rather than punching the shark, and making my peace with this mortal threat, was a saner and more sustainable response. If I could accept my diagnosis and mortality, I'd be liberated to live a full and joyful life for however long I endured.

Soon after this epiphany, I'm scrolling Instagram and come upon a post of Mick diving with sharks, alongside a famed marine conservationist and 'shark whisperer' Cristina Zenato. Here is Mick literally patting sharks, confronting his fears, staring down his demons, for a two-part National Geographic documentary *Save This Shark*. Cosmic confirmation that I'm on the right track, perhaps. Zenato has reviewed the footage of Mick's shark encounter and claims it wasn't an attack, confirming that the shark simply got tangled in his legrope and tried to get away. 'You guys just crossed paths,' she says.

'That's the way I look at it. It was an encounter and it's time to move on,' Mick replies. But how do I move on?

I used to worry I'd forget I had cancer, would wake up and remember and go through the shock and trauma and anxiety all over again. But the reality is, I never forget I have cancer. It's not always front and centre in my mind, but my fundamental, base state is forever altered in ways difficult to articulate. An acute sense of impermanence, an ever-present awareness of the fleeting nature of existence. A kind of spiritual tinnitus, a constant, subtle ringing in my ears, a knowing rather than a sound. This is all temporary. My time here is finite.

Intellectually, we all know we are going to die, but that knowledge is a very different thing to feeling it in your bones. Yet our ability to relegate this truth to the deep recesses of our consciousness is one of the great feats of human intellect and ego.

Life, it has been said, is like getting in a boat and heading out to sea knowing it is going to sink. Despite this inevitability we still manage to react with shock and distress every time a boat sinks. I've also heard it said, by someone far wittier than me, that life is a sexually transmitted terminal illness. The origins of this quote are still hotly contested, between anonymous, eighties graffiti artists, and authors Margaret Atwood and Marilyn Duckworth.

When you first acquire the unshakeable knowledge of the inevitability of your own death, say by receiving a diagnosis of incurable cancer, the mind struggles to cope, because most of us have never deeply contemplated our mortality. Going through that struggle, sitting with that anguish over time, feels like passing through a furnace of knowing – deeply painful but you come out the other side stronger, yet more malleable, like tempered steel.

In this regard, cancer can be seen as a superpower that might, if you allow its transformative effects, inoculate you against many of life's stressors. That's not to say there is no longer any struggle or suffering, but rather you can accept the struggle and suffering as an inescapable, inseparable part of life, the price we pay for the miracle of having a life at all.

Lying in Shavasana (the corpse pose – a yogic practice specifically to prepare for death) at the end of another yoga class, our teacher says, 'Every day around 380,000 babies are born. Every day around 160,000 people die. We are living in the largest transit lounge in the universe.'

I take a strange, inordinate comfort in these words. We're all just coming and going. Who am I to rail against the timing of my departure? I've already experienced one of the most privileged lives in the history of human existence – with more joy, love, travel, culinary delights, sensual pleasures, music and art and literature from around the world and throughout history at my fingertips than 99 per cent of humans who have ever walked the planet.

If you have lived a middle-class lifestyle in the modern developed world, you have gorged on material riches and technological wonders and medical marvels and everyday conveniences. Compared to most humans throughout history, we live lives of inconceivable wealth and comfort. Yet all that the entire evolution of human society has gifted us rarely translates into commensurate, greater happiness.

What, then, is missing from our lives? A sense of inter-connectedness and a common good? A deep awareness of the fragility of our existence, our precarious toehold on this life?

Terminal cancer patients given guided psilocybin trips commonly report a blissful awakening to this interconnected-ness, a complete absence of fear in the face of death. They are able to live out their final weeks and months deeply at peace, liberated to have the kind of profound, intimate conversations with loved ones we would all wish for in our final days or weeks.

As Ian Gawler says, 'An awareness of our mortality is entirely compatible with a will to live.' By truly accepting our mortality, rather than struggling to hold that mortal terror at bay, we are freed to live with presence and peace for however long we have left. Oncologists often report on the deep peace terminal cancer patients experience when they come to a complete acceptance of their prognosis. But some physicians seem to take this as a solemn duty to eradicate any sense of hope from their patients' consciousness. Gawler argues it is possible, even beneficial, to be able to hold both views simultaneously: an acceptance of our mortality along with a determination to live.

I've spent around 90,000 words trying to articulate what it's like living with advanced cancer. Yet there's been an almost perfect simile right under my nose the whole time. Living with my diagnosis is a bit like living through the COVID-19 pandemic – the shifting of reality, the confrontation with mortality, watching old ways of life recede into history, adjusting to a new normal, the collapse of a comfortable world view and dreams for the future. Daily press conferences and case numbers analogous to my monthly blood tests and oncologist's appointments and PSA scores. When the numbers go up, so too do the rumblings of anxiety. While we all feared escalating case numbers would send us back into lockdown or the virus clusters erupting and spreading unchecked, I worry about an elevated PSA sending me back to the oncology day unit for a shot of my ADT or more chemo, or risking cancer's spread.

A mate asks me how I'm coping with COVID stress, and I have to stop and think about it because, honestly, I don't give it a lot of time and thought. It's as if I've already been immunised against the anxiety and dread of the pandemic. I don't say this with any smugness. As someone reliant on a functioning health system, the consequences of letting it rip, as some economists and right-wing commentators delight in championing, could be disastrous. I'm sympathetic to the devastating impacts of lockdown on people's mental health and livelihoods but somehow, I seem to be moving through it all relatively unscathed. Despite my diagnosis and past chemo, I don't see myself as immunocompromised. With everything I've been doing to support my health, I suspect my immune system is coping just fine. And though I have my reservations about the state of oncology care, I believe in the sound evidence of medical science. I've had my double dose of Astra-Zeneca and my Pfizer booster.

Just as well I don't have a bucket list because the last couple of years have been a shitty time to try to cross things off it, unless your bucket list includes making sourdough, bingeing Netflix, hoarding toilet paper and starting a veggie patch. I've become used to the sensation of my world shrinking, so lockdowns hold few fears. Early in the pandemic I realised I couldn't afford to go on the collective journey of fear and anxiety we were being corralled into. I could choose a different, inner journey of deeper peace, acceptance, surrender. My meditation practice has deepened, and that place of peace and stillness feels like something I can access whenever I need to.

When my results are good and my oncologist is expressing his incredulity at how well I'm doing, I still harbour ambitions of achieving a miraculous, long-term remission. But then I think it would be a shame to survive stage four cancer only to live through societal collapse brought on by the pandemic and climate change and the rolling series of crises it's likely to unleash. It's hard to be healthy on a sick planet.

Cancer has also primed me for the necessity of living in the moment, as hackneyed and abused as that phrase has become. I read somewhere recently that depression is dwelling in the past, anxiety is dwelling in the future, and the antidote to both is living in the present. Simplistic perhaps, but it rings true for me in managing my diagnosis. Most of the time, my present is pretty bloody pleasant. I've just about mastered the three-hour workday. I take delight in eating healthy food. When the surf's good I surf, haunted by all those days I drove past pumping waves because of some pressing deadline.

I can't get too worked up about people outraged at the prospect of putting a new and rapidly developed vaccine in their bodies. Try an hour-long chemo-infusion of actual poison. Or a radioactive tracer dye that carries a one in 200,000 chance of death.

Plenty of people have done it tough through the pandemic, but spare a thought for ME! I haven't been able to see my psychedelic therapist for months! With all non-essential travel from Queensland into New South Wales strictly limited through much of 2021, I've had to postpone my highly antic-ipated psilocybin therapy again and again. After the joys of the MDMA session, and the exciting research results for psilo-cybin to address existential dread, PTSD and depression, this is a major frustration. A rising PSA and a return to the ravages of ADT on my mental health only raises the stakes. After six years of this, even intermittent hormone therapy has taken a cumulative toll that I never fully recover from in the breaks from medication.

So, in late 2021, with great relief I'm finally able to travel into northern New South Wales for the purposes of mental health care. My psychedelic therapist is a qualified psychol-ogist, so he can provide a letter verifying I have a legitimate mental health appointment (without specifying that this particular therapy involves scoffing a hearty serve of magic mushrooms).

I figure I shouldn't drive after my session so a friend in northern New South Wales offers to drop me at my appointment. It's a grey, rainy day, ideal for tripping on shrooms. My mate Harry delivers me to that same quaint cottage around 10 am and will return to collect me at 4 pm. I ponder what the intervening six hours might entail. The research around psilocybin is so compelling, my expectations are high. I'm ready, quite literally, to have my mind blown.

I'd been anticipating a one-on-one session with my therapist as I experience the mushroom's potent therapeutic powers for the first time. But Jose emails me a few days before to say another client has also booked in, which will reduce the cost of my session by several hundred dollars, which is welcome news. I'm introduced to my fellow psychedelic adventurer, Brad, who will be undergoing MDMA therapy today, and Jose gives us his customary briefing about the protocols of the session. We're to follow his instructions at all times, remain on the property, open ourselves up to the experience and not resist the direction it may take us.

Brad's a first-time client, with a shaky, nervous energy that speaks of past trauma. Jose prepares our doses and I'm handed a small cup containing 4.5 milligrams of dried gold tops, and begin chomping my way through them, washed down with water. I wouldn't eat them for the flavour, and I won't be adding them to a risotto any time soon, but they're not too off-putting. I soon swallow the lot and settle in for the ride.

I don the eyeshades and the noise-cancelling headphones and make myself comfortable on a day bed by an open window while Jose's psychedelic soundtrack begins to cast its spell. Jose suggests I might want to remain lying with the eyeshades and headphones on, or I might feel like engaging with nature and stare out the window at the trees or wander in the garden. I should follow my urges as they arise.

Brad, meanwhile, has taken his MDMA and laid down on a mattress on the floor opposite me. While I wait for the shrooms to take effect, it seems Brad is already feeling the therapeutic powers of his 'medicine'. Soon, even through the headphones, I can hear him grunting and panting and wailing and when I raise my eyeshades to see what's going on, he's writhing and contorting on the floor as if gripped by acute stomach cramps or possessed by demons. As the shrooms begin to kick in, this makes for an unsettling accompaniment to my own increasingly warped view of reality.

I try to focus on my breathing, the wafting, ethereal music, the kaleidoscopic images beginning to swim through my consciousness. But Brad's noisy contortions keep pulling me out of my own experience. After about an hour of this, I'm quite enjoying the pretty visuals but am growing increasingly disturbed by the distraction. Jose checks in and quizzes me about my experience but for some reason I'm loath to complain. I try to describe the visuals as best I can, but I'm surprised how lucid I feel, that I am able to hold a coherent conversation at all.

'It sounds to me like you are in the foyer but haven't yet entered the theatre,' he observes. He recommends a top-up and prepares me another 4.5 milligram dose. That's a total of 9 milligrams. Given that experienced psychedelic adventurers refer to 5 milligrams as a 'heroic dose' I wonder what I am letting myself in for. But I'm keen to go deeper, desperate for the big psychic breakthrough I've been anticipating and to escape the intrusions of my troubled neighbour.

As the second dose kicks in, I gaze out the window as the trees dance in a strong breeze, their leaves forming pretty, geometric patterns, my altered consciousness deciphering some grand choreography in their random movements. If I stare at anything with a repeating pattern, like the rug on the floor or tiles on the wall, they soon begin morphing and distorting like a Salvador Dalí painting. Order out of chaos, and chaos out of order. This is all quite fun but some way short of the annihilation of the ego or the overwhelming confrontation with some higher power I'd expected. I'm well versed by now in the importance of set and setting, to hold a conscious intention and create a safe and supportive environment. My intention is to confront my mortality and liberate myself from any fear of death. But my setting isn't feeling particularly safe and supportive, as Brad continues to loudly battle unseen forces.

I've been counting on this experience to deliver the final piece in the puzzle in my quest for equanimity, and a dramatic climax of sorts for this book. Another lesson in the dangers of expectations. The experience is interesting and mostly enjoyable, but I'm surprised and a little disappointed I don't feel something more . . . profound.

'I picked you as someone who could handle their medicine. You've had an enormous dose,' Jose says, as if this is a badge of honour. He credits my meditation practice for my relatively mild response to the therapy. Perhaps I'm further advanced in my acceptance of my mortality than I realise, he suggests. This seems both good and bad news – good that I might be closer to making my peace with death, but bad that this experience might not provide the dramatic narrative climax and transcendent mind expansion I've been craving.

At one stage, I step outside to escape the unsettling atmosphere, and gaze about at my lush green surrounds from the front porch as gentle rain patters down around me. A chicken scratches in the yard. The pool looks like it needs a clean. On my first visit here, this whole setting seemed quite magical, but now there's something almost a little melancholic about it and I question what I'm doing here spectating someone else's spectacular unravelling. I'm almost ready to ring my mate Harry to come and collect me, but I figure I'll ride it out, adhere to the protocol and see where the experience takes me.

I try to cultivate compassion for Brad's anguish. Perhaps he has something to teach me. When I step back inside, Jose appears to be delivering Brad some new therapy, with a strange V-shaped pipe. 'Amazonian snuff,' Jose explains when I look inquiringly at the curious procedure. He puts a small amount of a yellow powder in one end of the pipe and instructs Brad to place one nostril over it, while he blows in the other end of the pipe to administer the dose. Amazonian snuff is a dried and powdered mix of several South American herbs, plants and native tobacco. It's used by shamans in sacred rituals to detox the mind and body and clear your 'energetic field', and

348

can induce vomiting, sweating and diarrhoea. Brad begins sneezing violently. I beat a hasty retreat to the front porch.

I ride out the remainder of my trip happily enough, enjoying the visuals but awaiting the profound transcendent insights that never come. One powerful thought that emerges through the kaleidoscope is that I've been so self-absorbed and introspective in my cancer journey I haven't been aware enough how this all impacts upon my family. My emotional rollercoaster has affected Kirst and the kids more than I'm comfortable admitting. A powerful image arises of embracing my family, wrapping my arms around them in a tight huddle, the beloved 'family cuddle' we enjoyed when the kids were little. That insight alone is worth the price of admission.

Jose checks in to see what's occupying my consciousness and I tell him 'family'. A wave of emotion hits me as I say the word. 'We were happy,' I blubber, suddenly sobbing. 'Why couldn't this happen to a couple who already hated each other.' There's an anger there I didn't realise I was holding and a comforting sense of release along with the deep sadness. I'm out the other side now without ever really feeling like I entered the theatre, the gentle warping of reality gradually easing.

My mate Harry arrives on schedule, and I'm almost relieved to jump in the comforting cocoon of his late-model SUV, a little underwhelmed but still grateful for the experience. Perhaps the fungi's teachings will be integrated gradually over time, the therapeutic effects more slow reveal than fireworks show. I suspect this may bring my psychedelic adventures to a conclusion, or at least a substantial pause. I'm more inclined to pursue my meditation practice as a path to liberation.

In the weeks since my psilocybin therapy, I do feel a subtle mental looseness that sometimes feels like a disturbing fragility and at other times more like a welcome flexibility or dexterity, less attached to my earthly circumstances, more open and accepting of change and uncertainty. One night, a week after the trip, unable to sleep, I'm wracked by a sudden and dramatic meltdown in the middle of the night, as if releasing my own pent-up trauma. The ravages on my physical body, mental health, marriage, family life, career. My body no longer feels like mine, as if it's some macabre Frankenstein experiment. The shrivelled genitals. The hard, sensitive buds under my nipples where man boobs threaten to sprout. My stolen sexuality. My wild mood swings. I'm swamped by heavy, full-body sobbing with a heaving chest, gulping for air like a fish out of water.

Kirst is awakened by my histrionics. 'What's going on?' she asks, both mildly grumpy and genuinely concerned. In that strange twilight realm, not wholly asleep or awake, we somehow manage an emotional, blame-free, midnight heart-to-heart. I share my distress at what's become of my vanishing masculinity. I apologise for the way my brooding presence has impacted the family, the necessity for her to be the stoic one forever holding things together for the kids, weathering my mental health storm.

'I don't want you to always have to be the strong one. I want you to be able to let go sometimes. When I'm off ADT and I say I'm okay, please believe me. That's your chance to look after yourself,' I plead.

Suddenly, Kirst's the one sobbing, chest heaving, collapsing into my embrace. We hold each other, both crying, releasing the pain and anguish of the past seven years. Finally bonded instead of separated by our grief. Oddly, I feel calmed by Kirst's show of emotion, a wave of relief that she's finally letting go. Is this the fungi's healing properties playing out?

Sometimes I don't even know who I am anymore. The brooding, volatile presence on ADT? The Zen meditator off it? Some remnant of the me before my diagnosis? An evolving, new, non-binary entity shaped by the deep scars and lessons of the past seven years? All of the above?

I don't know how this story ends, apart from the ultimate, inevitable end. In the meantime, I'm here, alive, cracked open to the fullness of this experience. Breathing in, breathing out. The concept of quality of life in a medical context usually relates to our pain levels and our ability to perform daily tasks, wash, dress and toilet ourselves, work, exercise, enjoy a social life. But if I were to characterise my quality of life, the term 'high definition' comes to mind. Life, for better or worse, is rendered in fine, sharp, technicolour detail, my emotional range broadened – more potent joy, more crushing despair, more moments of deep peace and shocking intensity. Fully awake.

I visit my GP for a renewal of my mental health care plan, and he gives me the obligatory quiz to measure my level of distress. In the past four weeks, how much of the time have I felt hopeless?

(a) None of the time

(b) Some of the time

(c) Most of the time

(d) All the time

Reader, I'm happy to report, my answer is, (a) None of the time. I'm struck by the realisation this wasn't always the case. I ace the test, but that isn't really the idea with this test, where a high score indicates a high level of emotional distress.

'You haven't scored very highly,' my GP says, deadpan. 'The average person in the street would score higher than you.'

'It's preventative maintenance,' I tell him, grinning.

Just one of the perks of stage four cancer – no one quibbles about your mental health care plan.

John's known me for years, and survived throat cancer himself with a clean bill of health after radiation. He's deeply empathetic to my circumstances. There are school photos of his teenage sons on the bookcase, and a large, framed shot of John with a jumbo-sized barra on a fishing trip up north on the wall. He always bulk bills me so I'm not out of pocket.

I give him a quick update. My PSA's dropped sharply again even while off the ADT – from 5.5 to 0.78. Neither my oncologist nor I know what to make of it.

John's stoked for me.

'Yeah, it's great,' I agree, 'but it's also kind of weird. Like, I didn't even know if I'd still be here at this point and here I am, still surfing, fit and healthy.'

He looks up from his computer.

'I didn't think you'd still be here,' he says flatly.

This strikes me as an odd conversation to be having with one's doctor. In some parallel universe, have I already departed this earthly plane? What does it mean to outlive one's prognosis? Do I regard everything from this point on as a bonus? How do I plan for a profoundly uncertain future?

In her book *When Things Fall Apart*, American Tibetan Buddhist author Pema Chödrön argues we are all engaged in a futile search for what she calls 'solid ground', a sense of stability amid an inherently unstable existence; that there is, in truth, no solid ground to be found.

> To be fully alive, fully human, and completely awake is to be continually thrown out of the nest. To live fully is to be always in no-man's land, to experience each moment as completely new and fresh. To live is to be willing to die over and over again. From the awakened point of view, that's life. Death is wanting to hold on to what you have and have every experience confirm you and congratulate you and make you feel completely together.

By that measure I'm doing brilliantly. I have zero sense of feeling completely together, quite the opposite – more a sense of falling apart, cells disassembling, to be reassembled in some new form or to drift off into the ether altogether. Aren't we all just stardust? The death I welcome is that of individual identity, separation, the dictates of the ego and the erratic distractions of the monkey mind running the show. I dissolve. Everywhere but nowhere. Hopefully, when the time comes, there'll be no resistance, no grief, only liberation from the constricting armour of this earthly shell.

Our daughter makes it home for Christmas. We finally have that family cuddle. The kids are now sixteen and nineteen. We talk openly about my diagnosis, hormone therapy, the side effects of treatment. I explain that prostate cancer feeds on testosterone and the drug I'm on is the same one given to transgender teens transitioning from male to female. The kids are so across the concept of gender fluidity this makes sense to them. I apologise for my moodiness. 'No wonder. You're on blockers,' says Vivi.

There may not be solid ground, but there is the eternal, abundant force of love to sustain us, the sanctuary of the empty mind, the vast indifferent ocean to absorb our human foibles and dramas.

When I drop in, to a wave or a meditative state, for timeless moments there is no thought, just a gently humming sense of bliss and well-being that I am convinced has to be good for me. When I meditate, I picture a beam of white light pouring through the crown of my head, flooding my body with breath and awareness and a brilliant glowing aura of health, a delicious vibration that travels from the top of my head to the tip of my toes and back. In those moments, I don't feel like the wounded antelope limping across the savannah that has fallen behind the herd, waiting to be picked off by an opportunistic hyena. I feel like a brilliant, timeless, spiritual entity – untouchable, immortal. And in such moments, I am convinced things are somehow going to work out. What that looks like I don't know – if I manage to maintain good health until more effective treatments become available, or I achieve a miraculous, unexplained remission or I just manage to navigate a good death, at peace, fulfilled, able to offer comfort and solace to my friends and family in my final moments.

We're all dying, ships gamely heading out to sea only to inevitably sink. In the meantime I intend savouring this pitching, rolling, storm-battered and occasionally becalmed life on the high seas.

I'm all adrift. Untethered. Traversing a sea of uncertainty. Like Mick's shark, cancer didn't target me. We've just had an encounter, crossed paths. Nature doing what it does. Cells dividing. Oblivious, like the ocean.

ACKNOWLEDGEMENTS

So MANY PEOPLE HELPED make this story, and my continued good health, possible. If I overlook anyone, please know every act of kindness and compassion has made a difference and been deeply appreciated.

This book might never have happened without the support of my PhD supervisor, Dr Sally Breen. She encouraged me to apply for a creative writing PhD scholarship at Griffith University in the first place. Her brutal kindness in feedback and editing has elevated this work immeasurably. Her constant prodding to unlearn some of my journalistic discipline, to write more freely and personally and vulnerably, to 'let us in', as she urged me, has transformed my writing practice profoundly for the better. My co-supervisor Prof Nigel Krauth, with his vast academic experience and credentials, helped ease my acute case of imposter syndrome and convince me I had something worthwhile to say. The support of Griffith University and its creative writing community has provided an uplifting collegiate spirit throughout this process.

This is the tenth book publisher Alison Urquhart and I have worked on together, over twenty-five years and two publishing houses. As Ali helpfully pointed out when I expressed alarm at this news, it's just as well we started when we were nine. Her faith in me and this wild departure from my stock in trade of surf star biographies helped shore up my fragile self-belief. My former agent Jane Burridge (now enjoying a well earnt retirement) and her recommended replacement, Gaby Naher at Left Bank Literary, both offered invaluable support and kindness. Editor Meaghan Amor has performed a wonderfully sensitive edit with discerning suggestions and encouraging comments and just the right level of critique. Editorial assistant Grayce Arlov has chimed in with helpful guidance and wisdom. The combined effect of all this support is the sensation of having a crack pit crew keeping me on the track and on pace. Special thanks to Adam Yazxhi for a spectacular cover design (again!).

I'd like to thank all my healthcare providers over the past seven years for their care and expertise, particularly but in no particular order: all my treating physicians, who for professional and privacy reasons prefer not to be named, naturopath Sarah Franklin, physiotherapist Indiana Frankie, yoga teacher Mark Togni, the nursing staff at John Flynn Hospital Oncology Day Unit, Dr Stephen Bourne, Associate Prof Arun Azad, psychologist Michelle Stewart, massage therapists Brett Franke and Michelle Hill.

ACKNOWLEDGEMENTS

Extra special thanks to the wonderful Prof Suzanne Chambers for writing a very generous foreword, and for her unwavering belief that the voice of men living with prostate cancer needs to be heard loud and clear in any discussion of survivorship strategies.

For all kinds of big-hearted displays of support and compassion, special thanks to: Jock Serong, Al Mourad, Steve Snow, Dave Jenkins, my surfing tribe – especially Andy Kidd, Steve Hoskin and Marty Jackson – personal trainers Nadine King and Shiike Vanderwerf, University of Queensland exercise physiology students and staff for their cancer clinic and participation in the GAP4 Interval Study, the Gawler Foundation, Dhamma Rasmi Vipassana Centre, Ted Grambeau, Graham Lock, Graeme Murdoch, Rachel Torti, Captain Martin Daly and the crew of the *Indies Trader 3*, Neil Ridgway, Doug 'Claw' Warbrick, Brian Singer, Janet de Neefe, Maurice Cole, and Mind Medicine Australia.

For literary inspiration, that trauma and grief can be channelled into compelling narrative non-fiction, writerly thanks to Rick Morton, Jessie Cole, Ailsa Piper and Andrew Stafford. Much gratitude to my seventeen Patreon subscribers.

We've been blessed with generous support from both sides of our family, especially Kirst's dad Ken for the idyllic and therapeutic holidays and dinners, my dad for his many generous displays of support and ever-present concern, and my dear mum for assiduously catering to my dietary requirements during Melbourne visits.

Ultimately, overflowing love and gratitude to Kirst for standing by her man while being unflinchingly real and pragmatic about the challenges we face together. And Vivi and Alex for abundant love, pride, joy, keeping me on my toes, and the deep comfort of knowing my spirit or essence or legacy lives on through you. You're the best.

REFERENCES

INTRODUCTION

Kalanithi, P. (2017). *When Breath Becomes Air.* Vintage.

Sung, H., Ferlay, J., Siegel, R. L., Laversanne, M., Soer-jomataram, I., Jemal, A., Bray, F., (2021). Global cancer statistics 2020: GLOBOCAN estimates of incidence and mortality worldwide for 36 cancers in 185 countries. *CA: A Cancer Journal for Clinicians,* 71(3), 209–249. https://doi.org/10.3322/caac.21660

CHAPTER 2

Baguley, B. J., Skinner, T. L., Leveritt, M. D., & Wright, Olivia R. L. (2017). Nutrition therapy with high intensity interval training to improve prostate cancer-related fatigue in men on androgen deprivation therapy: a study protocol. *BMC Cancer,* 17(1). https://doi.org/10.1186/s12885-016-3022-6

REFERENCES

Leano, A., Korman, M. B., Goldberg, L., & Ellis, J. (2019). Are we missing PTSD in our patients with cancer? Part I. *Canadian Oncology Nursing Journal, 29*(2), 141–146.

Moreno-Smith, M., Lutgendorf, S. K., Sood, A. K. (2010). Impact of stress on cancer metastasis. *Future Oncol, 6*(12). 1863–1881. https://doi.org/10.2217/fon.10.142

Pranjic, N., Bajraktarevic, A., & Ramic, E. (2016). Distress and PTSD in patients with cancer: Cohort study case. *Materia socio-medica, 28*(1), 12–16. https://doi.org/10.5455/msm.2016.28.12-16

Zuniga, K. B., Chan, J. M., Ryan, C. J., & Kenfield, S. A. (2020). Diet and lifestyle considerations for patients with prostate cancer. *Urologic Oncology: Seminars and Original Investigations, 38*(3), 105–117. https://doi.org/10.1016/j.urolonc.2019.06.018

CHAPTER 4

(2015). *White Horses, 13* (winter). https://whitehorses.com.au/product/issue-13/

CHAPTER 8

Johnson, C. (2012, December 1). Letter claims 'evidence' of Gawler's fight with cancer. *The Age.* https://www.theage.com.au/national/victoria/letter-claims-evidence-of-gawlers-fight-with-cancer-20121130-2ameu.html

CHAPTER 9

Servan-Schreiber, D. (2010). *Anticancer: A New Way of Life.* Scribe Publications.

CHAPTER 11

Hart, W. (1987). *The Art of Living: Vipassana Meditation as Taught by S. N. Goenka.* Harper & Row.

CHAPTER 14

Baker, T. (2007). *High Surf.* HarperCollins.

Cormie, P., Atkinson, M., Bucci, L., Cust, A., Eakin, E., Hayes, S., McCarthy, S., Murnane, A., Patchell, S., & Adams, D. (2018). Clinical Oncology Society of Australia position statement on exercise in cancer care. *The Medical Journal of Australia, 209*(4), 184–187. https://doi.org/10.5694/mja18.00199

CHAPTER 16

Begley, S. (2017, March 24). Most Cancer Cases Arise from 'Bad Luck'. *STAT.* https://www.scientificamerican.com/article/most-cancer-cases-arise-from-bad-luck/

Byrne, J. (2019, October 24). Depression in oncologists: For many, a closely guarded secret. *Healio.* https://www.healio.com/news/hematology-oncology/20191017/depression-in-oncologists-for-many-a-closely-guarded-secret

McFarland, D., Hlubocky, F., Susaimanickam, B., O'Hanlon, R., & Riba, M. (2019). Addressing Depression, Burnout and Suicide in Oncology Physicians. *American Society of Clinical Oncology Educational Book, 39*, 590–598.

Paiva, C. E., Martins, B. P., & Paiva, B. S. R. (2018). Doctor, are you healthy? A cross-sectional investigation of oncologist burnout, depression, and anxiety and an investigation of their associated factors. *BMC cancer, 18*(1), 1–11.

Shanafelt, T., & Dyrbye, L. (2012). Oncologist burnout: causes, consequences, and responses. *Journal of Clinical Oncology, 30*(11), 1235–1241. https://doi.org/10.1200/JCO.2011.39.7380

Tulsky, J. A., Arnold, R. M., Alexander, S. C., Olsen, M. K., Jeffreys, A. S., Rodriguez, K. L., Skinner, C. S., Farrell, D., Abernethy, A. P., & Pollak, K. I. (2011). Enhancing communication between oncologists and patients with a computer-based training program: a randomized trial. *Annals of internal medicine, 155*(9), 593–601. https://doi.org/10.7326/0003-4819-155-9-201111010-00007

CHAPTER 17

Baker, T. (2019). *The Rip Curl Story*. Ebury Australia.

Queensland Poetry. (2017, November 16). *2017 Australian Poetry Slam – QLD champion Viv Baker*. [Video]. https://www.youtube.com/watch?v=wbur22yzmXE

CHAPTER 18

Bays, B. (1999). *The Journey*. Atria Books.

Rhee, H., Gunter, J. H., Heathcote, P., Ho, K., Stricker, P., Corcoran, N. M., & Nelson, C. C. (2015). Adverse effects of androgen-deprivation therapy in prostate cancer and their management. *BJU international, 115*, 3–13. https://doi.org/10.1111/bju.12964

Zoladex reviews. *Ask A Patient*. https://www.askapatient.com/viewrating.asp?drug=19726&name=ZOLADEX

CHAPTER 19

Simpson, J. (1988). *Touching the Void*. Perennial.

CHAPTER 22

Ramos, J. A., & Bianco, F. J. (2012). The role of cannabinoids in prostate cancer: Basic science perspective and potential clinical applications. *Indian Journal of Urology, 28*(1), 9–14. https://doi.org/10.4103/0970-1591.94942

Singh, K., Jamshidi, N., Zomer, R., Piva, T. J., & Mantri, N. (2020). Cannabinoids and prostate cancer: A systematic review of animal studies. *International journal of molecular sciences, 21*(17), 6265.

CHAPTER 23

McCartney, D., Arkell, T. R., Irwin, C. & McGregor, I. S. (2021). Determining the magnitude and duration of acute Δ⁹-tetrahydrocannabinol (Δ⁹-THC)-induced driving and cognitive impairment: A systematic and meta-analytic review. *Neuroscience & Biobehavioral Reviews, 126*, 175–193. https://doi.org/10.1016/j.neubiorev.2021.01.003

Strom, Marcus. (2021, April 21). Scientists put the stopwatch on cannabis intoxication. The University of Sydney. https://www.sydney.edu.au/news-opinion/news/2021/04/12/scientists-put-stopwatch-on-cannabis-thc-intoxication-lambert-drug-driving.html

CHAPTER 24

O'Hagan, A. (2020). *Mayflies*. Faber.

Symonds, D. (Director and Producer). (2021, July 20). Cancer: A Story of Hope. *Catalyst*. [Television series episode]. ABC Television. https://www.abc.net.au/catalyst/cancer-a-story-of-hope/13460750

CHAPTER 26

Australia's first psychedelic clinical trial commences recruitment. (2020, February). St. Vincent's Hospital. https://www.svhm.org.au/newsroom/news/australia-s-first-psychedelic-clinical-trial-commences-recruitment

Kalanithi, P. (2017). *When Breath Becomes Air.* Vintage.

Leonard, A. (2015, November 20). How LSD Microdosing Became the Hot New Business Trip. *Rolling Stone.* https://www.rollingstone.com/culture/culture-news/how-lsd-microdosing-became-the-hot-new-business-trip-64961/

Pollan, M. (2019). *How To Change Your Mind.* Penguin Press.

CHAPTER 27

Griffiths, R. R., Johnson, M. W., Carducci, M. A., Umbricht, A., Richards, W. A., Richards, B. D., Cosimano, M. P. & Klinedinst, M. A. (2016). Psilocybin produces substantial and sustained decreases in depression and anxiety in patients with life-threatening cancer: A randomized double-blind trial. *Journal of psychopharmacology, 30*(12), 1181–1197.

Mitchell, J. M., Bogenschutz, M., Lilienstein, A. et al. (2021). MDMA-assisted therapy for severe PTSD: a randomized, double-blind, placebo-controlled phase 3 study. *Nat Med, 27,* 1025–1033. https://doi.org/10.1038/s41591-021-01336-3

CHAPTER 28

Chödrön, P. (1996). *When Things Fall Apart: Heart Advice for Difficult Times.* Shambhala Publications.

Discover a
new favourite

Visit **penguin.com.au/readmore**